Who Knows the Reach of God?

Homilies and Reflections for Year A

Breaking Open the Word

Who Knows the Reach of God?

Homilies and Reflections
for Year A

Corbin Eddy

NOVALIS

© 2001 Novalis, Saint Paul University, Ottawa, Canada

Cover design: Blair Turner

Cover art: sculpture by Julie Campagns, photographed by Wally Moss

Layout: Suzanne Latourelle

Editor: Bernadette Gasslein

Business Office:

Novalis
49 Front Street East, 2nd Floor
Toronto, Ontario, Canada
M5E 1B3

Phone: 1-800-387-7164 or (416) 363-3303
Fax: 1-800-204-4140 or (416) 363-9409
E-mail: novalis@interlog.com

National Library of Canada Cataloguing in Publication Data

Eddy, Corbin, 1942-
    Who knows the reach of God? : homilies and reflections for year A

Includes bibliographical references.
ISBN 2-89507-174-8

    1. Church year sermons. 2. Sermons, Canadian (English)
3. Catholic Church--Sermons. I. Title.

BX1756.E36W42 2001   252'.6 C2001-903625-6

We acknowledge the financial support of the Government of Canada through the Book Publishing Industry Development Program (BPIDP) for our publishing activities.

*to the people of
St. Basil's Parish,
Ottawa*

Table of Contents

Table of Contents

Table of Contents

Introduction

You may know the humorist and writer Garrison Keillor. The author of numerous books, he's the host of *Prairie Home Companion* on American public radio and is especially famous for his stories from his hometown, Lake Wobegon. In his book *We Are Still Married*, he writes about the meaning of life:

> To know and to serve God, of course is why we're here, a clear truth that, like the nose on your face, is near at hand and easily discernible but can make you dizzy if you focus on it hard. But a little faith will see you through. What else will do except faith in such a cynical corrupt time? When the country goes temporarily to the dogs, cats must learn to be circumspect, walk on fences, sleep in trees and have faith that all this woofing is not the last word. What keeps our faith cheerful is the extreme persistence of gentleness and humor. Gentleness is everywhere in daily life, a sign that faith rules in ordinary things; through cooking and small talk, through story telling, making love, fishing, tending animals and sweet corn and flowers, through sports, music and books, raising kids—all the places where the gravy soaks in and grace shines through. Even in a time of elephantine vanity and greed, one never has to look far to see the campfires of gentle people. If we had no other purpose in life, it would be good enough to simply take care of them and goose them once in awhile.[1]

"Taking care of people and goosing them once in awhile" is a pretty good description of how I have understood much of my ministry, although "goosing" is not the word I would have chosen! Stirring up gentle people's campfires is another wonderful metaphor. In working with individuals and communities, I believe in a positive approach.

---

[1]   Garrison Keillor, *We Are Still Married* (New York: Penguin, 1990), p. 218.

I have found that the Christophers' motto, "It is better to light one candle than to curse the darkness," is right on the mark.

I believe it is so much more constructive to serve those who actually participate in the life of the parish as conscientiously and as creatively as possible than to moan about those who, for whatever reason, are not regular members of the assembly; to affirm faith where it can be discovered rather than to complain about its lack elsewhere; to build on positive elements of the culture rather than to decry its less positive aspects.

For the most part, the homilies in this collection are reworked versions of those preached at Saint Basil's Roman Catholic Church in Ottawa, where I served as pastor for eight years before accepting my present position at Saint Mary's Seminary in Baltimore. They reflect the style and tone of my relationship with the people and the culture of that particular parish community. In reworking them, I have included background material that would not have been in their original preached version. Although they reflect their oral beginnings, most are now too long and too complex to serve as actual homilies. They have been filled out to provide material for homilists and cate-chists who may find possibilities in them for their own preaching and teaching, as well as to offer more background material for those who use them for personal prayer and reflection.

In stirring campfires, taking care of people and, yes, goosing some of them once in awhile, I have found pastoral work to be a wonderful and gratifying experience. In my new responsibilities, I am working with the next generation of pastors, praying and believing that they will find parish ministry as affirming and life-giving as it has been for me.

Last Lent, for example, I had a very interesting discussion with a man who had returned to the regular practice of his faith just a year or so earlier. Seemingly out of nowhere, he felt stirrings of faith and found himself drawn back to the church. Once he began coming for awhile, the liturgy itself became very important to him. He spoke of the biblical texts and the rituals marking the turning of the liturgical year as very interesting and helpful to his own personal rhythms.

His year was no longer divided only into winter, spring, summer and fall, but was marked by the expectation of Advent, leading up to the fulfillment of Christmas, followed by Lent, the solemn prelude to the dark anguish of Good Friday that is transformed in the glory of Easter. A very articulate man, he was able to describe how birth and death and resurrection, beginnings and endings and renewals, were observed and celebrated in word and sacrament. His experience of the church's liturgy made him feel that he belonged, not just to a neighbourhood and a place, but to a larger order of things, a universal sequence of life and death and rebirth.

Going to church, even belonging to it, did not solve life's problems for him, but gave him a sense of living in a larger context, of being part of something greater than what he could see through the tunnel vision of his personal concerns. He told me that he looked forward to Sunday because it meant going to church. What once was strange now felt not only natural, but essential.

Needless to say, I was delighted that the parish liturgy was providing this kind of service to him and was convinced once again that the "source and summit of the Christian life" has a great deal to offer people of our own time and is well worth our efforts.

As you read the homily-reflections in this volume, there is no substitute for direct exposure to the biblical texts themselves, as organized by the lectionary and cited before each entry. This is especially true because they are so parish-specific. These texts are the source of the reflections that follow. And, to get a real feel for what is being said, there is no substitute for identifying the Sunday or feast being celebrated within the liturgical cycle.

The scriptures are proclaimed publicly as an act of worship within a liturgical context. Here in the liturgical assembly they come alive. There is in liturgy a new hearing of a living word. What Vatican II describes as "full, conscious and active participation" is greatly enhanced by personal preparation of the assigned texts and an appreciation of the liturgical year.

Whatever else might be said about the preparation of homilies, it is essential that preaching be appropriate to the present time and to the assembly of people actually gathered on a particular Sunday. As an interpretation of the scriptures for today, a homily needs to be *hearable*.

It brings the texts forward and invites the assembly to a new or fresh hearing of God's Word.

The Bible itself derives from a continual rehearing and reinterpretation of its own traditions in new settings and for new generations of believers. In the New Testament, for example, letters are directed to the concrete circumstances of specific persons and communities. Likewise the four gospels arise out of four different experiences, four different stages of early Christian development. Recognizing and respecting new settings and new circumstances are properly, even inescapably, integral to a genuine honouring of God's living word. The effective and realistic hearing of God's word in and through these ancient texts calls for ever-renewed interpretation and creative application.

The desire to be immediately relevant, however, should not suggest the abbreviation of careful study of the text in its original context. The homily cannot be divorced from the biblical tradition itself. The preacher's role is to see that the principle of fidelity to the scriptures is not abandoned in the daily life and worship of the church.

The effort to understand a text in its original historical, literary and theological contexts does indeed create distance between the Bible and the assembled parish community. The preacher may grow impatient with biblical study, considering this phase a "long way from a good homily."

The time of study, however, can be most fruitful. By holding the text and the parishioners apart for awhile, the homilist may be able to hear each more clearly and interpret each more honestly. When the two finally meet or intersect in the homily, neither the text nor the assembly will be consumed by the other. They will stand together in creative tension.

As an ancient collection of books, the Bible invites the homilist back into its own world(s) to properly understand the original meaning of a particular text. Because such a text is the church's scripture, it challenges the homilist to pull that meaning forward into our own world to address us here and now. Set on a particular Sunday or feast, biblical texts find their place in the church's "liturgical world" and, in a dynamic partnership with the rites, contribute towards shaping the spiritual and missionary world of Christian communities who gather to hear and to celebrate. The liturgy as a whole is formative of the church.[2]

These homilies/reflections correspond to the lectionary of Year A which, especially in Ordinary Time, finds its centre of gravity in the Gospel of Matthew. The following introductory comments about Matthew's gospel may be helpful.

At some time around AD 80–90, a learned Christian recast and reworked the traditional materials at his disposal into what has come down to us as the Gospel of Matthew. This work was necessitated by a severe crisis in the author's own community. Stringently Jewish in its origins, Matthew's audience had experienced the trauma of the destruction of Jerusalem and its temple in AD 70. With the loss of its ritual traditions as well as loss of control over the land, the Torah gained great prominence in Jewish life, but was interpreted in various ways by various groups among the Jews.

One group sought guidance in the Torah for living in what they believed would be a short interim period before God would vindicate his people and bring in a new age.

With the Torah as its source, another group sought to develop a Judaism that could be lived without temple or land, one that could exist and be lived in any place at any time.

Speaking from his group, Matthew presents Jesus as the Torah's fulfillment and definitive interpreter. Jesus fulfills and even transcends its categories and promises in his own person. Matthew's point was that if you want a sure interpretation of the Torah, look to the teaching and to the person of Jesus himself.

It's no wonder that these groups soon found themselves in real tension one with another. Their differences proved irreconcilable. Strong divisions arose even within families.

As time passed and God did not intervene in a definitive apocalyptic way, the first group virtually disappeared. Left were rabbinic Judaism and early Christianity; both have continued to evolve even to our own time. The division of church from synagogue was under-

---

2   See Normand Bonneau, O.M.I., *The Sunday Lectionary: Ritual Word, Paschal Shape* (Collegeville: Liturgical Press, 1998) and William Skudlarek, *The Word in Worship: Preaching in a Liturgical Context* (Nashville: Abingdon, 1981).

standably painful and bitter. Accusations and insults were hurled in both directions. It is just such a combative environment that gave rise to the particularly tough rhetoric attributed to Jesus in Matthew's gospel. Subsequent interpreters have labelled Matthew anti-Jewish and certain passages of his gospel have fuelled anti-Semitism even to our own day.

In his commentary on the gospel, Daniel Harrington urges that Matthew be read carefully and critically in the context of the late-first-century crisis facing all Jews, and that readers resist imposing on his gospel categories of a later time when Christianity and Judaism had become separate religions. Matthew's gospel is not anti-Jewish. Combatants on both sides were Jews. Nor is it anti-Semitic. Combatants on both sides were Semites.

> In Matthew we are only at the beginning of a transition from Christianity understood as a movement within Judaism to its being conceived as distinct from and over and against Judaism. Matthew and his fellow Christians still considered themselves Jews and sought to show that their identity as followers of Jesus was compatible with their Jewish heritage. It must, however, be admitted that the text of the gospel has anti-Semitic or anti-Jewish potential and that it has been used by anti-Semites through the ages as "theological" justification for great evil…. Historical study of Matthew can give Jews and Christians today important insight into the context of and reasons for the eventual parting of the ways between them and their long history of conflict over and against one another. The aim of such study is not to try to erase the distinctiveness of either Judaism or Christianity. The aim, instead, is for both Jews and Christians to look at a turning point in the history of both movements and to ask themselves whether theological differences necessarily demand conflict and eventual separation. They did in the past. But do they have to in the future? Can Christians and Jews perceive themselves as partners along the way rather than as opponents? Can we be with one another rather than over and against one another? Can we Christians work out a positive position vis-à-vis Jews for a

time and place different from those of Matthew and his apocalyptic and early rabbinic rivals?[3]

It seems to me that this point is well worth bringing in when
preaching the gospel and in adult Bible study connected with Year A.
The "Year of Matthew" may even provide a good opportunity for
inter-faith study and dialogue with a local Jewish synagogue.

Matthew is a rabbinical writer, a master of rich allusive stories that
draw on the ancient themes of Judaism and interpret them afresh. He
is a wise and experienced teacher, steeped in the law (Torah) and
traditions of Judaism, and has been a leader of its people in Antioch,
the greatest city of Rome's Asian empire.

At every turn Matthew highlights prophecies with their fulfill-
ments. In the gospel itself, the teaching of Jesus, stretched out over
Ordinary Time in our lectionary, is organized into five great sermons
reflecting the five great books of the Hebrew Torah, texts of supreme
importance for Israel. Throughout the gospel, Jesus is presented as the
embodiment and full expression of Israel's highest ideals and hopes.
Thought by some to have been a rabbi himself, Matthew draws on an
extraordinary wealth of traditions and stories and expresses that wealth
in a richly poetic way.

He searches the scriptures for clues to the identity and mission of
Jesus. He has inherited his method and language from the synagogues,
from deep wells of tradition unknown to many Christians. Jesus is
identified with Moses as leader and teacher, with the great biblical
kings, even with Israel itself, but in a way that transcends the events,
aspirations and categories they represent. Even more than a new
Moses, a new David or a new Israel, Jesus is seen as their ultimate
fulfillment. He stands in continuity and in discontinuity at the same
time. The very Law itself has been brought to its fulfillment by the
stately and commanding presence of Jesus, whose standing puts even
Moses in the shadows.

Who can this Jesus be? Who must he be?

---

[3]   Daniel J. Harrington, S.J., *The Gospel of Matthew* (Collegeville: Liturgical
Press–Michael Glazier, 1991), pp. 21-22.

Matthew draws an answer from Judaism that puts the ultimate break with Judaism beyond doubt.

Jesus is God-with-us, here and now.

"All authority," says the risen Jesus, "has been given to me in heaven and on earth.... And remember, I am with you always, to the end of the age." The gospel begins and ends with the affirmation that Jesus is the promised Emmanuel, "God-with-us."

In his spiritual and ethical teaching, Jesus' methodology is essentially to stretch his hearers' imagination even beyond the Torah as a way to challenge their capacity for generosity and commitment. Matthew's Jesus prizes the faculty of wonder above all. He consistently calls his hearers to an increasingly sensitive and magnanimous vision of human potential. He resists anything that would belittle the possibilities of ordinary people.

"It used to be said ... but I say," characterizes his approach to morality and spirituality.

In other words, stretch yourself, or let yourself be stretched in your understanding of life, in your relationships, in what seems fair, in everything.

"Jesus told the crowds all these things in parables; without a parable he told them nothing," characterizes his teaching style. In other words, let your imaginations be your guide. C.H. Dodd beautifully captures Jesus' sense of purpose and direction in his definition of a parable: "A parable is a metaphor or simile drawn from nature or common life, arresting the hearer by its vividness or strangeness and leaving the mind to sufficient doubt of its precise application to tease it into active thought."[4]

"Just as you did it to one of the least of these brothers and sisters of mine, you did it to me," captures the content of God's ultimate judgment. Guess what? In serving the least, you are serving the King of the Universe. Awesome! Wonderful! Imagine!

Finally, the disciples in Matthew's telling of the story not only represent the companions of the earthly Jesus, but serve as paradigms or models for all time. Whereas the disciples in Mark frequently misunderstand Jesus, those in Matthew do understand, but in an

---

[4] C.H. Dodd, *The Parables of the Kingdom* (New York: Scribner's, 1961), p. 5.

ongoing and growing way—as befits disciples. While not "perfect," they exhibit "little faith," which, even though it often fails, is real nonetheless. By calling the disciples "brothers" and "little ones," Matthew fosters their identification with members of his own church. He forbids the titles of his Jewish rivals such as "rabbi," "father" and "master." He sends into the world not rabbis and teachers and masters, but *disciples* to make *disciples* of the nations. It is in their littleness that the disciples share in the power of the risen Lord and are charged with leading others into the teachings and ethical challenges with which they themselves are struggling.

> This beautiful gospel stands at the beginning of the New Testament canon and has been a source of inspiration and teaching for every generation of Christians since the first century. Its commanding sweep of Jesus' life from the turbulent and wondrous events of his infancy to his final commissioning of the disciples on a mountaintop in Galilee, its strong emphasis on Jesus' teachings as in the famed Sermon on the Mount and its orderly structure quickly made it a capital influence on the church.[5]

Now for some words of thanks.

As was the case with *Who Knows the Colour of God? Homilies and Reflections for Year C*, the starting point for this book was a series of tape recordings of Sunday liturgies at Saint Basil's Church in Ottawa that were made by Ron Warren for use within our own faith community, and later transcribed by Michelle Rocheleau.

That a book such as this exists at all is due to members of Saint Basil's and their friends who wanted to keep and share these homilies, and who encouraged me to risk making them available to a wider faith community. It is due especially to Ron, who so faithfully recorded and catalogued them. It is my experience as a pastor at Saint Basil's and other parishes in the Archdiocese of Ottawa, however complex and challenging it was at times, that continues to be a wonderful source of energy and direction as I now work with pastors-in-training at Saint Mary's Seminary in Baltimore.

---

[5]   Donald Senior, *The Gospel of Matthew* (Nashville: Abingdon, 1997), p. 13.

I am even more conscious this year of my debt to Bernadette Gasslein of Novalis, who prepared and edited these homilies for publication. She herself was a member of Saint Basil's when many of them were preached. I am grateful not so much for her skill in polishing and preparing them for publication as for her challenging questions and comments accompanying those she sent back for more major revisions. Interestingly enough, none of those sent back were actually preached at the parish, but were newly composed—either because I had been away from Saint Basil's on that particular Sunday or because the content was so parish-specific that publication was not appropriate. Her comments that some of these newly composed pieces were not conversational enough, were too derivative, or were too abstract were right on the mark.

Finally, in a more general way, I am grateful for people behind the scenes who made it possible for me, in very busy parish settings, to study and to teach. In every instance, with their help and support, I was able to carve out significant time for personal study and reflection, which included homily preparation. I think especially of staff members Kathy Kennedy at Saint Patrick's, Fallowfield; Jan Lesage and Karen Dulude of Holy Redeemer, Kanata; and Florence Sutcliffe, Dawn Blakley, and Larry Kelly of Saint Basil's. In serving the people so effectively on the front lines, and making daily assessments of pastoral priorities (with good humour besides), their ministry to the community was also a great service to me. Their ministry of hospitality in the name of our parish mysteriously and wonderfully welcomed me, their pastor, with my own mix of gifts and limitations.

Getting back to Matthew: He reminds us often how real life is about such reciprocal hospitality—reaching and being reached, stretching and being stretched—recognizing others and being recognized as being in communion with Emmanuel, God-with-us.

"Whoever welcomes you welcomes me, and whoever welcomes me welcomes the one who sent me." (Matthew 10:40, Thirteenth Sunday of Ordinary Time A.)

May we all remain faithful to such a noble ideal. And may this year of Matthew be a blessing for the church.

Corbin Eddy
Saint Mary's Seminary and University
Baltimore, Maryland

September 21, 2001
Feast of Saint Matthew, Apostle and Evangelist

For further reading

Robin Griffith-Jones. *The Four Witnesses* (San Francisco: Harper Collins, 2001).

Daniel J. Harrington, S.J. *The Gospel of Matthew* (Collegeville: Liturgical Press-Michael Glazier, 1991).

John P. Meier. *Matthew* (Collegeville: Liturgical Press-Michael Glazier, 1980).

Donald Senior. *The Gospel of Matthew* (Nashville: Abingdon, 1997).

Uh-oh

First Sunday of Advent

Isaiah 2.1-5
Psalm 122
Romans 13.11-14
Matthew 24.37-44

Let us then lay aside the works of darkness and put on the armour of light. (Romans 13.12)

If the owner of the house had known in what part of the night the thief was coming, he would have stayed awake and would not have let his house be broken into. Therefore you also must be ready, for the Son of Man is coming at an unexpected hour. (Matthew 24.43-44)

Aren't those interesting images? Light as armour. The Son of Man as a thief.

There's a certain dizzying urgency in the experience of being robbed, especially in the dead of night. You hear a sound, you jump out of bed, throw on the lights and, blinking and squinting in the brightness, you try to figure out what to do next. It may be too late by this time, but light would have served as armour. When away from home, some people keep lamps lit in the house, even on rotating timers, as armour against potential intruders. They may even ask a neighbour to park in their driveway, so that it looks as if someone is at home.

Confronted by all of this, we still hear people talking nostalgically of simpler times when no one ever locked their doors, much less worried about timers on lamps or alarm systems. You may know families who even now refuse to lock their doors.

If the owner of the house had known in what part of the night the thief was coming, he would have stayed awake and would not have let his house be broken into. Therefore you also must be ready, for the Son of Man is coming at an unexpected hour. (Matthew 24.43-44)

There is a certain irony in the image as it appears here that is worth exploring on this First Sunday of Advent. Don't you find it strange that you are advised to protect your home from a potential thief and that therefore you must also be on the lookout for the coming of the Son of Man? Surely he should be welcomed, wouldn't you think? But it sounds like he's a thief.

In its context, today's text is drawn from the part of Matthew's gospel that describes Jesus' last words and actions in Jerusalem before his passion. It belongs to his prediction of coming disaster, including the destruction of the temple and of the whole city of Jerusalem. It is a prediction of violence and slaughter beyond description, beyond even the capacity of his hearers' imaginations. A whole civilization was to be stolen from the Jewish people. Precious cultural foundations would go up in smoke, disappearing forever.

Likening it to the deluge, when only Noah and his family were saved from God's judgment upon a helpless humanity, further emphasizes the seriousness of what is happening, By the time the gospel took its final form, these predictions had come to pass. Jerusalem had been destroyed. For Matthew's original audience, comprised mostly of early Christians with deep Jewish roots, the memory of this atrocity, which they themselves had experienced, would have been especially painful.

The point of these predictions and descriptions of disaster is brought out in the concluding verse, where we find the image we've been working with, including the warning to stay awake and the reminder that judgment comes upon the world and upon individuals as suddenly and unexpectedly as a burglar comes upon a victim.

What is ultimately so puzzling and mysterious is that God can in any way be discovered in the midst of all this destruction, that out of all this violence, stress and pain, purification is taking place. Horrible disasters, even prospective disasters, have life-giving potential. The Noah story is a precedent, as is the Babylonian exile.

I find that kind of theology very difficult to digest. It would perhaps be easy enough to jump ahead to the ultimate cataclysm when heaven and earth as we know them will pass away and a final purifying judgment will usher in a new heaven and a new earth. Ultimate justice will be done then, accounts will be settled and a new age will begin. All of that could happen at any moment, so be ready, the text may be suggesting. Once again, I don't find that persuasive and am not sure it's the only way to look at the text.

I certainly don't want to trivialize the passage or ignore its cosmic dimensions, but perhaps the metaphor of readiness for God as a thief has a broader and more universal application. In my experience, and I suspect in yours, purification is happening on an ongoing basis. Opportunities and even people are stolen from us as life takes its course. Judgment happens in these smaller, incremental break-ins to our security. The end of the world comes in forms large and small for different people at different times.

Robert Fulghum, in his book of the same name (*Uh-Oh*, New York: Random House/Villard, 1991) describes "Uh-oh" experiences. I'd like to suggest that even these small experiences have something to do with final judgment and that, for most of us, they "steal and reveal" in a cumulative kind of way. As he describes them, most of our break-ins are "uh-oh" experiences rather than 9-1-1 catastrophes, although we will experience those as well.

We say "uh-oh" to a small child who falls down or bumps his head or pinches her finger. It means that we know the child hurts, but we also know the hurt is temporary and that the child has the resources to handle the hurt and go about his or her business. The surprise and shock give way to handling the pain and moving on. The older we get, the more experience and knowledge we have, the more able we are to distinguish momentary difficulty from serious trouble, "Uh-oh" from 9-1-1. We grow daily in the "Uh-oh" mode.

Readiness for "Uh-oh" experiences is a frame of mind. It says expect the unexpected. It not only expects surprises in the night, but counts on them as signs of life, dimensions of vitality, interesting, even exciting, invitations.

Under various circumstances, "Uh-oh" can be translated as "Here we go again" or "Now what?" or "You never know what's going to happen next." It might mean "So much for plan A" or "Hang on, we're coming to a tunnel" or maybe even "You can't unscramble an egg" or "A hundred years from now it won't make any difference."

"Uh-oh" is more than a momentary reaction to small problems. It's part of an approach, an attitude, a perspective on life and the universe. It's part of an equation, which summarizes Fulghum's view of the varied ways in which we grow and learn. I find his equation a very clever and helpful Advent way of thinking: "Uh-huh" + "oh-wow" + "uh-oh" + "oh, God" = "ah-hah."

Can you name an experience that goes with each component? Listen again:

"Uh-huh" + "oh-wow" + "uh-oh" + "oh, God" = "ah-hah."

The final "Ah-hah" reflects discovery, genuine insight derived from the ways in which we process the twists and turns in our lives, unexpected intrusions into our normal ways of thinking and behaving. The equation gives God permission to steal away certain presuppositions and assumptions about how things have been and are always going to be. Even elements that seem essential may be stripped away.

Most of the time in our lives, our various universes don't tumble down all at once. There may be an occasional 9-1-1, but it's usually the falling away of small bits and pieces revealing what is essential and, yes, looking ahead to that great day when God will be all in all.

To you, my God, I lift up my soul, I trust in you;
Let me never come to shame.
Do not let my enemies laugh at me.
No one who waits for you is ever put to shame.
(Entrance Antiphon, First Sunday of Advent)

Can We Make
More Room in the Inn?

Second Sunday of Advent

Isaiah 11.1-10
Psalm 72
Romans 15.4-9
Matthew 3.1-12

I know that you've often heard the explanation of how the purple vestments of Advent and the rather austere, sometimes even penitential tone of the prayers and readings are designed to call us to repentance. In word and symbol the season critiques certain aspects of the culture, and proposes alternative ways of seeing things and of acting upon what we see.

Within this overall framework, Advent is often characterized by a certain amount of homiletic carping. I'm sure that there are pulpits in this city buzzing at this very moment about Santa showing up in the middle of October and Jesus being "the reason for the season."

For my own part, I usually try to avoid that kind of preaching: first, because people expect it and tune out immediately, and second, because I'm not sure I agree with most of it and don't think it does any good anyway. I have always tried instead to highlight the generosity, festivity, tradition and family consciousness that endure as positive characteristics of the Christmas season. I have invited people to recognize the Spirit at work in all of that, to exercise a certain discretion and balance, but to enjoy the festival of lights honouring the Light of the World to which it ultimately draws our attention.

This year, however, in looking ahead to the Advent season, I came across an article about the whole business—or busyness—of the season; both describe it accurately. Although the article is clearly negative, its robust, even in-your-face language reminded me of lines that prophets such as Isaiah or John the Baptist might have used in their own time.

> The Christmas feast, as generally celebrated, offers salvation to largely comfortable Christians by combining xenophobia with conspicuous consumption. The holidays, as we experience them, are ... a deadly aberration that eviscerates the central meaning of Christmas. Cynical commercialism dominates the season, demonizes poverty, exalts excessiveness, exploits guilt-ridden people, forces those who can least afford it into hopeless competition with the moneyed elite. The result is increasing misery for the marginalized, the poor, the lonely, the homeless, the separated, the divorced, the gay, the lesbian, the ill, the despised and dying people, for whom, arguably, God's self-disclosure in Jesus is intended. Christmas, even or especially in its "Dickensian" guise, has become a celebration of family values with a vengeance. These values are largely those of an affluent white, conservative, privileged, suburban, elite, for whom virtue lies primarily in tax cuts, reduced government, reliable alarm systems to protect our homes, a sound investment portfolio, membership in a Catholic or Protestant parish. Such critiques cannot be cavalierly dismissed. There's a kind of secular eschatology at work in our culture, which says that this is the end.[6]

Wow. Tough, isn't it? I hope you won't tune me out completely if we look at that statement, gently and conversationally, in two parts: xenophobia this week and conspicuous consumption next week.

What is xenophobia? To tell you the truth, I wasn't all that sure, so I looked it up. From a negative point of view, xenophobia is a fear of anything that is too different from you; anything that is too different from your way of being. It's reticence to get very close, for example, to Moslems, or Hindus, or Buddhists or African Americans or Asians. It can include fear of older people or teenagers, or even of cancer patients, or people with AIDS. Some men are afraid of very competent

---

[6] Nathan Mitchell, *Assembly*, December 1995.

women. In general it's a fear, however unconscious, of people with whom you are not at home. Sounds human enough, doesn't it?

As with all things human, xenophobia has a more positive side, a nesting tendency that makes us want to find or create a place where we can be comfortable and at home. Christmas brings this out in some people in very powerful ways.

I was thinking about that in terms of my own life experience. There were two years in seminary when I didn't get home for Christmas. We celebrated Christmas Midnight Mass as well as the Mass at Dawn and the Mass during the Day, after which we were welcomed into the homes of nearby Catholic families for the afternoon and evening. The host families could not have been more gracious, but it was perhaps this very graciousness that reminded us even more strongly that we weren't really at home. The family things associated with Christmas in the households with which I was so graciously included were not *our* family things. There was no Christmas Eve *tourtière*; the tree was Scotch pine, not spruce or balsam. It was cold outside, but there was not nearly enough snow on the ground for a real Christmas—at least for my tastes. Adventure and new mind-expanding (even mind-boggling) experiences are fine, but Christmas is a day to be at home.

I suspect that, for many of us, this resonates with reality. We have certain intimate personal Christmas needs. We have probably had our share of Christmas ups and downs that highlighted our awareness of those needs: a death in the family, separation or divorce, the awkward coming out of a gay cousin, a granddaughter whose hair has suddenly turned fluorescent chartreuse and has pierced her tongue …

Is xenophobia the downside of our Christmas need for comfort, even a certain psychological "peace and quiet"? There's nothing wrong with that, but perhaps we do need the prophetic voices of the season to help us make more room in the inn.

It's not a question of denouncing Christmas and the family values attached to it for so many of us. Rather, we must make sure that we recognize and respond as well to broader and deeper family connections that we recognize in faith. We are celebrating, after all, the mystery of the incarnation in which the eternal, creative Word of God takes flesh in human nature. Christmas celebrates the always-coming Christ as brother to the whole human race.

> "Bear fruit worthy of repentance," [the Baptist cries.] "Do not presume to say to yourselves, 'We have Abraham as our ancestor'; for I tell you, God is able from these stones to raise up children to Abraham." (Matthew 3.8-9)

As in everything important we need the "wisdom, understanding, counsel, might, knowledge and fear of the LORD" (Isaiah 11.2) to "welcome one another, therefore, just as Christ has welcomed you, for the glory of God" (Romans 15.7).

John the Baptist
at the Door of the Mall

Third Sunday of Advent

Isaiah 35.1-6, 10
Psalm 146
James 5.7-10
Matthew 11.2-11

"What did you go out into the wilderness to look at? A reed shaken by the wind? What then did you go out to see? Someone dressed in soft robes? Look, those who wear soft robes are in royal palaces." (Matthew 11.7-8)

It's strange how deserts aroused, and still arouse, a certain fascination. From the earliest times, Christians have imitated their Jewish forebears in going out into the desert to seek a level of reality that eluded them in ordinary society. When we walk a landscape of mirages, the senses are humbled. When we live in a land of precious little water, life's fragility arises out of the sand. Even artistic depictions of the desert usually included mounds of bones that point to spirits which have moved on. The holiness attributed to the desert relates to the holiness that it has traditionally drawn out of people. It is a forgotten place that invites us to remember the sacred. A journey to the desert is a journey to the self. The desert turns controllers into believers. There is no place to hide, and so we are found.

In *Dakota*, Kathleen Norris describes how certain people have come to love living under the winds and storms of the big open sky. They have come to prefer the treelessness and isolation, becoming "monks of the land," knowing that its loneliness is an honest reflection of the essential human loneliness. Willingly embracing the desert fosters not emptiness and despair, but stark, uncompromising realism about life and our place in the world.

John the Baptist lived in the desert. At times he hung around at places where the wilderness bordered ordinary life. He spoke vigorously about new possibilities for ordinary people and, surprisingly enough, large numbers of these folks found his teaching fascinating and compelling. It was challenging, to be sure, but had an inescapable inner truth and realism. Out to the desert went these ordinary people to see and experience a prophet, the forerunner of the kingdom of God, one who was, according to Jesus, the greatest person ever born, but whose mission was to point beyond himself to something even greater. These crowds that went out to meet him weren't looking for a "downer"—nor did they find one. However radical and challenging his message might have been to their status quo, what they experienced was an "upper." John the desert preacher was refreshingly life-giving.

Today the presence and message of John the Baptist as a living word in the liturgies of Advent suggest that we need to picture him standing at the border of the wilderness looking at us. The same word invites us to move out a bit to meet him there. If John were to wander in and wait for us at the entrance to our parking lot, or—even better—at the local shopping mall, how would we respond? What would this strident, monkish, ascetic soul have to say about how we observe the celebration of the coming of the messiah?

Last week I referred to a quote from Nathan Mitchell. Many of you commented that, for all its robust negativity, it was pretty good. I suspect you were saying that it had a stark desert realism, which Mitchell seems to be suggesting can help us look at both the positive and negative sides of our Christmas consumption.

Positively, much of the consumption around Christmas revolves around giving gifts and hospitality, both of which are clearly life-giving. We want our friends and loved ones to have something special. We want to find creative ways of contributing to their well-being. We want to share our homes and our favourite recipes with family and friends. Giving is fun. It's more blessed to give than to receive. The Bible itself says so, doesn't it? And surely Christmas is an appropriate time for all that!

It is possible, however, for all this positive Christmas goodness to be twisted and confused. While I hate to single out a specific commercial, I'm sure you've seen the one that tells people to "Give like Santa, save like Scrooge." A perfectly contented Santa, a perfectly delighted Scrooge and a perfectly decorated Christmas tree in a perfectly appointed living room serve as a perfect backdrop for a perfect mountain of gifts.

First of all, few of us live in homes like that. Few of us can afford mountains of gifts, but the commercial is subtly suggesting that we should stretch in that direction, as towards a desirable goal. I think that we need to positively consider other alternatives. Not only are they better objectively; they're also more desirable—and more fun!

Let's take the Christmas tree in the commercial as an example. When it comes right down to it, if you live in a family, would you even *want* a Christmas tree like that? Wouldn't you prefer one that has bits and pieces of Grandma's stuff, along with homemade goodies that the kids and grandkids brought home from school? Isn't it still fun to have a party to string popcorn and cranberries for garlands?

In affirming the positive wonder and beauty of the gift-giving and festivity attached to Christmas celebrations, we need to be more discerning, to plan better, and to make good choices. As a result the whole experience will be more fun and more life-giving for our families and enable us to reach out to the less fortunate in a time of special solidarity.

Let's try to imagine ourselves in a nearby shopping centre. At this time of the year, it looks like a cathedral filled with decorations and the music, language and spirit of Christmas. Is it possible to enjoy all that without spending more money than we consider appropriate, than we think we can afford, than we have? There are even opportunities to contribute to the Salvation Army or the food bank.

C.S. Lewis wrote a classic story about Exmas and Christmas. It takes place on the island of Niatrib—which is almost Britain spelled backwards. Every winter the Niatribians celebrated a festival they call Exmas. They packed their marketplaces even in dreadful weather, but as the celebrations drew near, they became pale and weary. Some missed the fun altogether because they were exhausted, or sick from overeating and drinking, or depressed from being in debt. Does that sound like any fun?

I hope that we can all enjoy the festivities of the season, but with discriminating Christian good taste. Have fun!

The Sign

Fourth Sunday of Advent

Isaiah 7.10-14
Psalm 24
Romans 1.1-7
Matthew 1.18-24

The Lord spoke to Ahaz, saying "Ask a sign of the LORD your God; let it be deep as Sheol or high as heaven." But Ahaz said, "I will not ask and I will not put the LORD to the test." (Isaiah 7.10-12)

Ahaz, who comes to life for us in the text from Isaiah, was king over the southern kingdom of a divided Israel. The northern kingdom retained the name Israel, while his southern kingdom was called Judah. The great eighth-century political crisis Ahaz was facing was a political alliance between Syria and Israel to resist Assyria's imperial expansion. The plan was to attack Judah and reduce Ahaz to a puppet ruler who would co-operate in the anti-Assyrian struggle. To protect his position Ahaz wanted to ally himself with Assyria, thus balancing the forces but pitting Judah against Israel, sister nation against sister nation.

Clearly opposed to this plan was the prophet Isaiah, who seems to have been convinced that the Syrian–Israelite alliance was doomed to fail at any rate and that there was something intrinsically destructive about Israel and Judah being in opposition. More than political considerations were at work, however. From Isaiah's point of view, only God is sovereign; only God can be trusted. Pragmatic political alliances are at best temporary expediencies and hold no potential for real security. Ahaz should remain neutral.

To intensify his prophetic message, Isaiah spoke for the Lord and invited Ahaz to ask for a sign as confirmation that his message was divinely inspired. Ahaz refused to ask, but a sign was nevertheless promised, probably involving both the birth of the child and the name assigned. The name "God is with us" confirms the truth Ahaz was implicitly denying by his political decisions. Some scholars suggest that Isaiah ironically parodies the formal announcement of the birth of a royal son who, unlike Ahaz, would carry on his dynasty in faith and right judgment. In a Christian context this clearly has had messianic overtones and is seen as ultimately fulfilled in Jesus himself.

What is it about Ahaz' situation, the quality of his personality and the prophetic challenge to him offered by Isaiah to "ask for a sign" that has such perennial value and that roots it so strongly in the Advent–Christmas spirit? Here's what I suggest.

For Ahaz to ask for a sign, for Ahaz to pray, something would have to give. It's not reverence for God, but his unwillingness to risk giving up control that keeps him from presenting himself to the Lord in faith. Everything is clearly a mess, but at least he's in charge of the mess. He's afraid: afraid to move, afraid to grow, afraid to change. Isaiah is clearly frustrated and goes out on a limb. Something in all of us is afraid to pray because if we expose ourselves to God, if we try in an act of worship to recognize God's sovereignty over us, something in us may have to give. Genuine prayer requires a certain flexibility, readiness for a sign, readiness for an invitation to grow and change, perhaps even deeply.

Isaiah is clearly exasperated and may even be stretching his own limits. Speaking for the Lord, he says, "Ask for a sign. God will prove that he's there for you. Ask God for a sign. If you want an earthquake, ask for an earthquake. God really is present and God is powerful. Ask for a bolt of lightning from the sky if you want. Ask for a sign if you don't believe that God can transform your world. God will prove himself to you."

Picture Ahaz' response. "Oh, no!" he says. At this stage he seems to get very pious and continues, "I don't play with God. I don't test God. I'm not going to ask for a sign." In fact, he asks for nothing, refusing to address God in any way.

Ahaz reflects something very deep in human nature, which we may even discover in ourselves. We've all had experience, for example, with a person who suffers from some kind of addiction or somebody who is really messed up and absolutely refuses to talk about it or to seek help, to see a doctor or a counsellor because they are afraid. If they take that kind of a step, they may have to change—and there's a certain security in the control they think they have. What if they prayed, stood before God in all their truth? Maybe someday, but not today.

Is this leaving well enough alone or leaving badly enough alone?

Think of any area in your own life that seems better left alone. The Advent scriptures have been speaking of readiness for something new, of a renewed call to holiness, to righteousness, to conversion of heart. Do any of us really want a call like that? Or are we more comfortable where we are? Yes, we're religious and faithful and pious to an extent—but let's not push this thing. Yes, there's generosity in all of us, but let's not push it.

"I'm doing quite fine, thank you, dear God. Please, not one more word out of you."

The Christian tradition sees the birth of Jesus as the ultimate sign that Ahaz is looking for, even though he cannot admit it or deal with it. Arising out of his own race and family is "God-with-us." Yes, this stretches Isaiah's original direction, but the Advent liturgy sees Isaiah's ultimate goal reached in Jesus. He is God's image and likeness restored, God-with-us, the great sign of what we, even in the midst of our personal and political struggles, are invited to be and become.

In spite of the fact that we're not sure that we're ready for the sign, in spite of the fact that calls to holiness and righteousness sound a little scary, in spite of the fact that a certain distance from God is more comfortable than the prospect of transformation, the sign is given.

Once more the story is told, the invitation offered. Once more the sign is given to which we, ready or not, respond, "Amen."

Hail, Joseph

Christmas Eve (Vigil of Christmas)

Isaiah 62.1-5
Psalm 89
Acts 13.16-17, 22-25
Matthew 1.1-25

There is such an extraordinary contrast between the Ahaz of the Fourth Sunday of Advent and the gospel figure of Joseph.

Today's is the same gospel text featuring Joseph that we heard on Sunday, but this time it includes the full genealogy of Jesus. The names roll along with great dignity and formality. Especially because I focused only on the text from Isaiah last Sunday, I can't resist giving Joseph his due: maybe not equal time, but some quality time just the same.

Speaking of genealogies, did you ever notice that Genesis 2.4 reads as follows? "Such is the story [literally, the genealogy] of the heavens and the earth at their creation." Matthew's new genesis, new beginnings, uses that kind of language. To regard his list as an archival document would be to misunderstand its form and to miss it as a way of understanding and recapitulating ancient events and prophecies, of interpreting events rather than just talking about them.

Notice that there are three sets of 14 generations: from Abraham to David, from David to the deportation to Babylon, and from the deportation to Babylon to the Messiah. We begin with our common father in faith, move through the ideal king to the age of the great prophets to the coming of the Messiah who, as the gospel unfolds, will sum up the entire story in himself.

Scholars also note that beyond presenting a theology of history, the genealogy has cosmic overtones. Calculated as six groups of seven (the number of days in a week), the coming of the Messiah initiates a seventh week, bringing all creation to Sabbath fullness.

In the birth of Jesus, both history and cosmology are renewed from within. In Jesus, whose name means "one who saves his people from their sins," and Emmanuel, which means "God is with us," there is clearly a fresh start.

In all of this it is Joseph who, responsive to the prophetic voice of an angel, facilitates God's will. Although not the father of the Messiah, Joseph is ready to stand "in God's place." In sharp contrast with a cynical Ahaz to whom Emmanuel is initially promised, stands Joseph, open and trusting. For him there are no political considerations, no need for pretense or posturing, only a desire to be righteous under God and under God's law. Unlike Ahaz, Joseph is clearly at God's disposition, ready to welcome "the sign."

Most of us are quite used to praying the "Hail Mary." Fewer of us are used to "Hail Joseph." As we prepare for the Christmas feast and in the spirit of Matthew's mystical genealogy, I'd like to share with you the following prayer, which is my own adaptation of a prayer to Saint Joseph composed in French by Father Olier in the early 17th century. It just seems to fit with today's vigil liturgy.

Hail, Joseph, image of the Eternal Father;
Hail, Joseph, guardian of the Eternal Son;
Hail, Joseph, temple of the Eternal Spirit;
Hail, Joseph, beloved of the Trinity.

Hail, Joseph, spouse and companion of the Mother of God.
Hail, Joseph, friend of angels.

Hail, Joseph, believer in miracles.
Hail, Joseph, follower of dreams.

Hail, Joseph, lover of simplicity.
Hail, Joseph, exemplar of righteousness;

Hail, Joseph, model of meekness and patience;
Hail, Joseph, model of humility and obedience.

Blessed are the eyes that have seen what you saw.
Blessed are the ears that have heard what you heard.
Blessed are the arms that have embraced what you embraced.

Blessed is the lap that has held what you held.
Blessed is the heart that has loved what you loved.

Blessed is the Father who chose you;
Blessed is the Son who loved you;
Blessed is the Spirit who sanctified you.

Blessed is Mary, your spouse, who honoured and loved you.
Blessed is the angel who guarded and led you.
And blessed be forever all who remember and honour you.
Amen.

Prayer to St. Joseph
Father Jean-Jacques Olier, 1608–1657
Founder of St. Sulpice

Light with a Capital "L"

Christmas: Mass during the Night

Isaiah 9.2-4, 6-7
Psalm 96
Titus 2.11-14
Luke 2.1-16

The people who walked in darkness
have seen a great light;
those who lived in a land of deep darkness—
on them a light has shined. (Isaiah 9.2)

The glory of the Lord shone around them, and they were
terrified. (Luke 2.9)

As many of you may know, I like to jump on the train and go to
New York City for a few days after New Year's. Along with going to
good sales and good theatre, I sometimes even get to go to church like
a normal person. There's a church just off Times Square that celebrates
Twelfth Night, the Feast of Epiphany, on January 6 in grand style.

Last year, in the midst of my shopping, I picked up a flyer from a
large mid-town Protestant church. It included a former pastor's reflections on his ministry at that church in 1972. Some of us remember the
Christmas bombings of Vietnam that year. For his part, the minister
recalled how, on that particular Christmas Eve, the weather was typical
for New York in December: cold, wet and all around miserable. He
recalled how, at that particular Christmas Eve service, even more
people than usual poured into the church from the soggy streets. They
squeezed into the pews, lined the walls and sat on the floor. Most of
them were strangers to him, strangers of all races and descriptions.
Some, he was sure, were agnostics or atheists, men and women who
would not set foot in a church on a bet. Others, he was sure, were
Jews and Moslems, even Buddhist and Hindus.

Since it was his first year at this church and nobody had warned him of the possibility of such a gathering, he found his initial contact with the congregation a bit disconcerting. "Who are these people?" he asked himself. "What are they doing here?—out of nowhere! Why this troubled, war-torn night—why this Christmas night?"

Then it dawned on him—why not? He simply took a deep breath and let the service unfold.

The special music may have had something to do with the crowd; perhaps it was the wonderful story, maybe just the warm place. The service progressed, and the time came for the lighting of candles. That this would be a candlelight celebration had been advertised on the church's outdoor notice board for weeks. As the ritual progressed, the pastor sensed that everyone seemed to need to be a part of that. They didn't all sing the hymns and carols, but they all wanted to light a candle. They needed to have a flame in their hands on that cold, wet Christmas Eve, a flame that demanded a certain amount of care and attention. Watching them, he realized it no longer mattered who they were. The strangers were welcome. They were friends. Mysteriously, in mid-town Manhattan, they were at home ... in this "little town of Bethlehem."

> ... yet in thy dark streets shineth
> the everlasting light.
> The hopes and fears of all the years
> are met in thee tonight.

There's nothing denominational or sectarian about lighting candles. You surely don't have to buy into any particular religious tradition to understand the foundational meaning underlying the lighting of candles or even our more basic rituals such as sharing broken bread and a common cup, or bathing in water, or being anointed with oil.

These hundreds of burning lights in hundreds of human hands brought this young minister, on this particular Christmas Eve, a larger sense of who he was and what he was about than he had previously imagined. In the spirit of Jesus himself, he was hosting an event, a service of proclamation and prayer that reflected the gospel's own call to universality. Rather than being stunned or distracted by this large and diverse assembly, he took a breath (of the Spirit?) and decided to enjoy the experience as a signal of divine potential for healing and reconciliation in the world, which Jesus himself represents.

Here in our own parish, this Christmas Eve assembly is probably more diverse than it is on any other occasion. Peace be with you, men, women and children. Be of good will. Be of good cheer. Welcome to Bethlehem. Did you know that the name Bethlehem means "house of bread"? Welcome to the lighting of candles and the breaking of bread.

Of course we recognize that there's more to the reign of God than the lighting of candles and the breaking of bread, but it's a start. Sins are hard to forgive, wounds are hard to heal, wars are hard to stop, opinions are hard to change, prejudice is hard to overcome, but lighting candles and breaking bread are a start.

"Jesus Christ is the light of the world." "Jesus Christ is the bread of life." "Glory to God in the highest."

Christmas faithfully comes back every year to stir up the ashes and embers of our dreams of peace and good will for all people. Christmas presents a feast of lights centring on Jesus himself as a light with a capital "L." Bethlehem presents a house of bread calling all the world to holy communion.

We gather here at midnight to affirm the Eternal Word made Flesh; Jesus Christ the Light of the World; the Way, the Truth and the Life. We light the candle, we sing the hymns, we hear the story, we share the bread and cup, so that, enlightened and nourished, we can serve peace and goodwill as members of the Body of Christ, whose memory we celebrate and whose name we bear.

> All ye, beneath life's crushing load,
> whose forms are bending low,
> who toil along the climbing way
> with painful steps and slow,
> Look now, for glad and golden hours
> come swiftly on the wing;
> O rest beside the weary road
> and hear the angels sing.

"It Came upon a Midnight Clear," v.3
Edmund H. Sears
1810–1876

Universal Presence

Christmas Day

Isaiah 52.7-10
Psalm 98
Hebrews 1.1-6
John 1.1-18

In these last days [God] has spoken to us by a Son, whom he appointed heir of all things, through whom he also created the worlds. He is the reflection of God's glory and the exact imprint of God's very being, and he sustains all things by his powerful word. (Hebrews 1.2-3)

We have seen his glory, the glory as of a father's only son, full of grace and truth. (John 1.14)

These wonderful texts for Christmas Day are the climax, the summit, of the Christmas liturgy. In the earliest tradition of the celebration of Christmas in Rome, this was the Christmas Mass. These texts were proclaimed—not the familiar stories of Mary and Joseph, singing angels, bustling shepherds, a moving star and travelling sages, but a profound statement of theology.

God's word has always been creative and re-creative of this world and all worlds. The eternal Word pre-exists the historical Jesus, but in him is fully expressive. The eternal Word speaks everywhere, but in him speaks "grace upon grace": the Way, the Truth and the Life. If Christians want to know what love is, we look at Jesus; if we want to know what power is, we look at Jesus; if we want to know what mercy is, we look at Jesus; if we want to know what God looks like and what God wills for us, we look at Jesus. In Jesus we find the fullness of revelation, but even the word "fullness" implies an affirmation that we discover and acknowledge God and God's presence elsewhere as well: in fact, in the whole created world.

Precisely because the incarnation is understood as the summit of the unfolding of God's presence, it is only logical that our spiritual and religious tradition invites us to discover God everywhere else. God is more than the world, but God is profoundly present in the world, not only in special historical moments, but everywhere and always. God is always here and now, waiting to be discovered.

In the famous story of the call of Moses, this truth is clearly revealed. When Moses, trying to get a handle on the Almighty, asks God, "What is your name?" God's response in the original Hebrew is *ehyeh asher ehyeh*, most commonly translated as "I am who I am."

The Hebrew word *ehyeh* means not just I AM in the sense that "I exist." The word is more alive than that. It means I AM REAL. I AM ALIVE. I AM HERE. I AM PRESENT. God's holy name suggests a universal active presence in a universal now. Didn't many of us learn in catechism that God is everywhere; that God is, always was, and always will be? Think of it! Isn't it wonderful to think of God's intimacy and accessibility in that way? God is right here and right now. God's holy name itself, God's revealed name points not to a faraway, transcendent, heavenly deity, but to an intimate, immanent, earthly presence that is immediate and accessible to all. God's name even suggests that the divine presence is an *unavoidable* aspect of every life experience. The divine name even has overtones of incarnation. It leans towards God's taking flesh in the now of human lives, which we celebrate in this wonderful feast.

Chief Seattle (1854), who comes out of a tradition that predates the coming of Christianity to North America, is clearly in harmony with this kind of theological reflection:

> You must teach your children that the ground beneath their feet is the ashes of our grand fathers ... the earth is our mother. Whatever befalls the earth, befalls her children. This we know. The earth does not belong to humans; humans belong to the earth ... All things are connected like the blood which unites a family. We humans did not weave the web of life, we are merely a strand in something bigger than ourselves.

In similar fashion, Psalm 29 recognizes the voice of God in the awesome power of a storm moving in from the sea.

The voice of the LORD is over the waters;
The God of glory thunders,
The LORD, over mighty waters ...
The voice of the LORD breaks the cedars ...
The voice of the LORD flashes forth flames of fire.
The voice of the LORD shakes the wilderness ...
The voice of the LORD causes the oaks to whirl. (Psalm 29.3-9)

I received a card from a friend with the following reflection
written by that famous author, "Anonymous":

I am the wind that breathes upon the sea,
I am the wave on the ocean,
I am the murmur of leaves rustling,
I am the rays of the sun,
I am the beam of the moon and stars,
I am the power of trees growing,
I am the bud breaking into blossom,

I am the movement of the salmon swimming,
I am the courage of the wild boar fighting,
I am the speed of the stag running,

I am the strength of the ox pulling the plough,
I am the size of the mighty oaks,
And I am the hope and dreams of people,
who, looking to the future,
praise my beauty and grace.

Although it probably wasn't stressed a whole lot, many of us
learned that basic theology as children in the questions and answers of
our catechism. "Where is God? God is everywhere." But—we add—
especially in Jesus.

O little town of Bethlehem,
How still we see thee lie;
Above thy deep and dreamless sleep
The silent stars go by.
Yet in thy dark streets shineth
the everlasting Light;

The hopes and fears of all the years
Are met in thee tonight.

Of the Father's love begotten, e're the worlds began to be ...

And heav'n and nature sing;
And heav'n and nature sing;
And heav'n, and heaven and nature sing.

Listening to Joseph's Angel

Feast of the Holy Family

Sirach 3.2-6, 12-14
Psalm 128
Colossians 3.12-21
Matthew 2.13-15, 19-23

The infancy narratives of Matthew's gospel invite us to enter into the mystery of Emmanuel, God-with-us. If we take up Joseph's perspective, we discover that we are invited to experience expectation, dreams, visions and angelic visitations. And yet, awkwardly enough today, on the Feast of the Holy Family, with him we confront the mystery of evil head on.

Throughout Matthew's Christmas story, however poetically expressed, nothing is clearer than the humanity of Jesus and the human reality of the world into which he is born. God discloses his being in Jesus' humanity. Jesus is Emmanuel, God-with-us. If this experience is to be genuine or authentic, he must become a survivor who mysteriously escapes catastrophe, a brother to the poor and to refugees, a person who lives on the edge of society.

Christmas has a dark side. Emmanuel has a dark side, and no one knows that as well as Joseph. God-with-us shares the experience of the children of Auschwitz, of the children of Hiroshima and of disadvantaged children of every continent and island of every age. In our own schools he shares the life of such children whom we may even be able to name—not far from the security and family feeling of which we are proud in this beautiful place and community.

The Christmas story does not shield us from dealing with a world out of order but, rather, thrusts us into its midst. Human experience is full of contradictions. In fact, the universal experience of suffering, evil and misfortune is perhaps more evident than the reality of universal love. While this is not a cheerful thought for the Christmas season, for many people, Christians among them, it is not just a thought, but a lived experience. It's part of the history of our larger human family.

Most of us have experienced a certain amount of turmoil and trouble in the midst of so much goodness and beauty to enjoy in our lives. The experience of so many others, however, is quite different. In the midst of so much turmoil and trouble, there is potential for beauty and goodness. Joseph lived like that, but along with so many others, he had an angel at his side saying: "Keep on believing. Go here for now. Go there for now. But keep on believing."

If you have seen *Life Is Beautiful,* you will know that it's a fantastic film about a Jewish father and son who, separated from their wife and mother, are prisoners of the Nazis. The father's solution is to make it a game, to laugh and sing his way through it, hoping against hope to survive.

Some seminarians I know went to El Salvador, where they had a life-changing experience. Amazingly, the storms of history and the storms of nature combined could not crush the people. Isn't it surprising that there is often more hope, joy and energy among oppressed peoples than among their grim and driven oppressors?

Most of us have not had experiences like that, but I'd like to suggest that there are Christmas angels at work among us just the same. Let me name a few of them.

There's the angel of indignation. The fact that people are indignant about all kinds of life and justice issues such as the globalization of the economy, the pollution of our environment, inadequate funding for AIDS research, the issues of abortion and capital punishment and so many other issues that warrant the attention of society, signals enduring energy for life and goodness, the presence of an angel. Proactive movements, as well as post-decision protests are signs of hope and new possibilities. Especially when apparent or temporary defeat fails to stifle hope in people of good will, we can detect the presence of the same angel who told Joseph to take the child and his mother to Egypt and wait for another chance, another opportunity, another call. Perhaps not today, but another chance will come.

There's the angel of conversion. The genuine openness that we find in so many people to grow and to change is itself a wonder. The story is told, for example, of two boys who got into a fight many years ago. One was rich, lived in a fine house and had the best of food. The other boy was poor, his clothes were ragged and he had little to eat. Not surprisingly, the rich boy won the fight. The poor boy complained: "The only reason you won is that you're rich and fat. I'm poor and skinny." This fight remained a part of the rich boy's memory bank for the rest of his life. The rich kid was Albert Schweitzer, musician and Bach specialist, theologian, medical doctor and missionary in Africa, Nobel laureate, stubborn defender of the dignity of human persons, one of the real giants of the 20th century.

There's the angel of quiet personal commitment. In spite of and even because of headlines, there continue to be people who are committed to being "family people" in ways that range from the global to the interpersonal. We honour our parents; we respect our history and our heritage. We drive our neighbour to her eye appointment; we are blood donors; we take our turn delivering food to the needy; we are members of Amnesty International; we run for office; we teach in the seminary. We listen to Joseph's angel and live in hope.

A Christmas card I saved from last year contains good advice for Christmas, or anytime for that matter. It's by "Anonymous"—the same name as Joseph's angel!

This Christmas

Mend a quarrel.
Seek out a forgotten friend.
Write a love letter.
Share some treasure.
Give a soft answer.
Encourage youth.
Keep a promise.
Find the time.
Forgive an enemy.
Listen.
Apologize if you were wrong.
Think first of someone else.
Be kind and gentle.
Laugh a little.
Laugh a little more.

Express your gratitude.
Gladden the heart of a child.
Take pleasure in the beauty and wonder of the earth.
Speak it again.
Speak it still once again. Speak your love.

Even if you don't feel like it,
Do it anyway.

To the extent that we maintain this kind of spirit in ways great and small, whether with our own families or with the family of nations, is the extent to which we are alive in Christ and listening to Joseph's angel.

A Real Workout

Solemnity of Mary, the Mother of God

Numbers 6.22–27
Psalm 67
Galatians 4.4–7
Luke 2. 16–21

Anyone who has ever lived with a person whose first language is different from their own will be especially conscious of the subtleties of words. Words do more than just express thoughts or concepts. They are multi-dimensional.

In various contexts, the same simple word can have any number of different meanings, sometimes clearly related, sometimes less so. To say, for example, that something is "cool" could mean any number of things. The weather is cool; her attitude towards me is cool; that ring in his nose is cool. Try finding a single word in another language that would translate all three of the above "cools."

For these reasons, the world of biblical translation is so complex and interesting and so obviously important for a proper understanding of the content and spirit of the ancient texts. Today's gospel offers an excellent example of this. Let's look carefully at one verse: "Mary treasured all these words and pondered them in her heart." This is a translation into English from the Greek, which may itself be a translation from Aramaic.

"Mary treasured all these words." We might think this would mean to esteem them highly, value them, prize them. "To ponder them in the heart" would be to think about them with a certain amount of affectivity, a certain amount of emotion. Either way it would be mental-spiritual work.

One of the altar servers got here a little early last night and I read this same verse to her and asked her what she thought it meant. Just as I suspected, she thought that Mary was thinking very hard. As we talked a bit more, she suggested that Mary may have been praying. We might say she was meditating, but the language of prayer and meditation doesn't capture the vigour of the original any better than deep thinking, although it is potentially more affective and emotional.

I'm not an expert in the ancient languages, but because of my ongoing curiosity about such things, I'm discovering that "spiritual" activities are far more "physical" in these languages than in ours. Take "treasure and ponder," for example. I read that you don't treasure something in your mind; you grasp it and hold it and protect it with your hands. When you ponder something, you roll it around, you turn it over and over so you can come into contact with every aspect, feel every texture, see every colour. Treasuring and pondering is a real workout! It leaves you breathless.

The gospel portrays Mary with the shepherds gathered around. Either she or Joseph must be holding the child Jesus. In her prayer, she grasps what is happening to them, she seizes the moment, she rolls the experience around in her heart, in her maternal bosom. The prayer of treasuring, pondering, holding and feeling actively engages the whole person of a woman like Mary who has just given birth. She must have been out of breath! Mary was fully engaged in the process of being a person, of understanding that and living it to the full.

Before I went to Israel on sabbatical a few years ago, I had the occasion to watch a documentary on ordinary life in the Holy Land. I was particularly struck by the sight of a woman walking down a narrow street with a large clay jar balancing on her head. As another woman greeted her and she smiled it was evident that she didn't have all her teeth. I wondered if that's what Mary looked like. I wonder if she didn't look more like that woman than our traditional Christian depictions of her in iconography or statuary.

I sometimes think that even our liturgical tradition can do a disservice to the real life experience of Mary, as it does to Jesus'. We struggle with the real humanity of Jesus; I have a feeling we do the same with Mary. We speak today, for example, of the Solemnity of Mary the Mother of God. We celebrate the Immaculate Conception and the Assumption of the Blessed Virgin Mary into heaven. All these feasts and designations try to grasp and celebrate some aspect of her absolutely unique role in God's plan, but, in the meantime, we separate her from the rest of us. It is remarkable how, despite all that, Christian people, especially suffering and struggling people, have turned to her throughout the ages as a friend and advocate who will understand them.

Think for example of the prayer "Hail, Holy Queen," which some of us learned as children. Beneath its rather florid language lies a deep sense of humanity and the confidence that Mary knows what this humanity is all about.

> Hail Holy Queen, mother of mercy,
> our life, our sweetness and our hope.
> To thee do we cry, poor banished children of Eve.
> To thee do we send up our sighs,
> mourning and weeping in this valley of tears.
> Turn then, most gracious advocate, thine eyes of mercy towards us
> and, after this our exile,
> show us the blessed fruit of thy womb, Jesus.
> O clement, O loving, O sweet Virgin Mary.

That prayer could only have come from a struggling human soul that was seeking to connect with Mary's own soul and Mary's own experience. "Show us the blessed fruit of thy womb, Jesus"—the Jesus whom you treasured and pondered, whom you held in your lap as an infant and who was placed in your lap, bruised and bloodied in death. "*Ave Maria. Ave Pietà.*"

> When the fullness of time had come, God sent his son, born of a woman, born under the law, in order to redeem those who were under the law, so that we might receive adoption as children. And because you are children, God has sent the Spirit of his Son into our hearts, crying, "Abba! Father!" (Galatians 4.4-6)

How wonderfully the text from Galatians relates to what I've been trying to say. This is the New Testament's first reference to the woman we know as Mary, clearly one of us, sharing the human condition, learning to pray, being filled with the Spirit to treasure and ponder life's wonders. At the beginning of another New Year, we would all do well to invoke her protection as we pray, as we prayerfully roll around and massage our own unique opportunities to live with courage, integrity and grace.

Imagine Mary herself giving us today's New Year's blessing from the Book of Numbers:

> The Lord bless you and keep you;
> The Lord make his face to shine upon you
> and be gracious to you;
> The Lord lift up his countenance upon you,
> And give you peace.

A Rusty Licence Plate
Named Trust

Epiphany

Isaiah 60.1-6
Psalm 72
Ephesians 3.2-3a, 5-6
Matthew 2.1-12

I doubt that we would associate the word "crisis" with the Feast of the Epiphany, but crisis it is.

At its root, the word "crisis" means "turning point." In an acute illness, for example, a moment of crisis occurs when the patient's condition will deteriorate or improve. If the patient gets through this stage, she'll be fine, otherwise, it's all over. History has similar moments of crisis where decisions have to be made from which there will be no turning back. Perhaps in your personal life you can look back and point to such moments in your marriage, or in the life of your family.

Epiphany is crisis. Epiphany manifests the presence of God, a call to attention, a moment of decision. The wise men detect a new star, and it's moving: there's a crisis. They have to make a decision. When Herod realizes just what's up, there's a crisis. He has to make a decision.

Thornton Wilder, the famous American playwright, commented once about his own experience of growth and evolution in maturity and faith. "Maturity," he said, "means accepting crisis as the normal state of man and enjoying it, being inspired by it. Without tension, we'd still be in the treetops."

I remember hearing a story about a minister who was sitting in his car parked just in front of the hospital. He was trying to brace himself to get out and face the comatose victim of a tragic accident and his family ... or maybe, he thought, I should just let the pastoral care department look after it. (I can identify with the experience and

57

with the temptation.) Suddenly another car slowly drove by; its licence plate bore the one word he needed to hear: "TRUST."

A licence plate named "trust." He was stunned.

What do you call a moment like that? he asked himself. A word from God, an angel, or a goofy coincidence? He was ready to admit that it could have been any of the above, but he chose to call it an epiphany. For him, it was a manifestation. He was being called to grow and to change, to come down out of the treetops, to stand on two feet and to step forward. The word "trust" came to him as an invitation, a commandment, a manifestation of God's will. He got out of his car and went ahead to the emergency ward, confident that he was not alone. It was as if the star were guiding him.

The minister later found out that the driver of the other car was a parishioner of his, the assistant manager of the local bank and "trust" company who had simply slowed down to wave when he recognized his pastor. Eventually, when its time ran out, his parishioner gave him the old licence plate which, rusted edges and all, he still has on his bookshelf.

The star of Bethlehem and the licence plate named "trust" are examples of calls to movement, sparks of energy set off when crisis and readiness for hope come together. These two partners, the crisis itself and a readiness to move forward in faith, are at work. An attitude of readiness and preparation, openness to life, personal discipline and prayer made both the minister and the magi ready to embrace their crises, to follow their stars, however scary the direction in which they were being led.

Whatever supernovae, comets, or astrological conjunctions of Jupiter and Saturn may have occurred around the time of Jesus' birth, the meaning of the star goes beyond any such phenomena. The star is more like a licence plate called "trust" than a comet. A new star is a divine invitation to think differently and to be ready to move forward. It functions like the pillar of fire by night and the pillar of cloud by day that guided the Israelites through the wilderness. The star is part of the symbolic texture of the Christmas story, reminding readers of earlier stories of salvation, and suggesting links and connections to their own experience, to what is going on in their own lives. Licence plates inviting us to trust and other potential turning points, potential crises and invitations call us to participate in God's eternal and ongoing plan to move ahead for the life of the world.

Herod, for his part, could not even brace himself to look up at the star. He had fought his way to the top by whatever means he could and, with the help of the Romans, managed to cling to his throne for 33 years—no mean feat. Although he was known to have committed many ruthless acts, he had monumental accomplishments to his credit. In fact, visitors to the Holy Land encounter Herod everywhere they go. As one is guided about from south to north, viewing Masada, the Herodium, ancient portions of the temple platform in Jerusalem, to Caesarea, all the way to Caesarea Philippi one finds remains of Herod's phenomenal building activity. Herod lived in such a way that he could never admit to crisis, to the possibility of a real turning point. His thinking was one-directional. The coming of the magi and their story about a star was not an invitation to be heard and interpreted, but a problem to be solved. Herod was his own star.

Some of us will have the chance to see this story enacted in pageant form at a local elementary school. In a pageant I saw not long ago, one of the children, carrying a big stick that sported a glittering Styrofoam star at one end and ribbons hanging down, was leading the parade away from a grisly looking Herod and his courtiers to Mary, Joseph and somebody's baby sister who was Jesus for a day. Bathrobes and cardboard crowns abounded.

I sometimes wonder what is going through the minds of the audience and the child actors in such performances. What inklings of incongruity and irony they must all feel while watching such an awesome and terrifying story being played out in a school gym! Yet the relative innocence and youthful awe of the children also make the themes of searching hope against conniving evil, of acts of humble worship outwitting worldly power, seem strangely possible.

This year I'm going to picture a rusty licence plate named "trust" hanging amidst the ribbons beneath their glittering star. I'm going to try to realize once again that there are moving stars in my sky. Be on the lookout. You may see one yourself.

Who Are You? What Do You Want? Where Do You Think That Will Get You?

Baptism of the Lord

Isaiah 42.1-4,6-7
Psalm 29
Acts 10.34-38
Matthew 3.13-17

Then Jesus came from Galilee to John at the Jordan, to be baptized by him. John would have prevented him, saying, "I need to be baptized by you, and do you come to me?" But Jesus answered him, "Let it be so now; for it is proper for us in this way to fulfill all righteousness." Then he consented. (Matthew 3.13-15)

Pheme Perkins, Professor of Theology and New Testament at Boston College, makes a suggestion that I've never seen before in her commentary on this text.[7] She suggests that, in Matthew's gospel, the dialogue between John and Jesus before his baptism reflects the practice of questioning candidates before baptism. She suggests that the liturgical tradition of questioning was already in place in Matthew's community at the time of the writing of the gospel. She notes that Matthew's gospel has also handed down the liturgical formula for baptism, "in the name of the Father and of the Son and of the Holy Spirit." It, too, reflects the practice of the ancient church. In preparation, as it were, for this "sacramental event," John and Jesus were

---

    7   Pheme Perkins, *Epiphany, Proclamation 5, Series A* , (Philadelphia: Fortress, 1992), p. 15.

engaged in a process of discernment around issues of identity and sense of purpose and direction.

We're all quite familiar with the baptismal promises, which we renew during the Easter Season and again on this feast (Do you reject sin? … Do you believe in God? …). Another equally important set of questions is posed much earlier, when people are formally accepted as candidates for baptism in the *Rite of Becoming a Catechumen*.

Who are you?
What do you want?
Where do you think that will get you?

At the very beginning of the rite, the assembly meets prospective candidates at the doors of the church and ask these questions. Perkins seems to be suggesting that John and Jesus are asking similar kinds of basic questions—questions so basic that we presume we have answers for them. If I'd asked you those questions as you approached the church doors this morning, you probably would have been puzzled. But if I had, how would you have answered?

"Who are you?" Would you answer: "I'm a retired civil servant"; "I'm a single mom"; "I'm a teacher"; "I'm Mary Ann"?

"What do you want?" Would you answer: "A word of inspiration"? "Grace"? "Holy communion"? "An hour to myself"?

"Where do you think that will get you?" Would you answer: "Through another week"? "Peace of mind"? "To heaven when I die"?

Of course, there are no right or wrong answers to these profound and perennial questions, but here's how our liturgical tradition proposes they should be answered.

"Who are you?" "John." In other words: "Here I am." The question is not about role, occupation or state in life. It's not about what a person does, but about who the person is. It's about the foundational uniqueness and dignity of every person. The rite expects the person to have a good sense of self with the kind of courage and integrity that it takes to present one's self to the community with confidence.

"What do you want?" "Faith." In other words: I know that I can never be absolutely sure of myself. I know that I'll never have all the answers and that I can't manage the world or create happiness or fulfillment for myself. I have to learn how to believe in and to trust myself, others and God. I want to be able to let go and live. I'm coming to realize that this is what being human is all about.

"Where will that get you?" "Eternal life." In other words, I know people who are pretty sour and grumpy most of the time. Some even have a hard time getting up in the morning to face the day. I can't imagine that they want to live forever, but I do. My faith makes life a wonderful adventure and I want it to go on forever.

We probably don't think of our religion in such simple categories. They are, however, the foundational personal and spiritual questions and answers upon which everything else stands.

John the Baptist, in his own time, finds it very difficult to imagine that the Messiah would be dealing with life at this level, that he would be engaged in this kind of discernment. He should be above all that. Jesus rejects John's protest that his baptism is not for him. Instead of making distinctions about their respective roles, Jesus places them both under God's plan: "Let it be so now; for it is proper for us in this way to fulfill all righteousness." These are Jesus' first words in the gospel: a "let it be," an "Amen" to his own life as an adventure of trust: trust in God and in the ultimate fulfillment of God's righteousness, even in the midst of life's tensions and ambiguities. Jesus dissociates himself from John's sure and fiery rhetoric that we heard during Advent. He looks more like an ordinary human who humbly and voluntarily associates himself with the people. He stands in solidarity with the poor, the sinful, the outcasts who are presenting themselves to John for his baptism. That Jesus submits himself to a penitential baptism is consistent with Emmanuel—God-with-us, the name given to him by the angel in Joseph's dream, which is so important to the whole gospel. "To fulfill all righteousness" suggests a willingness to be in motion, to be counted with limited, even sinful, human beings who find within themselves a desire to move towards God. "To fulfill righteousness" is to be involved in an ongoing process of questioning, discernment and conversion. In standing before John, Jesus associates himself with this process. There Jesus affirms his own sense of himself and of his mysterious, unfolding destiny.

In Jesus' experience of being baptized, God's own call confirms the rightness of his decision. As he rises out of the water, the Spirit of

God and a voice from heaven confirm the beginnings of the new creation and the new passage from slavery to freedom that his life and death will bring about.

> And when Jesus had been baptized, just as he came up from the water, suddenly the heavens were opened for him and he saw the Spirit of God descending like a dove and alighting on him. And a voice from heaven said, "This is my Son, the Beloved, with whom I am well pleased." (Matthew 3.16-17)

Christians have often been tempted to the heresy towards which John was leaning. They have wanted to bypass Christ's humanity in favour of an exalted divine Son of God. They have needed to explain away the baptism of Jesus. They have found it hard to believe that Jesus struggled with all the personal and psychological problems of the rest of humanity and could authentically enter into the experience of such a baptism. If he didn't have these experiences, however, how could we possibly be expected to "follow him"? If he didn't have these experiences, he would not have saved us from within. He would not have been true to who he was, true to his name, Emmanuel.

> Who are you?
> What do you want?
> Where will that get you?

A fourth and final question is posed to the candidates in the Rite of Becoming a Catechumen: "Are you ready to move ahead and to follow Christ?" This time, however, the question is clearly focused in the prologue to the rite. Let's use it this morning and move right into the renewal of our own baptism in Christ.

> God gives light to everyone who comes into this world; though unseen, God reveals himself through the works of his hand, so that all people may learn to give thanks to their Creator.

> You have followed God's light and the way of the Gospel lies open to you. Set your feet firmly on the path and acknowledge the living God, who truly speaks to everyone. Walk in the light of Christ and learn to trust in his wisdom. Commit your

lives daily to his care, so that you may come to believe in him with all your heart.

This is the way of faith along which Christ will lead you in love towards eternal life. Are you prepared to make your journey through life under the guidance of Christ?
I am.

And so: Do you reject sin, so as to live in the freedom of God's children?
I do.

Do you reject the glamour of evil and refuse to be mastered by sin?
I do.

Do you reject Satan, father of sin and prince of darkness?
I do.

Do you believe in God, the Father almighty, creator of heaven and earth?
I do.

Do you believe in Jesus Christ, who was born of the Virgin Mary, was crucified, died and was buried, rose from the dead and is now seated at the right hand of the Father?
I do.

Do you believe in the Holy Spirit, the holy catholic Church, the communion of saints, the forgiveness of sins, the resurrection of the body and life everlasting?
I do.

God, the all-powerful Father of our Lord Jesus Christ, has given us a new birth by water and the Holy Spirit and forgiven all our sins. May he also keep us faithful to our Lord Jesus Christ forever and ever.

Amen.[8]

---

[8] *Rite of Christian Initiation of Adults,* Ottawa: Canadian Conference of Catholic Bishops, 1987.

Behold the Lamb of God

Second Sunday in Ordinary Time

Isaiah 49.3, 5-6
Psalm 40
1 Corinthians 1.1-3
John 1.29-34

John the Baptist presents Jesus to the crowds and proclaims: "Here is the lamb of God who takes away the sin of the world."

In just a few moments, you will hear the same words addressed to you: "This is the lamb of God who takes away the sins of the world. Happy are we who are called to this table," and as the eucharistic bread is being broken and the eucharistic wine is being poured out into cups for communion, we will all be singing, "Lamb of God, you take away the sins of the world, have mercy on us. Grant us peace."

Only in John's gospel is the title "Lamb of God" applied to Jesus; it appears 29 times in the mystical Book of Revelation. Let's probe and ponder that rich image and its implications for our lives.

The image of Jesus as Lamb of God gathers into itself various layers of ancient liturgical history and practice. It's the language of sacrifice.

You'll remember how, after the second time Moses came down from the mountain with the tablets of the law, a lamb was slaughtered and sacrificed on an altar the Israelites had built. The blood of the lamb was poured out on the altar and sprinkled on the people as a covenant sealing. The people entered into communion with God through the blood of the lamb whose flesh was shared in a feast. Whatever their differences, they were blood brothers and sisters. They were one family under God. The altar was their family table; their sharing of food was covenant bonding. Jesus himself is the lamb of the new covenant.

It's also important to remember that Abraham offered a ram, which substituted in the sacrifice for Isaac, his son. In the story of Jesus and God, his Father, no angel holds back the proceedings. There is no substitute. Jesus himself is the lamb of sacrifice.

At the time of John the Baptist and Jesus, the blood of Passover lambs was poured out in the temple, which was built on the very spot associated with the intended sacrifice of Isaac. According to John's gospel, the crucifixion of Jesus, the Lamb of God, was carried out on the Day of Preparation, the very day when these Passover lambs were being slaughtered. The eucharistic–sacrificial associations are very rich indeed!

The Qumran community associated with the Dead Sea Scrolls had another set of expectations to which John may also have been referring. In light of Israel's nomadic past, it has been suggested that John may have been thinking of the ram walking before the flock, overcoming obstacles to the pregnant ewes. The sheep had ways of shepherding their own. The ascetical John may have dreamed about the "ram of God," a warlike Messiah figure, who would rescue and save his flock from danger and oppression. In his subsequent life and teaching, Jesus clearly rejected this point of view, which may have disappointed John. As the liturgy of Holy Week reflects, Jesus grew to think of himself in terms of the suffering servant, the lamb led to slaughter described by the prophet Isaiah.

Whatever his meaning at the time might have been, John the Baptist points to Jesus and says: "This is the one. This is the Lamb of God who will be the source of mercy and peace for you. It's in his story, in his person, in his life-blood that you will be saved."

I had a remarkable experience this week with a woman who's in the process of growing into a deeper awareness of the direction and meaning of her own life. She's about my age, perhaps a little younger; I've known her for 15 years. She's the mother of three daughters, the youngest of whom is just finishing high school. She has brain cancer and there's nothing more the medical profession can do for her except be there to help her die in peace. (That's actually a lot.)

In the course of our conversation, she told me that she's beginning to realize that, although she would love to see her girls grow up and would love to meet her grandchildren, that's just not going to happen. She's decided that her legacy to them is going to be dying well. She's going to use her sickness and suffering and make her way of dying a gift.

She said, "You know, Father Eddy, they listen to me now that I'm dying in a way they didn't before." She is choosing to recognize her brokenness as a strength, not a weakness, as an asset, not a liability, and is offering it to her family as a word about life, about values, about perspective. Wow! I was blown away.

After our conversation, I gave her holy communion. "This is the lamb of God, the body of Christ," I said. "Amen," she replied. "Amen" is right! She was entering into the mystery of Christ's own sacrificial death.

We read today in Isaiah 49 about being formed in the womb to be God's servant, to fulfill God's purpose. We see Christ in the text, but we see ourselves as well. We hear Jesus being called "Lamb of God," and probably never thought of ourselves in those terms. I saw the Lamb of God in the eyes of my friend with cancer as I gave her holy communion that day.

For those who break and share bread, who pour out wine and share a common cup, who respond to the invitation to share the body and blood of Christ, there are clear implications. For those who receive holy communion, who participate in the holy sacrifice of the Mass, there are unfolding consequences.

Ritual actions signal what we are called to become. As Jesus lived out his own life journey, he became the Lamb of God. We, in our own life stories, grow into that same role. In Psalm 40, we sang: "Sacrifice and offering you do not desire, but you have given me an open ear. Burnt offering and sin offering you have not required. Then I said, 'Here I am, I delight to do your will, O God. Your law is within my heart.'"

How the full meaning of our liturgical life will unfold in our unique personal stories is always mysterious. None of us yet knows the full meaning and implication of the "Amens" we say to the body and blood of Christ each Sunday. None of us knows for sure what our communion with the Lamb of God will look like, but as the eucharistic bread is broken today and as the "Lamb of God" is sung, we recognize the broken body of Christ and our own call to sacrificial brokenness in communion with him. As the eucharistic wine is being poured out and we sing our litany, we recognize his life-blood and our own. In faith we affirm the profoundly sacrificial content of the eucharist and of the deepest meaning of our own lives. In faith and humility, we move forward. We approach this altar once again, with reverence, with respect, with serenity, with hope, with courage.

Life in the Prophetic Perfect Tense

Third Sunday in Ordinary Time

Isaiah 9.1-4
Psalm 27
1 Corinthians 1.10-13, 17-18
Matthew 4.12-23

"As soon as I saw that light," she said, "I was as good as home."

A sister who is a friend of mine took early retirement and is now working in a neighbouring diocese where she spends her time travelling to small parishes, encouraging them in their projects of liturgical renewal, developing parish councils, or offering opportunities for adult faith growth. These meetings typically take place in the evening, so she was getting quite used to driving home in the dark. On one particular wet, soggy, gray November evening, just before winter broke in upon us, the meeting was going so well that the time passed quickly. Suddenly it was 10 o'clock—more than time to go home. One of the men in the group said, "Sister, I know a shortcut. If you go down this way and then turn that way and just watch for this and then cut across country, you could save almost a half hour." You can probably already guess what happened. Guess again. It was worse. She got into the car and set out, turning right where she thought she was supposed to turn right. It was one of those little two-rut paths, the kind with grass growing in the middle. She turned in, went a ways, thinking to herself, "This is cross country, all right," and then, sploosh. Down she went.

She was not only stuck, but hung up, all four wheels turning in the breeze—all alone in the dark. It was starting to snow softly, beautiful in its own way, but she would appreciate that beauty better at another time. She waited in the car for half an hour and nobody came by, so she got out and started walking. It was past 11, it was snowing, her car was hung up and she was walking. After about two hours in the mud she saw a farmhouse ahead, its lights still on.

I'm sure she's reading the liturgical texts this Sunday with better eyes than ours, which may never have experienced such darkness. She knows how our minds and bodies work together. It was dark outside, but she was feeling an inner darkness, plus fear and stupidity. Then she saw the beam of light. Just the sight of that light was already warmth and comfort. It didn't matter how stupid the people who let her in might have thought her to be—out alone on a night like that, taking a shortcut "cross country." She knows first-hand how transforming a beacon of light can be.

As soon as she saw that light, she was as good as home.

> There will be no gloom for those who were in anguish. In the former time, [the LORD] brought into contempt the land of Zebulun and the land of Naphtali, but in the latter time he will make glorious the way of the sea, the land beyond the Jordan, Galilee of the nations. (Isaiah 9.1)

Today Jesus describes something like my friend experienced, but in larger spiritual categories. Standing in the very place referred to in the prophet, he quotes directly from Isaiah, describing the gloom, anguish and alienation which so often and for so long had characterized life in that place. The "Galilee of the nations" to which he is referring had a long and difficult history of oppression: this one, that one, the other one in charge. Syrians, Babylonians and Egyptians had all had their turn at being in charge. The people had been wandering in the dark for a long time.

Jesus moves out of the hill country, the relative security of Nazareth, and makes his home, the centre of his ministry, in the very place of promise, Capernaum by the sea. The mixed cultural and ethnic environment of this commercial and trading town seemed well-suited to his style and approach.

Jesus' first word in and for that place, for those sitting in the "region and shadow of death," is "Repent, for the kingdom of heaven has come near." Notice that he doesn't say "Repent and the kingdom of God will come near," or "If you repent, the kingdom of God will come near." No: "Repent, for the kingdom of heaven *has* come near."

The author of a commentary on this text from Matthew was describing the tense of the verb in this very important verse. In another familiar translation, it's rendered: "Repent! The kingdom of heaven is upon you." The commentator noted that the tense of the verb is the prophetic perfect, which is very difficult to translate. The prophetic perfect tense: Have you ever heard of such a thing?

We studied a lot of grammar in school and were quite clear about imperfect, perfect, even pluperfect and future perfect, but prophetic perfect? That the kingdom of God is "upon" you or the kingdom of God is "near" you is the best we can do in translating the prophetic perfect tense.

I don't think much grammar is taught anymore. Some of us quasi-dinosaurs think that's too bad. Anyway, brace yourselves for a quick lesson or a quick review. All the perfect tenses have something to do with the past, but are not past in the same way, or equally past. "Past is a many splendoured thing." Let's take an example.

"I was fishing." That's the imperfect tense. It's in the past but describes an action that didn't take place in an instant but continued for a period of time.

"I caught a fish." That's the perfect tense. It happened at a particular moment in the past and was over.

"I had been fishing for over an hour before I caught anything." That's the pluperfect tense.

"By two o'clock, I will have been fishing for three hours." That's the future perfect. It looks forward to looking backwards, if that makes any sense.

Enough of that. Now for the prophetic perfect tense. The kingdom of God is upon you. That's the prophetic perfect.

The kingdom of God came? No. The kingdom of God was coming? No. The kingdom of God had come? No. The kingdom of God will have come? No. The kingdom of God is near, so near, that it's "upon you." The prophetic perfect tense.

An example is the only way to get our heads around this. Let's pretend that Christmas is two days away. This three-year-old girl is beside herself. She's so excited and so anxious for Christmas to come that, in fact, Christmas is already here for her. Christmas is "upon" her. In a way, Christmas is already accomplished in her. To say that Christmas is "upon" her is to use the prophetic perfect tense.

Another example. One year, when I first started teaching in the seminary, it was getting close to Thanksgiving, which is a very big deal for many American families. We were supposed to be dismissed Wednesday after class and be back Sunday night, but the long-range weather forecast was so poor that the rector decided we would dismiss after classes Tuesday and not be back in class until the following Tuesday. Whatever the weather was, the seminarians would not have to be on the road on Wednesday and Sunday, the two heaviest traffic days in the whole year. I had an exam scheduled for Wednesday morning, the last class before the break. Made sense to me. What was I to do about my exam? I put a note up on the board that it would be rescheduled for Monday, which was the last class before the break. Still makes sense except that the note didn't go up until Saturday evening and some of the students didn't see it until after Mass Sunday. They lived Sunday afternoon and evening in the prophetic perfect tense. The exam suddenly became very real. The exam was upon them.

There's tremendous intensity in the prophetic perfect tense: energy, excitement, flowing adrenaline. In the prophetic perfect, one lives with such strong expectancy that the future is drawn into the now and, mysteriously, is already accomplished. Living in the prophetic perfect tense isn't natural for most of us. Perhaps it's best understood at the level of grace.

The light is on. Live as if you were already home, because you are. Home is upon you.

The lights are up. Live as if Christmas were already here, because it is. Christmas is upon you.

The note's on the board. Live as if the exam were already here, because it is. The exam is upon you.

Repent! Live as if the kingdom of heaven were already here, because it is. The kingdom of heaven is upon you.

A New Look at Old Blessings

Fourth Sunday in Ordinary Time

Zephaniah 2.3; 3.12-13
Psalm 146
1 Corinthians 1.26-31
Matthew 5.1-12

When Jesus saw the crowds, he went up the mountain; and after he sat down, his disciples came to him. Then he began to speak and he taught them, saying:
"Blessed ..." (Matthew 5.1-3)

The beatitudes, with which the Sermon on the Mount begins, are surely among the most beloved verses in the whole Bible, clearly among Jesus' most treasured sayings.

It's dangerous to have friends who are scholars. One of them passed me an article from the *Catholic Biblical Quarterly*,[9] which is forcing me to rethink the way I have always read, understood and preached this text.

I had always thought of and interpreted the beatitudes as "wisdom sayings." Each one makes sense. Each one reflects a deep level of human life and experience, however paradoxical. Take poverty of spirit, for example. Simplicity, humility and openness to others are clearly more attractive in human beings than being "full of oneself." Nothing is a bigger turn-off than the person who flaunts wealth, power and prestige. As regards wealth, money can't buy happiness and you can't take it with you anyway, so to be too attached to it and preoccupied with it is misspent energy. You see? I could develop a whole homily around this approach to just one beatitude as a wisdom saying.

---

[9]   Mark Allan Powell, "Matthew's Beatitudes, Reversals and Rewards of the Kingdom," *Catholic Biblical Quarterly*, Vol. 58, July 1996, p. 58.

Mourning may be a bit more challenging, but isn't it true that much of life is about moving on and suffering the losses that are part of that movement? To be able to be in touch with pain, to accept it, even to savour it, reflects reality and draws us to deeper maturity. To reach your 30th birthday or to see your four-year-old daughter off to school for the first time involves passages, of which mourning is an aspect. Another way to look at it would be to recognize mourning as the other side of love. Developing close relationships is risky business. We mourn only because we treasure the preciousness of that which we have lost. There's something very human and beautiful about that. Presiding at funerals right here in this church has given me many opportunities to look out over a congregation of mourners and see something truly blessed in the experience.

Meekness is something else. I saw a very haunting photograph some years ago, which I wish I had cut out. Armoured tanks and troops were moving across the fields in the background, perhaps in the Ukraine. In the foreground was an elderly lady with a miniature icon in her hand. She was praying. Where was the power? The accompanying article recalled the 1970s visit to the Soviet Union of a seminary professor who declared that the church there was irrelevant, because the only people in them were "little old ladies." Many, looking back now, thank God for the fortitude and courage of the little old ladies who bet on the stronger of two gods and won. Their existence and quiet presence provided a continuing, visible, political rebuke to the Soviets. Blessed are the meek, they shall inherit the earth.

Understanding the beatitudes as wisdom sayings let me see being pure in heart as having a certain single-mindedness, strong basic commitments and clear priorities. To be merciful meant recognizing the limits of justice, being able to let go of old hurts and grudges, and coming to real freedom in the process. Hungering and thirsting for righteousness and making peace reflect an ongoing energy and zest for social justice and for healing and reconciliation in our families, in our communities and in the world. To be ridiculed, laughed at, even persecuted in ways large and small may come with "beatitude territory," and mark maturity and depth commitment—truly admirable.

Spiritual attitudes and approaches such as these lead to real happiness, lead to the kingdom of heaven, lead to communion with God.

It's not even a question of getting to heaven at some future time. If you live this way, you will already be discovering the presence and power of the kingdom of God on a daily basis. Of course, I still believe all of this is true, but I'm discovering that it may not be what the beatitudes themselves are saying.

The author of the gospel, a Jewish Christian himself, is addressing his work to a community that, for the most part, shares his heritage. His references to the Old Testament, his choice of words that reflect Old Testament precedents, his way of shaping and crafting his material and the literary devices he uses arise from his Hebrew tradition, in which he is very skilled indeed. One of the most characteristic elements in Hebrew writing is that of parallelism and balance. Look at the beatitudes again and note that there are eight in the third person ("they") and one in the second person ("you"), addressed directly to the disciples. One clear possibility regarding their parallel structure would be to think of them as two sets of four, with a concluding remark. The first four refer to the poor and dispossessed, the second four to those who are working towards justice on their behalf. The blessings in the first set refer to reversals, which God will work on behalf of the poor and dispossessed. In the second set, the blessings are rewards for those who are involved in God's work among them even now. Let's explore that way of understanding the beatitudes in a bit more detail.

According to Mark Powell's article, to which I referred earlier, the poor in spirit are the genuinely poor and dispossessed. They are so poor and have been poor for so long that they have no spirit left. They have lost heart and are on the verge of giving up. Those who mourn are the lonely, isolated and abandoned ones who find no cause for joy. The meek are not so much the humble, but the humiliated, who have no human dignity accorded to them and no access to the resources necessary for a life of dignity. Those who hunger and thirst for righteousness are those who are literally starving for justice. These are desperate people, living at the margins of society. Their situation is not "spiritual," hence admirable, but dreadful, hence unconscionable.

These poor, mourning, meek and hungry people are so in real life. They are those who have no reason for hope, no reason for joy, no access to the resources of this world, no access to justice. In the kingdom of heaven, this simply cannot be. In the kingdom of heaven, these people must and will be vindicated. In this reading of them the first four beatitudes are not about spiritual virtues lived out by believers and the corresponding blessings coming to them as rewards, but about real-life situations that the kingdom of heaven cannot tolerate and which must be reversed. The first set of beatitudes reflects Jesus' conviction that God will turn this around. The blessings promise a reversal in their state of affairs.

The second stanza of four beatitudes refers to those persons who, even in the present, are working towards bringing about this reversal. In a sense, they are agents of the kingdom of heaven. The merciful are those who value mercy over sacrifice, who don't blame the poor for their own condition, who do not judge lest they themselves be judged, who eat with outcasts, who give money to the poor and put right what is wrong. The pure in heart are those whose inner life matches their outer life, who, in their faith and religious practice, are free of hypocrisy, who don't pretend to be pious and do nothing. The peacemakers are those who are actively committed to *shalom,* which involves dignity, integrity, civility, community and justice for all. These are persons whose goal in life is active co-operation with God's will for the well-being of society and all of creation, persons who recognize and welcome the kingdom of heaven.

Misunderstanding, even persecution, may well come to those who "stick their necks out" in support of justice for those who have no reason to hope, no reason for joy, no access to the resources of this world or to justice. The blessings of this second set of beatitudes are rewards for those who share already in the kingdom of heaven by living as God intends, working towards the removal of the ostracism, hunger, disease and debt that characterize the lives of those who are poor in spirit, mourning, meek and hungry for righteousness.

The last beatitude is a direct challenge to the disciples.

> "Blessed are you when people revile you and persecute you and utter all kinds of evil against you falsely on my account. Rejoice and be glad, for your reward is great in heaven, for in the same way they persecuted the prophets who were before you." (Matthew 5.11-12)

In this last beatitude Jesus identifies himself with the kingdom of God and with all who have stood for the kingdom throughout history. Ironically, he knows that living in terms of the last four beatitudes means he'll wind up among those who live the situation of the first four. By welcoming and responding to the kingdom of heaven by being merciful, pure in heart and a peacemaker, he will die among the poor, mourning, meek and hungry. The cross already awaits him, as does the resurrection in which he will experience God's great reversal and will signal the "blessing" involved for all who associate with him as disciples. Already at the outset of his preaching the meaning of his life, death and resurrection are previewed.

I find these reversals and rewards, in what for me is a new way of reading the beatitudes, to be persuasive and even more challenging than my former way of approaching them. What do you think?

Salt Makes the Tomato

Fifth Sunday in Ordinary Time

Isaiah 58.6-10
Psalm 112
1 Corinthians 2.1-5
Matthew 5.13-16

"You are the salt of the earth... You are the light of the world."
(Matthew 5.13-14)

I remember Pearl Dunn, a member of our parish who was a resident at one of the local nursing homes for the last 11 or 12 months before she died. She was very gentle and open, and was always ready to think and to talk.

She wasn't very tall and seemed to get even smaller as her physical stamina diminished. She only complained once in a while about food. It's true that good food is so very important in such institutions. Her diet was restricted and, among other things, was salt-free. I was visiting her in August when she said, "Can you imagine a nice ripe tomato, all neatly sliced on your plate, but no salt? Salt makes the tomato. I used to like to fix a roast of beef at home and cook it so that it would still be pink. It was even better the next day and made a fine sandwich—but without salt? That Mrs. Dash stuff is no good either."

I remember meeting another lady in the hospital. I was visiting her roommate and she was overhearing our conversation and our prayers. As I was getting ready to leave, she called me over and we had quite a chat. She was in her early eighties and hadn't been to church for years. She had gotten quite fed up with a lot of the fussing and pettiness in the congregation to which she belonged and wanted to tell me all about it, because deep in her heart she was homesick, and was thinking about giving the church another try. I hope she did. Once again, as I was leaving—trying to leave—the lady I had initially come to visit called me back to her bedside. "Isn't she a salty old thing?" she remarked, loud enough for her neighbour to hear.

Salt brings out what's best. It heightens the experience. Salt makes the tomato; it makes the roast beef sandwich; it makes a fun conversation; it perks things up. Can we see giving zest to things, bringing out the best, drawing forth the "flavours" inherent in persons and situations as part of our mission in life? Perking things up?

> You are the light of the world. A city built on a hill cannot be hid. No one after lighting a lamp puts it under the bushel basket. (Matthew 5.14-15)

You may have seen photos or even reproductions of oil lamps from the ancient world. They're shallow little things, almost like covered saucers. They had a handle for carrying and a hole in the top into which the wick was placed. People would place these lamps as high up in the room as possible so that the light would reflect with maximum effect. Lowering them would reduce their efficiency. Even in this church building, we can imagine that a single candle, properly placed, would give enough light for us to move about safely, offering confidence and security, even in the middle of the night.

"This little light of mine, I'm going to let it shine." Another song we sang as children had to do with asking Jesus to make me a sunbeam.

Can you see yourselves as light?

You may remember Craig Kielburger, the rather salty and very bright 13-year-old who went to India and Pakistan in connection with one of Prime Minister Chrétien's "Team Canada" trade promotion tours. He actually upstaged the prime minister one day with his insistence that Team Canada had to be about more than trade. Craig's interest was in human rights, particularly child labour.

I watched him being interviewed by Dan Matheson on Canada AM. Dan was discussing the issue, but was trying to turn the conversation to more personal, psychological issues. He was curious about Craig himself. He wanted to know more about Craig. "What are your interests? Hobbies? What is your family like? Where did you get all this spunk and determination?" In other words: "Who are you and what makes you tick?" Craig responded that he wasn't at all interested in talking about himself—a distraction from what he was about. He wanted to talk about child labour in the developing world. "Who cares what my hobbies are?" he seemed to imply. He wanted to talk about issues, more specifically about this issue, the issue of child labour in these countries that Team Canada was visiting.

Craig was certainly not afraid to express himself, to stand for something, to "let his light shine before others." I have a feeling that I was not the only one that morning who, "seeing his good works, gave glory to our Father in heaven."

There's a lot to be said for being bright and salty, isn't there?

"But ..."

Sixth Sunday in Ordinary Time

Sirach 15.15-20
Psalm 119
1 Corinthians 2.6-10
Matthew 5.17-37

[The LORD] has placed before you fire and water;
stretch out your hand for whichever you choose.
Before each person are life and death,
and whichever one chooses will be given. (Sirach 15.16-17)

Two Sundays ago, we looked briefly at parallelism, a very common Hebrew literary or rhetorical device. There is balance and symmetry in the writing for the sake of both emphasis and clarity, and sometimes for paradox and surprise. Listen again to the two verses and note carefully the symmetry:

[The LORD] has placed before you fire and water;
stretch out your hand for whichever you choose.
Before each person are life and death,
and whichever one chooses will be given.

The symmetry is clear, but the meaning, I suggest, is ambiguous. Paradox and surprise are in store for us. Fire and water: choose one. Life and death: choose one. Is fire life and water death—or can both be either? Fire is life and death. Water is life and death. How and why should we choose between the two?

It strikes me that we choose both. We choose fire and water, death and life in different ways and at different times. Sometimes fire is life and we choose it. Sometimes fire is death and we choose it. Sometimes water is life and we choose it. Sometimes water is death and we choose it. Fire is energy, love and light. It is also purification and destruction.

Water is energy, life and refreshment. It, too, is purification and destruction.

The issue here is not fire and water, life and death, but the reality of human choice, the reality of and need for divine wisdom in making good choices, which can be exhilarating and painful at the same time. Life and death feature in every choice. Every choice implies a "yes" to one possibility and a "no" to others. In every serious choice, there is a movement towards one thing and a movement away from something else. On the one hand there is positive energy, and on the other, purification, for which fire or water could be an apt metaphor.

We humans have the capacity for pondering our choices. Our capacity for analysis and discernment is central to the way in which we are gifted by the creator. In all of this we grow in wisdom through honest, living and ongoing partnership with God and with each other.

This whole wonderful and mysterious process is particularly close to Matthew's heart, arising as he does out of a Jewish cultural context. The Sermon on the Mount pictures Jesus himself engaging in this activity, weighing matters, discussing possibilities, even fussing over "What if?" questions—which, my Jewish friends have taught me, is a favourite activity for Jews even to this day.

Perhaps you have heard the saying "Two Jews, three opinions"? Such a witticism is quite understandable if you're used to interpreting and arguing over the ramifications of biblical texts such as the fire/water–life/death verses from Sirach.

There's a wonderful story about a Jew who, for whatever reason, was alone on a desert island. Only months later was he found and rescued. He was quite proud of his ingenuity and survival skills. He seemed in no big hurry to leave the island before showing his rescuers how he had survived. He showed them where he slept, where he cooked, where he fished, where he gathered edible berries, even green vegetables, if you can imagine. He even showed them the synagogue he had built. There was no congregation, but he was homesick, so he built a synagogue. Everybody was amazed and congratulated the man on both his skills and determination to make the best of what must have been a dreadful situation. The island wasn't large, but its terrain was uneven and as they were leaving in the boat, one of his rescuers noticed another little building just over a small hill. He asked: "What is that little building over there?" "Oh, that's the synagogue I don't go to."

Even almost 2000 years ago, Matthew, the name given to the author of the gospel, lived out of a Jewish heritage that was similarly philosophically and religiously combative. Jesus himself functioned in that world and very often it is in that spirit that we need to take his combative discussions with the scribes and Pharisees. The relationship between Matthew's Jewish–Christian community and the Jewish community, however, was anything but "good sport" competition. Instead it was very tense and difficult, as we will see more fully as the gospel unfolds. With Jerusalem and its temple destroyed, the Jewish faith was at the point of crisis and transition. The growing Christian movement was understood to be heretical and divisive, dividing even families.

It is still necessary, however, to note the positive side of a certain combative spirit within the Jewish community that continues to be normal, a very ordinary way of entering into the dynamism of being open to the mystery of God. Would that many of us had that kind of energy around life in the spirit.

In today's gospel, Jesus says, "Do not think that I have come to abolish the law... You have heard that it was said: 'You shall not murder' ... But I say to you ... You have heard that it was said: 'You shall not commit adultery.' But I say to you ...."

The operative word is "but." This is the word which sets up a new set of parallel verses that move our thinking and discussion about fire and water, life and death forward into specifics.

I haven't killed anybody, *but* do I love life? I haven't committed adultery, *but* is my marriage good? What does the law require? What is the will of God? What does the kingdom of heaven demand? What is true wisdom? How in some kind of humanly reasonable way can I keep all these things together? With fire and water, death and life. What is the difference between hopeless idealism and real–life hope? They've always said such and such, *but* is this all there is to it? The Bible says such and such, *but* what does that mean? What does it involve?

To simply read the Bible and act accordingly is clearly out of the question in the tradition represented by both Sirach and Matthew's gospel. True obedience to the law as well as adherence to wisdom move beyond any perfect understanding or precise observance of legal niceties to the ultimate intention of the law, to the ultimate and final will of God, who is at the foundation of both law and wisdom.

The fire and water metaphors of Sirach and the concrete questions of the Sermon on the Mount prompt fussing and fuming, a life-and-death discussion about life and death. We are at our best when, with great commitment and energy, we enter into the conversation. We discover God in the conversation.

The Holiness Code:
Too Close for Comfort

Seventh Sunday in Ordinary Time

Leviticus 19.1-2, 17-18
Psalm 103
1 Corinthians 3.16-23
Matthew 5.38-48

"You shall be holy, for I the LORD your God am holy."
(Leviticus 19.2)
"Be perfect, therefore, as your heavenly Father is perfect."
(Matthew 5.48)

In whichever testament you read, if you're reading carefully, you'll be blown away from time to time. Commands to be holy like God or perfect like God are a bit much! The holiness code and holiness sayings such as these would make any mortal uncomfortable. Being one with the Lord whose name you bear may be just too close for comfort! Our preferences would be to act humanly—yes, with a certain justice and generosity, but humanly. Let's do our best to be fair and decent, then let's call it a day.

Such reasonable moderation is not in the picture. "You scratch my back, I'll scratch yours" is an utterly inappropriate norm or lifestyle. As realistic as it may sound, it doesn't work anyway. Effective living and genuine morality go far beyond *quid pro quo* calculations. Gestures of healing and reconciliation are, in fact, most effective (clearly of God) when they go beyond common sense and prudence. De-escalation of war, diffusion of conflict, or evening the score simply never happen globally, nationally, or personally without somebody doing something "unreasonable." Somebody has to step in, break the circle of *quid pro quo* reciprocity and believe that the potential for real life lies in precisely such activity.

"You have heard that it was said: 'You shall love your neighbour and hate your enemy.' But I say to you: Love your enemies and pray for those who persecute you, so that you may be children of your Father in heaven; for he makes his sun rise on the evil and the good, and sends rain on the righteous and on the unrighteous." (Matthew 5.43-45)

Let's take a look at a concrete example of someone who was called to live this invitation quite literally in her own life and circumstances. A journalist in the south Bronx reported the following:

My attention is arrested by one of the most unusual memorials that I have seen in the South Bronx. In bright white paint against a soft beige background is a painting of a large and friendly looking dog, his tail erect, his ears alert for danger. Above, in yellow letters, I read "Moondog," which appears to be the nickname of the person who has died. "Gone is the face ... Silent is the voice ... In our hearts we'll remember," reads the epitaph.

As I am on the sidewalk copying these words, a plump Hispanic woman rises from the stoop nearby and comes up to my side.
"Is this where he died?" I ask.
"Yes," she answers. "He was shot right there, inside the door."
"Why was he killed?"
"He was protecting a woman who was pregnant."
"Did the woman live?" "The woman lived. She's fine."
"How old was the man when he died?"
"He was almost 21."
I ask her how he got his nickname.
"He loved dogs. He used to bring them home." Her voice is jovial and pleasant.
"Did you know him well?"
"He was my son," she says.[10]

---

[10] Jonathan Cozal, "Amazing Grace," quoted in *Spiritual Literacy,* Frederick and Mary Ann Brussat, eds. (New York: Scribner, 1996), p. 424.

What does God look like? What is true holiness? What is perfection? You've seen it right here! We're talking radical morality, radical letting go, radical openness to reconciliation—to God's own perfection. We're talking a radically divine way of being human, which has in fact divine potential, since we are created in the divine image.

Another example, though perhaps less personal, is no less real. It is the story of another woman of faith and conviction.

You may remember that Casper Weinberger was the American Secretary of Defense during the Vietnam years. I remember hearing the broadcast report of a woman who hated him—at least she thought she did. She couldn't stand seeing his picture in the paper or listening to his reports on that seemingly endless conflict. Something happened to her one day. I guess we'd call it grace. As she was praying for peace in her morning prayer, there he was in her consciousness. She prayed for him and her perspective changed. She saw that, in spite of his cold appearance, arrogant style and apparent lack of wisdom, he was a human being. She could oppose his actions and still keep her heart open towards him. She saw how it would be even harder for him to be free of the role in which he was so obviously trapped, if she sent nothing but negative energy his way. Prayerful "love energy" might even help to set him free. An Orthodox Christian, she cut his picture out of the paper and placed it with her icons. When she lit her candle and incense for daily prayer, she included him with the "faces of God." She included "Good morning, Casper" in her prayers. She included him in the love and appreciation that she directed towards the God of heaven and earth. She recognized both her place and his in the wonderful possibilities of God's unconditional love.

You have heard that it was said ... But I say to you ...
Where charity and love prevail there is God.

We'll be singing that refrain at communion today: *Ubi caritas et amor, Deus ibi est.* Let's stretch its content to fit as full and expansive a "holiness code" as we can imagine for ourselves and for the world.

Taking a Lesson
from the Birds of the Air

Eighth Sunday in Ordinary Time

Isaiah 49.13-15
Psalm 62
1 Corinthians 4.1-5
Matthew 6.24-34

Strive first for the kingdom of God and his righteousness, and all these things will be given to you as well. So do not worry about tomorrow, for tomorrow will bring worries of its own. Today's trouble is enough for today. (Matthew 6.33-34)

A good perspective on life is perhaps a human person's best asset. The 18th-century literary figure Oliver Goldsmith, best remembered for his play *She Stoops to Conquer,* was always worrying about keeping his finances in order. With characteristic elegance, he is quoted as saying: "It is a melancholy consideration indeed that one's chief comforts often produce one's greatest anxieties and that an increase of our possessions is but an inlet to new disquietudes."

Sounds like an echo of Sirach or one of the other wisdom books, doesn't it? Thomas Aquinas wrote 500 years earlier:

A person must have a certain anxiety about the acquisition or preservation of external things. But if he does not seek them or possess them save in a moderate quantity—enough, that is, for the needs of a simple life—then the anxiety demanded does not conflict with the perfection of the Christian life.

Matthew's perspective about possessions and corresponding worries is not like either the melancholy consideration of Goldsmith or the spiritual moderation of Aquinas. Typical of the Sermon on the

Mount, it is more radical. It may be the kind of thinking to which Thomas Merton was drawn on his night watch rounds. I love this section of his *Sign of Jonas*. As a young monk in Kentucky, he was taking his turn as night watchman and during the course of the night was gazing out at the world from the abbey's tower. Beyond the questions of balancing human needs and priorities, he discovered a deeper, more profound sense of his place in the universe and in the reign of God. He took a lesson from the world of nature: "And now my whole being breathes the wind, which blows through the belfry and my hand is on the door through which I see the heavens."

He sees great forests as he looks around, as if for the first time, and seas of stars as he gazes heavenward. He experiences the sounds of countless living things, "choirs of millions and millions of jumping and flying and creeping things." He becomes aware of God in what he sees. "There is no leaf that is not in your care," he prays. "There is no concealed spring in the woods that was not concealed by you."

In the depths of the forest, in the immensity of the sky, and in the midst of the sounds of countless mysterious "critters," he discerns the presence of God and comes to terms with his own place in the universe.[11]

Although our own pace of life and set of responsibilities are quite different from those of a Trappist monk, something in his nighttime perspective on life from the belfry can resonate with all of us, can invite us to deepen our perspective. To live life in this context will always be a challenge.

A few years ago a parishioner asked me to accompany her to the apartment of a neighbour who had died, just to check the place. She felt awkward doing it alone. Her deceased neighbour's only nephew would be arriving from out of town the next day to make funeral arrangements. As we let ourselves in, we found a space quiet as a tomb with the exception of the tick-tock of a clock, which she must have wound shortly before her sudden death. Everything was in its place—chairs, tables, plants, books, pictures, a stove, a refrigerator. Only she wasn't. Her mail had piled up. I suddenly realized that mail doesn't stop when we die. Wandering from room to room, we observed some

---

[11]   Thomas Merton, *The Sign of Jonas* (New York: Harcourt Brace, 1953), p. 360.

fragments of her life: a piece of jewellery, a magazine opened to a page. We emptied the refrigerator. We watered the plants. Turning the key in the lock on our way out was a strange, almost eerie feeling, which you may have had yourselves on such occasions. She was gone and had taken nothing for the trip.

Our visit to her apartment made us think. We were both glad that the lady had been a gracious and generous person all her life, and we were confident that she was at peace. We were even a bit thankful that this sprightly and vigorous woman hadn't survived the massive stroke that took her life. In all of it, though, we were thinking about ourselves. She was older than both of us—but only by a few years.

> No one can serve two masters ...
> look at the birds ...
> consider the lilies ...
> strive first for the kingdom of God ...

The Sermon on the Mount proposes wide and deep perspectives on human relationships and ethical considerations. In this section, it offers correspondingly deep perspectives on personal matters, values and priorities.

What's left to us is to let it all sink in, or perhaps to allow ourselves to sink into it.

Learning by Doing

Ninth Sunday in Ordinary Time

Deuteronomy 10.12-13a; 11.18, 26-28, 32
Psalm 31
Romans 1.16-17; 3.20-26, 28
Matthew 7.21-27

There's a story told about Heinrich Heine. The German Jewish poet was standing with a friend before the great cathedral of Amiens. When the friend asked, "Why can't people build piles like this anymore?" Heine replied, "My dear friend, in those days people had convictions. We moderns have opinions and it takes more than an opinion to build a pile like this."

To tell you the truth, I'd never think of calling a cathedral a "pile"—but to each his own.

I do think, however, that this "pile founded on convictions" is a fairly common way of looking at Jesus' own use of the building metaphor in his parable. We should build our institutions on solid ideas, on strong convictions. We should build our lives on the true faith. As true as that may be, it is not the point of the parable.

Saying "Lord, Lord," with whatever degree of conviction, is not the foundation about which Jesus speaks. Jesus stresses not concepts or belief in the word itself, but actions in response to the word, or ethical behaviour that is consistent with the word.

> "Everyone then who hears these words of mine and acts on them will be like a wise man who built his house on rock ....
> Everyone who hears these words of mine and does not act on them will be like a foolish man who built his house on sand."
> (Matthew 7.24-26)

Notice that Jesus does not say that whoever hears these words and *believes* them is like a wise man who builds his house on rock. It is not about hearing these words and believing them, or being convinced about their truth or validity, but about acting on them.

What Saint Teresa of Avila called the "interior castle" is built on a lifetime of lived response to the word of God: in this case, to the ethical standards and ideals presented by Jesus in the Sermon on the Mount, of which this parable is part.

The New York Daily News ran an article about the person they were confident was the oldest active member of her profession. Sister Mary Claudia, a nurse at Saint Vincent's Hospital, was celebrating her 91st birthday and her 60th year at the hospital. Her responsibilities and workload had been cut back over the years, but there was a rumour going around that the spry old lady was finally going to retire. Indignant, she made a statement to the authorities: "Retire? Of course, I shan't. There are sick people in this institution and I shall stay to care for them. There's lots I don't know and lots I do. There's lots I can't do and lots I can. One thing I know: People in pain are more eager for human kindness than for medicine and I've still got lots of that to give."

I think that our own experience bears out the wisdom in this woman's life-building project. She has built solid foundations by a life of habitual discipline and service that no one can deny or take away from her. The winds may blow as they please, but she's solidly founded. She has a real sense of place in this world and is able to live her life out of her own reality, gracefully and generously. She's at home in her skin and, as such, is a wonderful contributor to the ongoing building-up of her community and her profession.

Let's look at another way of being at home in community. It's often been said that there's a big difference between a house and a home. There's a difference between a housekeeper and a homemaker. Being a homemaker is less about things and more about people. It's less about tidiness and more about the inevitable untidiness of family life and relationships. House is a building; home is a community.

Rabbi Harold Kushner, author of the well-known book *When Bad Things Happen to Good People,* has other equally worthwhile works to his credit. He reworks the building metaphor in another way. The following incident is reported in *When All You've Ever Wanted Isn't Enough.*

I was sitting on a beach one summer day, watching two children, a boy and a girl, playing in the sand. They were hard at work building an elaborate sand castle by the water's edge, with gates and towers and moats and internal passages. Just when they had nearly finished their project, a big wave came along and knocked it down, reducing it to a heap of wet sand. I expected the children to burst into tears, devastated by what had happened to all their hard work. But they surprised me. Instead they ran up the shore away from the water, laughing and holding hands and sat down to build another castle. I realized that they had taught me an important lesson. All the things in our lives, all the complicated structures we spend so much time and energy creating, are built on sand. Only our relationships to other people endure. Sooner or later, the wave will come along and knock down what we have worked so hard to build up. When that happens, only the person who has somebody's hand to hold will be able to laugh.[12]

Real living means developing the capacity to recognize and affirm relationship-building projects that have lifelong value and potential—character-building, home-making, family-building, community-building.

We learned a lesson in our infancy that we should never forget as we grow up. It is far, far easier to knock something down than to build it up. As infants, we came equipped with the convulsive movement of hand and foot that easily topples a pile of blocks. Only with repeated efforts and concentration did we learn to take up one block after another and build a pyramid. We learn by doing. We learn maturity not by following a certain infallible course of action, but by taking risks and chances; we learn to be friends not by analyzing or believing in friendship, but by being friends. We learn family not from psychological or sociological theory, but by being family. For the most part, analysis grows out of experiences that build on one another.

---

[12]   Rabbi Harold Kushner, *When All You've Ever Wanted Isn't Enough,* quoted in *Spiritual Literacy,* Frederick and Mary Ann Brussat, eds. (New York: Scribner, 1996), p. 424.

Building an interior castle requires more than the solid convictions which Heine saw in the cathedral he so admired. An interior castle is never a finished pile, but a work in progress.

To be consistent with Matthew's very Jewish approach to wisdom and ethical teaching, let me conclude with an extended Jewish proverb. I think it provides a good summary of the process of right living. Notice how it begins and ends with doing. Thinking and believing are found throughout the process, but it begins and ends with doing. I think you'll find in it a good process for interior castle-building.

> We are here to do,
> And through doing to learn;
> And through learning to know;
> And through knowing to experience wonder;
> And through wonder to attain wisdom;
> And through wisdom to find simplicity;
> And through simplicity to give attention;
> And through attention
> To see what needs to be done.

Probe the Possibilities

Tenth Sunday in Ordinary Time

Hosea 6.3-6
Psalm 50
Romans 4.18-25
Matthew 9.9-13

"Let us press on to know the LORD;
his appearing is as sure as the dawn;
he will come to us like the showers,
like the spring rains that water the earth." (Hosea 6.3)

Do you remember those lines from Hosea, the first reading from today's liturgy? Don't they sound sincere, positive and beautiful? "Let us press on to know the Lord."

The passage unfolds in a sharply worded response attributed to God himself, which seems quite out of place. God's words are words of ironic exasperation. He's tired of their prayers. He wants deeds. Their sentiments aren't enough. God wants action. There is an almost sarcastic parody of what is, in the prophet's judgment, lip-service rather than authentic moral fidelity.

In the gospel, Jesus clearly cites this text. He quotes from the prophet Hosea, but the second half of the parallel construction is different.

Hosea says, "I desire steadfast love and not sacrifice, the knowledge of God rather than burnt offerings." Notice the symmetry and balance.

Jesus quotes only the first line and moves on: "I desire mercy, not sacrifice. For I have come to call not the righteous but sinners." Note a symmetry and balance that don't quite work. The match isn't good. He's both in sync and out of sync with Hosea.

In his time, Hosea was up against what he considered morally ineffectual religious practice: lots of words and ritual activity, but no action in real life.

The gospel text describes how, in the time of Jesus, his adversaries are critical of his actions, his associations with sinners like Matthew who, as a tax collector for an occupying power, has betrayed both his people and his God. Jesus' association with him would bring down any proper prophet's wrath.

The contexts of Hosea and the Gospel of Matthew are not quite the same, but have clear parallels. Following on the Sermon on the Mount, Jesus demonstrates in word and deed what this "blessedness" looks like in practice. In his own life and choices, he lives out the consequences of what he has said about the very nature of ethical living, of a particular style of life and its relation to the kingdom of heaven. "He talked the talk; now he's walking the walk," as strange and uncomfortable as that might be.

In calling Matthew, Jesus demonstrates what is involved in the way of life he has been preaching. In calling a tax collector, he is suggesting that believers need to go below the surface in their assessment of others. They need to be able to intuit the possibilities of the human heart and take corresponding risks. Matthew's profession and way of life gave no indication either of righteousness of action or purity of intention—anything but. Jesus called him anyway.

In the spirit of Matthew's gospel, let's see if we can't invent a little Sermon on the Mount-style saying, a little parallelism to account for this controversial choice.

It used to be said: "Give me the facts," *but* I say to you, "Probe the possibilities."

Thornton Wilder, the Pulitzer Prize-winning author of *The Bridge of San Luis Rey* and *Our Town,* presented ordinary human beings, flawed but lovable, in his works. They make the human race seem worth preserving. On a poster advertising the production of some of his lesser-known one-act plays, he was quoted as saying that to pass judgment on another person is "to stand apart from the human condition." Passing judgment involves "the assumption that the presence of evil in the world is each time an exceptional case." To pass judgment from the outside is to "assert one's own immunity." For Wilder, life is clearly a work in progress.

I think that we find the same conviction in Jesus, both in his words and in his deeds. Sin has touched us all. It is to the extent that human beings recognize that truth and to the extent that we are ready to stand up and seek and follow a higher path that we are truly human. Paul, in Romans 4, uses Abraham as an example of just such a person whose "faith was reckoned to him as righteousness."

If we let ourselves go, most of us are probably pretty good at passing quick judgments about people like Matthew. We even pigeon-hole people, put them in little boxes. Certain people are trapped by our minds and hearts; they're predestined; they're irredeemable. Although we wouldn't use that language, we have made them inhuman and incapable of change, and in doing so have dehumanized ourselves. With all our hearts we need to resist the temptation to limit faith, to cripple hope and to paralyze love.

In "It used to be said, 'Give me the facts,' *but* I say to you, 'Probe the possibilities,'" I proposed a Jesus-style wisdom saying. Let's try our hand at parables or metaphors to further develop our point. Here's one:

> The jailer of a small county jail once received a letter to an inmate who wasn't registered at his institution. While attempting to search his memory for the inmate's name, on the chance that the addressee may have been in the jail at some previous time, he turned the envelope over. A note scribbled in pencil on the back of the envelope clarified the situation. It read: "If not in jail yet, please hold until he arrives."

Whoever wrote that letter had a certain predestination in mind for the poor fellow to whom the letter was addressed. Jesus' critics had a certain predestination in mind for tax collectors and sinners like Matthew.

"It used to be said, 'Give me the facts,' *but* I say to you, 'Probe the possibilities.'" The galleries are too full of cynical observers who come at life from outside the action. They play no ball. They fight no fights. They make no mistakes because they attempt nothing. Down in the field are the doers. They make mistakes because they attempt many things. The cynic makes no mistakes, because he believes in nothing and tries nothing because nothing is worth his effort. He stands on the sidelines, judging, carping and criticizing, refusing any involvement with real life. I hope that you don't know anyone like that, but most of us have had to deal with such sorts over the years. Here's our second "parable."

It's a story about three men on a journey. No, it's not a priest, a minister and a rabbi, but you're on the right track. It's a Hindu and a rabbi and an agnostic cynic. A storm had brought them together.

While travelling in separate vehicles through the countryside late one afternoon, three men were caught in a terrible thunderstorm and pulled in at the same farmhouse. "The storm is supposed to last for hours," the farmer told them. "Why don't you stay for the night? I do have a problem, though. There's just one spare room in the house, but there's another room with a cot over the barn." "No problem," the Hindu replied, "I'll be fine out there." A few minutes later, there was a knock at the door. It was the Hindu. "I'm sorry," he told the others, "but there is a cow in the barn and according to my religion, cows are sacred and I can't intrude into their space." "Don't worry," said the rabbi. "Make yourself comfortable. I'll sleep out there." He went out to the barn. A few minutes later a knock came on the door. "I'm sorry to be a bother," he said, "but there are pigs out there. In my religion, pigs are considered unclean. I wouldn't feel comfortable sharing my sleeping quarters with pigs." "Oh, all right," said the cynic. "I'll sleep out there." He went out to the barn. A few minutes later there was a knock at the door. It was the cow and the pig.

Even though we can be a little like that ourselves, none of us really like people who, in Wilder's words, "stand apart from the human condition," or "assert their immunity" from the human condition. We know that there's no real life in being a critic from the outside, in avoiding solidarity with human reality. There's no real-life in cynicism that sees nothing but futility in efforts to call forth what is fresh and new.

In Matthew's gospel, Jesus is anything but a dispassionate critic; he is an active reformer. Jesus is Emmanuel, God-with-us, the God who enters in, the God who engages personally in real-life struggles, makes choices, takes risks and makes leaps of faith in calling people forward, people like Matthew, like you and like me.

"It used to be said, 'Give me the facts,' *but* I say to you, 'Probe the possibilities.'"

In Jesus we see what it is like to risk believing in the possibilities of human beings, to actively seek to encourage and even create new opportunities for human growth, development and conversion.

Go Up

First Sunday of Lent

Genesis 2.7-9, 16-18, 25; 3.1-7
Psalm 51
Romans 5.12-19
Matthew 4.1-11

After being baptized by John, "Jesus was led up by the Spirit into the wilderness to be tempted by the devil." I looked in the commentaries that I have in my own library, but there was nothing about Jesus being led *up*. I wondered whether "up" had anything to do with geography, or whether it may be hinting at something else. I may be suggesting something that's not really there, but it does make a good starting point for reflecting on the text.

I usually think of a desert or a wilderness as "down." We go up to a mountain, not up to a wilderness or a desert. The Spirit is leading Jesus *up*. Would the Spirit lead him down? The Spirit leads him up to be tempted by the devil.

"Then the devil took him to the holy city and placed him on the pinnacle of the temple." What must that have been like? Was it windy up there? How could he balance himself on something that sounds like the steeple down at Saint Pat's? How did he get up there without everybody seeing him?

Or "Again, the devil took him to a very high mountain and showed him all the kingdoms of the world." What mountain could that have been, so high that he could see all the kingdoms of the world?

Isn't it interesting, though, that with all the spatial language, the devil takes to these high places, but it is the Spirit who leads Jesus up.

It's very clear that the text has nothing to do with place. Its concern is sense of direction or point of view. We speak of upward mobility, of climbing the ladder of success, of getting a raise in pay, even moving into a higher tax bracket, which may not be so good after all ... but, in all of this, where are we actually going? Where are we headed? Are we going *up*?

The Spirit is leading Jesus upward, leading him Godward, and there is no way upward or Godward except through struggle and temptation. In its day Israel was "led up" out of Egypt to be tested in the wilderness for 40 years. Jesus likewise was led up into the wilderness and "in every respect has been tested as we are, yet without sin" (Hebrews 4.15). The temptations of the people of Israel throughout their history, which Matthew has Jesus recapitulating, are paradigms of all human temptation.

One of our problems with biblical stories such as this one is that they appear bigger than life. In this instance, I believe that the secret to making connections between the Jesus story and our own experience is to listen to how Jesus responds. In the midst of these fantastic moments, hear what Jesus has to say. His responses can provide a model for us in temptations great and small.

The devil, for example, suggests to Jesus that he can turn stones into bread. I don't know about you, but no one has ever suggested that I have that capacity. Listen, however, to Jesus' response: "One does not live by bread alone, but by every word that comes from the mouth of God." I can think of many temptations to place material well-being and comfort over values that may cause sacrifice, even pain; that statement would be the best of all possible responses: "One does not live by bread alone, but by every word that comes from the mouth of God." I should say that more often.

Nor have I been tempted to jump off a steeple to test God's ability or desire to protect and save me. Listen once more to Jesus' response to that temptation: "Do not put the Lord your God to the test." I have, however, been tempted to test God's patience with me, to test God's mercy towards me (even to test the patience and mercy of others). I have been tempted to travel beyond certain appropriate limits. Haven't you? "Do not put the Lord your God to the test."

I have never been taken to a high mountain, shown the kingdoms of the world and promised them all if I were to worship the devil. There have, however, been false gods clamouring for my attention and false priorities competing against what I know to be best. "Worship the Lord your God and serve only him." Wouldn't that be a good answer? "Away with you, Satan."

In the long silences and discipline of his Trappist Abbey, appropriately named Gethsemane, monk and author Thomas Merton knew what it felt like to "go up" into the wilderness. In a very deep and personal way, he struggled with temptations and demons such as these. In *The Sign of Jonas*, the continuation of his more famous *Seven Storey Mountain,* he describes taking his turn as night-time security guard. He makes his rounds throughout the monastery, coming at last to the roof, where he stops to rest and is moved to pray, trying, under the stars, to figure out the meaning of his life, trying to discern his vocation:

> God my God, God whom I meet in darkness, with you it is always the same thing! Always the same question that nobody knows how to answer! I have prayed to you in the daytime with thoughts and reasons and in the nighttime you have confronted me, scattering thought and reason...[13]

As he moves forward in his prayer, Merton discovers that the quest for certainty, the possibility of being absolutely sure of himself, was beyond him in this present life. As the Apostle Paul points out, "we see but dimly."

I remember being amazed as a little kid that my eyes could get "used to the dark." The fact is that our eyes can't get used to total darkness, but we can become accustomed to seeing dimly and moving ahead anyway. A kind of dimness is characteristic of the human condition. We humans never find full and complete answers to our most important questions. Merton goes on in his prayer:

> God, my God, whom I meet in the darkness,...While I am asking questions, which you do not answer, could it be that you are asking me a question which is so simple that I cannot understand... [always] the same question.

Just what is the question that he is hearing? Merton doesn't clarify that for the reader, but makes the suggestion that God's question to him and to all of us (even to Jesus in the wilderness) may be as simple

---

[13]   Thomas Merton, *The Sign of Jonas* (New York: Harcourt Brace, 1953), p. 365.

and as profound as "Can you live with your humanity?" "Can you see and function even in dim light?" "Can your eyes get used to the dark?"

God's question to Merton and to all of us (even to Jesus in the wilderness) may be as simple and as profound as "Can you live with your humanity?"

Especially when we find ourselves led up into the wilderness of temptation, competing voices will suggest competing answers to this fundamental question, voices of darkness—greed, lust and jealousy, pride, resentment and desire to get even, anger and pain over loss, abuse and rejection. Let these voices speak, noisy and boisterous in the night. Let them wear themselves out in their emptiness. Let them gradually recede into the background, creating space for the softer, gentler voices of the stars. These are the smaller and softer voices of peace, gentleness, kindness, goodness, hope, forgiveness and love. They might seem small and insignificant, barely audible, but they are there. Trust them. They are faithful. They can lead us up to say with Jesus:

"Not by bread alone can I live."
"I will not put the God of the universe to the test."
"I shall worship the Lord. God alone shall I serve."

In Touch with God:
A Life in Tension

Second Sunday of Lent

Genesis 12.1-4
Psalm 33
2 Timothy 1.8b-10
Matthew 17.1-9

Especially at the high points in Matthew's gospel, we experience a clear tension between two ways of understanding the spiritual life: what a living relationship with God is all about and what we can expect from such a relationship.

The first is peace, a deep sense of well-being or inner calm. In touch with God, I am well-grounded, in good order, in harmony with life. With God I am at home.

The second, strangely enough, sounds like just the opposite. In touch with God, I am motivated, challenged, dis-comforted. With God I am on a journey.

In spite of this seeming contradiction, it is necessary to see our lives in both ways. We can expect to experience God as both present and absent, as available and unavailable, as with us and ahead of us, as known and unknown, as intimate and distant, sometimes even all at the same time.

If God is personal, isn't such a dialectic to be expected? Doesn't a good marriage, a strong family community, or a long-lasting friendship bring with it both comfort and challenge, a sense of security and a sense of being stretched? Even within themselves, mature persons feel both at home in their skin and restless.

Faith is a way of living this tension, this experience of humanity, this mystery. In the transfiguration story, this tension, this dialectic, is operative.

Peter said to Jesus: "It is good for us to be here." Jesus does not respond. As the story unfolds, he reaches out and touches them saying: "Get up and do not be afraid."

Matthew sets the scene on a "high mountain." It was on a mountain, Mount Sinai, also called Mount Horeb, that Moses communed with God and received the law, and Elijah, at the mouth of a cave, heard God's "voice of silence." With Moses and Elijah present, something like that is happening here. It's big stuff!

Last week we heard that Jesus' third temptation took place on a very high mountain from which the devil showed him "all the kingdoms of the world and their splendour." On the mountainside Jesus delivered the Sermon on the Mount.

Only after Jesus had gone up onto the mountain did he cure the crippled, the deformed, the blind and the lame. It was from the mountain to which Jesus had called them that he sent the disciples forth to make disciples of others.

Situating the transfiguration on a high mountain marks its importance, placing it among the most significant moments of Jesus' life and ministry.

On this mountaintop, Jesus is in very good company. He is talking with Moses and Elijah, consulting with the experts. They know what faith and struggle are all about. They know what it feels like to be at home in their own skin and restless at the same time. They both know first-hand the dialectic of intimacy and distance, God's availability and unavailability. As their consultation unfolds,

> A bright cloud overshadowed them, and from the cloud a voice said, "This is my Son, the Beloved; with him I am well pleased; listen to him!" When the disciples heard this, they fell to the ground and were overcome by fear. Jesus came and touched them, saying, "Get up and do not be afraid." And when they looked up, they saw no one except Jesus himself alone. (Matthew 17.5–8)

Of course they were overcome with fear. Mountaintop experiences are awesome and bewildering. Life is awesome. The call to be with the likes of Moses, Elijah and Jesus is neither lightly issued nor lightly accepted.

As they were coming down the mountain, Jesus ordered them, "Tell no one about the vision until after the Son of Man has been raised from the dead."

The stakes are high. This "following Jesus" business is going to be quite a trip.

A month or so ago I was quite struck by a poem by George Herbert. He lived in England during the tempestuous reigns of James I and Charles I, and saw his country racked by conflict among Catholics, High Anglicans and Puritans. He was a member of a politically active family, but chose the life of a simple country pastor. He demonstrated his literary genius in *The Country Parson,* an extended essay on the joys and hardships of a pastor's life, and *The Temple,* a collection of poems.

One of those poems is entitled "The Collar." I may be wrong, but I read it as the clerical collar being a straitjacket or ball and chain for him that day. The political realities of the church at the time cornered him. Listen to his struggle and to the fresh invitation that arises from it.

> ... leave thy cold dispute
> Of what is fit and not. Forsake thy cage,
>   Thy rope of sands,
> Which petty thoughts have made and made to thee
> Good cable to enforce and draw,
>   And be thy law,
> While thou didst wink and wouldst not see.
>   Away; take heed:
>   I will abroad ... .
> But as I rav'd and grew more fierce and wild
>   At every word,
> Me thoughts I heard one calling, Child:
>   And I replied, My Lord.

Jesus came and touched him, saying, "Get up and do not be afraid." And when he looked up, he saw no one except Jesus himself alone. (Matthew 17.7-8)

The door of his cage was opened for him. The ball and chain were cut from his feet. The collar was no longer a straitjacket, at least for the time being. Without glossing over the fragility and brokenness of his experience, even within the professional ranks of the church itself, Herbert reaffirms the great values of faith and prayer. Real growth takes place in his experience at the edges or borders of his human reach—between the heart of his life and its limits.

For earlier disciples the metaphor of the mountain-top experience describes an awakening and a fresh call for them as they hear the divine affirmation of Jesus' own vocation. It calls them forward in their ongoing voyage of discovery whose precise destiny, dangers and purpose cannot yet be known for sure.

Jesus brought his disciples to the Mount of Transfiguration for the transformation of their consciousness of his destiny and theirs. Their moment of discovery does not alter the external circumstances of their lives in a lasting way, but it does alter their perspective. Their experience of God's affirmation of Jesus begins to change them from the inside out.

Their discovery of grace changes nothing but changes everything. Our own discovery can do the same.

Lord, let your mercy be on us, as we place our trust in you.

Let your steadfast love, O LORD, be upon us,
even as we hope in you. (Psalm 33)

Another Well-side Meeting

Third Sunday of Lent

Exodus 17.3–7
Psalm 95
Romans 5.1–2, 5–8
John 4.5–42

[Jesus] came to a Samaritan city called Sychar, near the plot of ground that Jacob had given to his son Joseph. Jacob's well was there, and Jesus, tired out by his journey, was sitting by the well. It was about noon. A Samaritan woman came to draw water. (John 4.5–7)

Another well-side meeting. There are plenty of them in the Bible.

Abraham is reported to have sent his servant to the well to sit there and wait until an appropriate woman might come to draw water, a woman who would be an appropriate wife for his son Isaac. The servant sat there and Rebecca showed up. A great dream passed to another generation. The story was told at water's edge, a covenant sealed at the well.

Isaac's son Jacob in his turn was sitting at a well waiting for an appropriate wife, who turned out to be Rachel. The dream moves forward from one well-side meeting to the next. The well is a deep water source, a life source over which dreams are dreamed, promises made and the future assured.

The ancients knew that water was life, and treasured it accordingly. Water was their future. The well at Sychar was a gift from God to Jacob, and for generations had been offering the gift of life to people and their flocks. The woman of Sychar was right to reverence the spot. When Jesus speaks of living water, she is right to question him.

"Sir, you have no bucket, and the well is deep. Where do you get that living water? Are you greater than our ancestor Jacob, who gave us the well, and with his sons and his flocks drank from it?" Jesus said to her, "Everyone who drinks of this water will be thirsty again, but those who drink of the water that I will give will never be thirsty. The water that I will give will become in them a spring of water gushing up to eternal life." (John 4.11-15)

These well-side stories of Israel's past make the story of Jesus and this woman especially poignant, especially rich in spiritual possibilities. Jesus, alone at the well with this woman, is both in sync and out of sync with biblical well-side precedents. Jesus is not looking for a wife, but he is in a stance of covenant-making. He is carrying a dream forward. He states very clearly at the beginning of the "interview" that he would like to meet her husband, which sets clear boundaries for their relationship.

The tradition of well meetings continues, but is transformed. Jesus *did* propose to her at well-side and she accepted. She was hooked. She left her jar right there and went into her village as the first missionary, the first herald of the Word, a disciple making fellow disciples. She was liberated. This man was not into arguing over mountains or pointing fingers and listing reasons for her unworthiness. He was different—invitational, generative—offering the gift of God, a spring of water flowing up from within herself and bubbling up forever and ever and ever to life everlasting. This nameless Samaritan woman becomes the mother of faith for a new generation of "new time religion." All in all, she's pretty amazed! Try to imagine what must have been going on in her mind:

> He told me everything I ever did. He received me with compassion and grace. Even though I am who I am and even though I tried to get him off track, he stuck with me. I told him that I have no husband and he read straight through me, but didn't turn me away. I had five and the man I'm with now is a nobody. He knew that already. I tried to avoid my own issues by turning the conversation to theology, you know, the mountain question. Who does what, where and when according to the rules. I was really trying to avoid my own issues, but he turned around and started talking about "spirit and truth," and about an inner well, a life-giving spring of water gushing up to eternal life that I might even be able to discover within myself. I could hardly stand it!

Pullman Car Hiawatha is one of Thornton Wilder's wonderful one-act plays. As it opens, the stage manager introduces each passenger by name and destination. We get to know them just a little better as they interact with the porter and with each other. Each is circumspect, guarded, revealing just a little bit of their story, just a little bit about their destination. We know only one lady on the train very well from the beginning. She's a little bit crazy and is completely transparent. She thinks out loud. During the night, one of the passengers is dying and God comes on the scene. All of a sudden we see with God's eyes and hear with God's ears. Everybody is thinking out loud. As the train rumbles forward, so do all these disparate individual thoughts and desires. Nobody's in their own little compartment anymore. All are on the same journey.

With God we are all transparent. With Jesus we are all the woman at the well. We come together here, along this Easter-bound journey as thirsty fellow-seekers of life and truth.

We celebrate the first scrutiny today with those among us preparing for baptism. The rite invites them to transparency before God, to be in touch with their deepest selves, with their successes and failures, with their hopes and fears. The rite invites them to enter into the spirit of the woman at the well, to be one with her in both her questions and aspirations. We can all join them in that process. We can think along with them, knowing that God knows, understands and fills our depths.

We can make the scrutiny prayer our own:

Lord Jesus,
in your merciful wisdom,
you touched the heart of the woman at the well
and taught her to worship
in spirit and in truth.

Now by your power
free us from sin;
draw us to the fountain of living water.

Touch our hearts with the power of your Spirit,
that we may come to know the one true God,
in faith and hope, which expresses itself in love.[14]
Amen.

---

[14] *Rite of Christian Initiation of Adults,* Ottawa: Canadian Conference of Catholic Bishops, 1987.

More Than Meets the Eye

Fourth Sunday of Lent

1 Samuel 16.1b, 6-7, 10-13a
Psalm 23
Ephesians 5.8-14
John 9.1-41

Jesus said: "As long as I am in the world, I am the light of the world." When he had said this, he spat on the ground and made mud with the saliva and spread the mud on the man's eyes [the eyes of the man born blind], saying to him, "Go, wash in the pool of Siloam" (which means Sent) ....

"I came into this world for judgment so that those who do not see may see, and those who do see may become blind." (John 9.5-7, 39)

What sayings! What commands! What invitations! What challenges! Since the earliest times of the church's history, this story and its invitations and challenges have been a part of our baptismal catechesis and baptismal celebration. Even today we recognize ourselves in the story and enter into it accordingly. It comes alive for us in our own liturgical celebration.

On the Fourth Sunday of Lent we gather around candidates for baptism whose eyes and other senses have already been marked, not with mud and saliva, but with the cross of Christ. These same candidates are in the process of gradually coming to see clearly; they are developing and deepening their vision of life in the spirit of the gospel, in the spirit of Jesus who is the Light of the World. All of us accompany them as they move toward baptismal purification and enlightenment. We move forward with them, recognizing, as we do so, our own need for a broader and deeper vision of life—*real life.*

At the Easter Vigil just three weeks from now, these men and women will be immersed in their own pool of Siloam, the baptismal pool. We will join them in spirit as we renew our baptismal vows and feel the water from that same pool as it is sprinkled over us. Together we will be "sent" into springtime, purified, enlightened, refreshed and renewed.

In the Lenten liturgies, the dynamic of the story of Jesus and the man born blind emphasizes not only its enduring relevance, but its ongoing vitality. It is lived again in the lives of any and all who feel the challenge and invitation to be a part of it. Together we are invited to engage in the ongoing process of recognizing areas of blindness within ourselves, and of the possibility of being purified and enlightened to see what needs to be seen. Finally, we are sent and empowered to live fully in light of what we see.

In her book *Pilgrim at Tinker Creek,*[15] Annie Dillard does a wonderful job describing how people learn to see, and what a terrific metaphor physical sight can be for a deeper and broader internal vision. Coming to sight and to clarity is clearly a process.

Parents, for example, hang funny little mobiles over the cribs of their infant children. The children see the objects moving about and learn how to reach for them, grab at them, and finally connect. Their perspective and capacity for judgment develop. When they get a little older they learn to play catch. How complex the act of throwing and catching a ball is! The child sees the catcher at a certain distance from herself and uses her hand, arm and whole body to propel the ball from here to there. Her eyes move her to co-ordinated action that takes a lot of concentration and practice.

If I place my hand in front of my face to block the sun's glare, my hand appears bigger than the sun because, from here, my hand in front of my face does cover the whole sun. But because I have experience with seeing and have developed a sense of perspective, I know otherwise. We develop vision. Only slowly do we learn to see rightly. We see things differently as we grow older and integrate experience.

---

[15] Annie Dillard, *Pilgrim at Tinker Creek* (New York: Harper and Row, 1974) Chapter 2, "Seeing."

When I visited a funeral home last week, the new widow said to me, "Everything looks so different now." I knew exactly what she meant. How do things look to you today? Is everything clear to you? In what ways do you lack clarity in your vision of life or in your sense of meaning and direction? In what ways does your faith help you to see beyond the horizon, or even to see the nose on your face more clearly, or to look in the mirror and see wonderful possibilities—even in that newly discovered wrinkle or developing second chin?

A very curious little girl was walking along with her mother one summer's night and, like most youngsters, every new sight—flowers, trees, houses, people—caught her attention. Finally, after it had gotten very dark, she looked up. She stared skyward for what seemed to her mother, used to her daughter's incessant questioning, to be a very long time. Wisely, she made no comment until she sensed that her little girl was ready. "What did you see up there, Sarah? What were you thinking about?" For a moment or two, the youngster seemed to search for words to describe her thoughts: "If the bottom side of heaven is so beautiful, what must the other side be like?"

Isn't that wonderful? The little girl is clearly being drawn beyond what her physical eyes can see. She has a perspective that must have delighted her mother.

When you look into the heavens, what do you see? When you look into the eyes of a loved one, what do you see? When you read the morning paper, what do you see? When our pastoral council and various parish committees look at our financial situation and consider possibilities for improved access to our church, what will we see?

There's more to life than meets the eye. A lot lies beneath the surface that can be seen only with what we used to call the "eyes of faith." What do the eyes of your own faith, hope and love see when you look at yourself, or look around you at your family, or our community, or our world, for that matter? Do you see only what's there, or do you see deeper, perhaps even hidden possibilities?

Our catechumens and candidates were asking each other these kinds of questions as they prepared for this liturgy. They recognized clearly that seeing rightly is a real journey. The blind man in the gospel was himself on a journey towards sight. First he saw with his physical eyes; then he saw that it is Jesus who healed him and was truly grateful, then he saw that such power must come from God. Finally he saw clearly enough to worship Jesus and to let everything else fall into place. We are being invited today to enter more deeply into that same movement. In this Lenten liturgy we engage ourselves in the process of coming to a similar spiritual awareness that would invite Christ not only to open our eyes, but to be our light—to be the Light of the World as he promised.

A couple of verses from a wonderful old Irish hymn capture this process in a poignant prayer:

Be thou my vision, O Lord of my heart,
Naught be all else to me save that thou art;
Thou my best thought in the day and the night,
Waking or sleeping, Thy presence my light.

Riches I heed not, nor man's empty praise,
Thou my inheritance through all my days;
Thou, and Thou only, the first in my heart,
High king of heaven, my treasure Thou art!

Ancient Gaelic
Translated by Eleanor Hull

Free the Dead!

Fifth Sunday of Lent

Ezekiel 37.12–14
Psalm 130
Romans 8.8–11
John 11.1–45

Thus says the LORD God: "I am going to open your graves, and bring you up from your graves, O my people.... I will put my spirit within you, and you shall live." (Ezekiel 37.12, 14)

Ezekiel was a remarkable man who had a keen mind and who deeply and faithfully loved his people. He had consistently and hopefully prophesied for years that Jerusalem was doomed to destruction unless the people repented and changed their sinful ways. His preaching, however, did nothing to turn their hearts back to God, but he kept preaching anyway and, sure enough, Jerusalem fell. What is more remarkable than his consistency and fidelity in preaching to a deaf congregation of sinners was his fidelity to them even after the fall of their beloved city. He went down to Babylon with them. He shared their experience of exile and began preaching again, this time a message of hope and promise, of dauntless, irrepressible hope and promise. A section of his famous visionary preaching is included in today's liturgy:

"You shall know that I am the LORD, when I open your graves, and bring you up from your graves, O my people..." says the LORD. (Ezekiel 37.13)

The picture of a massive cemetery or of a valley strewn with bleaching fragments of innumerable skeletons is not exactly a complimentary way of describing a community of people who think they're alive. There is clearly a lot going on in Ezekiel's metaphor. Though not dead, Israel in slavery is as good as dead, perhaps even worse than physically dead because of its paralysis, fragmentation and powerlessness to live in dignity and freedom. Even before the exile they were dead because of their consistently sinful ways.

As stubborn as he was about preaching disaster, Ezekiel was even more stubborn about preaching hope. His confidence that God could and would restore the people to their land and to their homes was unshakeable. God will make a living community out of their desiccated and dislocated bones. According to Ezekiel, God could not conceive of leaving his sinful and exiled people in the "sleep of death." God is life and mercy in abundance, life and mercy in action.

The account of the raising of Jesus' friend Lazarus is a symbolic story that complements Ezekiel's imagery. When Jesus heard the news of his friend's sickness, he said, "This illness does not lead to death; rather it is for God's glory, so that the Son of God may be glorified through it." Jesus said to Martha: "I am the resurrection and the life. Those who believe in me, even though they die, will live and everyone who believes in me will never die."

Death in this case, too, serves as a metaphor. For individuals as well as for communities, there are lots of ways of being dead, lots of ways of being entombed. The physical death of Israel was not the issue for Ezekiel, nor is the inevitable physical death of "all mortal flesh" the issue in John. Notice how Lazarus is first called from the grave, then unbound and set free. His coming back to life involves a whole lot more than just breathing again and finding that his heart is once more beating and his flesh is restored. His new life and liberation from the tomb invite his sisters and the whole community to faith in Jesus who is the resurrection and the life.

Just what can all this mean for the church today? How can these metaphors relate to our experience as a community and as individuals? In what way can bones be knit back together and dead people be set free?

In just a few moments we will be praying over members of this assembly who are preparing for Easter rebirth in baptism.

Lord Jesus Christ,
You commanded Lazarus to step forth alive from his tomb

And by your own resurrection freed all people from death.
We pray for these your servants,
Who eagerly approach the waters of new birth
And hunger for the banquet of life.
Do not let the power of death hold them back,
For, by their faith
They will share in the triumph of the resurrection.[16]

In this third scrutiny, we celebrate the raising of Lazarus from the dead as a metaphor for being called from the grave in other than physical ways. It points to the resurrection of Jesus. Surely there are lots of ways of being dead, and lots of ways and levels of being called back into life. The prayer refers to powers of death that can hold people back even now. The scrutiny recognizes that Jesus, our resurrection and life, has the potential, the energy and the grace to revitalize and transform them all.

People and communities are still being called from the grave. Unbinding and setting free is Jesus' favourite activity, and he does it in so many wonderful and awesome ways. Remember the woman at the well and the man born blind? Weren't they, too, being called from a kind of grave? Weren't they, too, being set free?

Wouldn't it be interesting to interview our candidates and catechumens about the life–death issues that they have faced in their own lives, about the banquet for which they hunger, about the powers of death that have done their best to hold them back from moving Godward—heavenward—towards fullness of life? I'll bet that they and all of us could come up with resurrection stories of our own, with stories of dry bones coming together, eyes and ears opened, tongues loosed to speak the truth, arms unbound for service, legs unbound for the dance. Do you see how the metaphors can be stretched into our own time and place?

In the playbill I was given at a recent opera performance, I read this story about Madame Ernestine Schumann-Heink, a world-renowned opera star from the 1940s and '50s. Early in her career, her

---

[16] *Rite of Christian Initiation of Adults*, Ottawa: Canadian Conference of Catholic Bishops, 1987.

marriage broke up. Sick, hungry and discouraged, reluctant to bring up her children in what she experienced as the very worst of worlds, she contemplated suicide. Not only did she contemplate it, she planned it and was on her way to carry out her plans in a horrible way. She packed up her little ones on a bitterly cold night and headed for the railroad tracks just outside Vienna. She knew the schedule. Cowering on the tracks with her children, she waited for the express train to come roaring down on them and bring her ultimate relief. Her little daughter said: "Mama, it's cold here. I love you. Let's go home." This little voice pleading from the darkness brought Ernestine to her senses. She abandoned her desperate plan, made another try at life and, within a few years, was acclaimed as one of the greatest singers of all time.

"Ernestine, come forth .... Unbind her and let her go." Schumann-Heink was called from the grave. She was raised from the dead by the voice of God calling to her in the words of a child.

It is not likely that many of us have experienced a resurrection so dramatic, but we are all called to life and freedom. I don't want to trivialize these wonderful metaphors, but I'd like to share something I came across last week that makes them a bit more life-size, at least for me. The name Malcolm Boyd may be familiar to you. An African-American Episcopal priest, over 30 years ago he wrote the book *Are You Running With Me, Jesus?* which became very popular. It was as if people were starving for a more intimate and familiar way of dealing with the Lord. Just a couple of years ago, he wrote *Go Gentle into that Good Night.* He dedicated it to his mother, who had died the year before and whom he had cared for personally. I believe he gives some good advice as he meditates aloud on the shortness of life and God's call to come alive every day:

> Act in freeing ways. Avoid rigidity. Speak to someone who appears forbidding. Tell the truth. Make the telephone call you have been afraid to make. Break the silence. Place on paper a letter that has been long on your mind. Ask the hard question. Come to life.

> In order to live more fully in the present and prepare for our ultimate departure, we can strive to be more open and vulnerable. We needn't worry about what other people think.

We should laugh uproariously if we feel like it. Go to a park and ride a swing, whether we are ten or seventy. Cry if we are moved and wish to. Respond with the fullness of our being to a poem, the sound of the wind, or the beauty of a cello. We can come alive.

While we are here, our lives can either be unhappy, self-destructive, unproductive and lacking fire, or celebratory, loving, creative and filled with spiritual energy. Choose.[17]

It's not exactly dry bones dancing or Lazarus coming out of a tomb, but it's real, isn't it? Smaller scale, but real! Speaking from experience, Boyd invites us at any age and under any circumstances to get it together and come to life. As I read these lines, I thought of Moses who so long ago challenged his own people in the name of God: "I place before you life and death. Choose life."

The wonderful biblical images and metaphors of today's liturgy offer the same invitation. Let's all choose to accept it!

---

[17] Malcolm Boyd, *Go Gentle into that Good Night* (Columbus, MS: Genesis Press, 1968), pp. 124-126.

The Cross-Shaped God

Passion (Palm) Sunday

Isaiah 50.4–7
Psalm 22
Philippians 2.6–11
Matthew 26.14–27.66

Now from the sixth hour, there was darkness over all the land until the ninth hour ... Jesus cried out with a loud voice and yielded up his spirit. And behold, the curtain of the temple was torn in two, from top to bottom; and the earth shook; the tombs also were opened and many bodies of the saints who had fallen asleep were raised, and coming out of the tombs after his resurrection they went into the holy city and appeared to many. When the centurion and those who were with him, keeping watch over Jesus, saw the earthquake and what took place, they were filled with awe, and said, "Truly this was the Son of God." (Matthew 27.45, 50-54)

What a picture! What a scene! There's a lot more going on in this story than the execution of a religious misfit or a political agitator.

Noon becomes midnight.

A crucified man, dying of asphyxiation, is not breathless. Instead he shouts a victory cry.

Jesus does not die but yields up his spirit, making it an offering, a free gift.

Temple offerings will never be the same. A final sacrifice has been offered in the blood of Jesus.

The foundations of the earth are shaken. The dead are shaken loose from their graves. The resurrection is already at work.

Roman soldiers keeping watch join in acclamation: "Truly this was the Son of God."

What a story indeed! Nothing will ever be the same. Even the earth is moved. Humanity at its deepest level is changed forever. With a cry of victory, the Son of God yields his spirit. He offers himself. He lets himself go. He pours out his life as a sacrifice to God for the life of the world.

In this story the cross is no longer an instrument of torture. The cross is a person. The cross is Jesus himself. Stretched between heaven and earth, reaching out to all creation, joining north, south, east and west, he draws the whole world to himself in a life-giving death that offers reconciliation and communion to all. What an event! Life for the world comes through the death of a cross-shaped God.

We who believe in Jesus are invited not just to look on, but to be reshaped through him, with him, and in him. We're invited to see the cross at work in our own bodies. We're invited to become cross-shaped ourselves as we stretch out our own arms and hands in self-offering and prayer.

Being "in shape" takes on a whole new meaning.

When I behold the wondrous cross,
On which the prince of glory died,
My richest gain, I count but loss,
And pour contempt on all my pride.

Were all the realms of nature mine,
That would be off'ring far too small:
Love so amazing, so divine,
Demands my soul, my life, my all.

Isaac Watts (1674–1748), alt.

The Easter Triduum

Broken Bread, Broken Bodies

Evening Mass of the Lord's Supper
Holy Thursday

Exodus 12.1-8, 11-14
Psalm 116
1 Corinthians 11.23-26
John 13.1-15

To gather at such a solemn moment is both a great privilege and a great responsibility. At the outset all of us need to assume responsibility for what we do here, to dedicate ourselves fully to the paschal process that the liturgy observes and celebrates.

> Now before the festival of the Passover, Jesus knew that his hour had come to depart from this world and go to the Father. Having loved his own who were in the world, he loved them to the end. (John 13.1)

We remember and celebrate Jesus' great three-day hour. We do not simply follow him along; rather, we see the meaning of our own life as reliving what he lived. We do so in the hour of our own lives. The texts, gestures and symbols for this great three-part liturgy open wonderful possibilities for our imagination, which I hope will guide and sustain us in our prayer.

The people of Israel were ready to pass through the sea from Egypt to freedom, ready for the angel of death to pass over their homes, marked as they were with the blood of the lamb. Their journey would be long and hard, but they would have a pillar of cloud by day and a pillar of flame by night to guide them. Their daily bread would be provided in the form of manna, a gift from heaven.

In our own movements and passages during this three-day hour we, too, experience signs of God's presence. We, too, have the blood of a lamb, manna from heaven, cloud and flame. We have broken bread and wine, flowing water and oil, cross and candle, towel and basin. I'd like to suggest that as we experience these symbols, we explore the mystery into which their meaning is inviting us. Together they define what God is doing with us in this invitation into the mystery.

Although First Corinthians and John's gospel present the Lord's Supper quite differently, there are clear common elements, common symbols.

"On the night when he was betrayed," Paul begins; John writes, "The devil had already put it into the heart of Judas to betray him."

"He took a loaf of bread; he took the cup," Paul reports; John notes, "And during supper Jesus, knowing that the Father had given all things into his hands and that he had come from God and was going to God, got up from the table, took off his outer robe and tied a towel around himself. Then he poured water into a basin."

In one telling of the story, he breaks bread and shares a cup. In the other, he washes feet. In both, he is signalling who he really is, what God is doing through him and in him, and how we, too, are to be drawn into the mystery.

"Do this in remembrance of me," he says in the first case and, in the second: "If I, your Lord and Teacher, have washed your feet, you also ought to wash one another's feet. For I have set you an example, that you also should do as I have done to you."

The temptation to miss the full significance of these commands, to miss their profound ethical implications, is real. Paul tells the story in the context of having to remind the Corinthians that without genuine care, consideration and service to the poor, their eucharist is a sacrilege. To use his very strong language, Christians at the table need to "examine themselves," "discern the body," "judge themselves," "wait on each other" lest they "eat and drink unworthily," even unto "condemnation."

Paul is definitely not the first or the last to express concerns that authenticity and ethical behaviour be consistent with what happens at the table. Isaac Watts, a very devout but independent thinker of the 17th and 18th centuries, wrote not only hymns, but other poetry that didn't quite make it into hymnals. The following is his reading of Paul's concern that what happens in the rest of life be consistent with what happens at the eucharist.

There are a number of us creep
Into this world to eat and sleep
And know no reason why we're born,
But only to consume the corn,

Devour the cattle, fowl and fish,
And leave behind an empty dish.
Then if their tombstone, when they die,
Be n't taught to flatter and to lie,

There's nothing better will be said
Than that "they've eat up all their bread,
Drunk up their drink and gone to bed."
There's nothing better can be said.[18]

Ouch!

You may have noticed a print of a famous artistic depiction of the Last Supper that hangs in the corridor right behind the sacristy. Jesus and the disciples are all lined up at the table. The haloes behind their heads figure prominently but, oddly enough, there's practically no food on the table. Jacques Prévert, a popular 20th-century French poet and satirist, pokes fun at depictions such as that, but in doing so challenges the distance he perceives between Christianity and the real tables of life. Let me read you his poem. Brace yourself. It's only five lines.

The Last Supper

They are at table
They eat not
Nor touch their plates
And their plates stand straight up
Behind their heads.[19]

---

[18] Isaac Watts, quoted in "What Are Your Plans?" J. Alfred Smith in *Minister's Manual*, James W. Cox, ed. (San Francisco, Harper Collins, 1997), p. 318.

[19] Jacques Prévert, quoted in *Divine Inspiration: The Life of Jesus in World Poetry*, Robert Atwan, George Dardess, Peggy Rosenthal, eds. (New York: Oxford University Press, 1998), p. 375.

Ouch again! What an indictment it is to suggest that holiness is in the haloes, not on the plates, that holiness is some mental, disembodied state, rather than real-life sharing of life and death. To miss the connection between broken bread and broken bodies, to miss the connection between a shared cup and shared commitment to sacrificial living is to miss the real presence of Christ. That's what Paul is signalling.

Let's look now at John's symbol. Foot-washing, too, is real presence.

In his book *The Active Life: A Spirituality of Work, Creativity and Caring,* Parker Palmer describes a remarkable experience.

> Twice in my life, I have experienced deep depression. Both times various friends tried to rescue me with well-intended encouragement and advice .... In the midst of my depression, I had a friend who took a different approach. Every afternoon at around four o'clock he came to me, sat me in a chair, removed my shoes and massaged my feet. He hardly said a word, but he was there, he was with me. He was a lifeline to me, a link to the human community and thus to my own humanity. He had no need to fix me. He knew the meaning of compassion.[20]

A friend was telling me about another friend who had told her yet another "foot story." His wife gave him a new pair of slippers for his birthday. She had given him the old set, moccasins lined with wool, 20 years earlier. The soles were fine, but they were starting to come apart. He reluctantly put them in the trash. She seemed to sense that he hated to part with them. An hour later he went into the kitchen and saw that she had taken them out of the trash. They were sitting in their usual place like old friends. He reflected on their shape and their aging, which in a way matched his own. He was a little rougher around the edges than he had been twenty years ago; the slippers had accompanied him all along the way. Only he could fully appreciate their being and their history. Sensing that, his wife couldn't stand

---

[20] Parker Palmer, quoted in *Spiritual Literacy: Reading the Sacred in Everyday Life,* Frederic and Mary Ann Brussat, eds. (New York: Scribner, 1998), p. 533.

seeing them in a green plastic bag with milk cartons and food scraps. She set out repairing and relining them. The new ones went back to Sears.

Did you ever think how your feet carry you around, how they bear the weight of your life, how they make possible your comings and your goings? To bathe them, to anoint them, to clothe them doesn't sound very churchy, but has profound spiritual and symbolic potential.

"If I, your Lord and Teacher, have washed your feet, you also ought to wash one another's feet. For I have set you an example, that you also should do as I have done to you." (John 13.14–15)

"Do this in remembrance of me." And so, we proceed.

Shaped Like God

Celebration of the Lord's Passion
Good Friday

Isaiah 52.13–53.12
Psalm 31
Hebrews 4.14-16; 5.7-9
John 18.1–19.42

Last evening, as we began this great service, the opening antiphon was, "We should glory in the cross of our Lord Jesus Christ, for he is our salvation, our life and resurrection; through him we are saved and made free" (Galatians 6.14).

To some of you, it may not have sounded appropriate, especially if you think of Last Supper, Crucifixion and Resurrection (and Holy Thursday, Good Friday and Easter Sunday) as three separate events that we are commemorating separately on three separate days.

The liturgy considers it differently. This is one great event, one great movement, one great mystery; we don't just commemorate the event, we participate in it. We are drawn into the mystery from different angles, from different points of view. There was no entrance antiphon or hymn today. We all entered in silence this afternoon to take up where we left off. Tomorrow night we will continue our celebration again as we gather in the courtyard for the paschal fire. We enter into Jesus' great "hour" from the perspective of distinct moments, using distinct but complementary texts, gestures and symbols as our point of entry, our gates. Last night we entered by way of towel and basin, bread and wine: foot-washing and a sacrificial meal. This afternoon we enter by way of the cross.

In one of William Butler Yeats' plays, a particularly vivid scene takes place in an Irish country cottage. The family members are all sitting together in the firelight of the kitchen where, on the wall behind them, a black wooden crucifix hangs. There is a knock at the door and, when it is opened, a little fairy girl dressed in green comes dancing in. She is singing a merry little song. She is the personification of the spirit of the forest, and the ideas and ideals represented by so many fairy tales and legends. Suddenly her eyes fall upon the crucifix. She stops her singing, hides her face and shrieks, "Take down that ugly black thing."

Nearly 300 years had passed before the cross came into use as the chief emblem of Christianity during the reign of the Emperor Constantine. According to tradition, on the eve of a crucial battle, Constantine saw a flaming cross in the heavens bearing the inscription *In hoc signo vinces*, "In this sign conquer." The emperor, a recent convert to Christianity, made the cross his standard to be crafted and carried by the Roman legions. This *Labarum*, as it was called, remained the standard of the Roman army until the downfall of the Western Empire in 476. It was made like a banner, bearing the embroidered monogram of the first two Greek letters of the title *Christos*. Superimposed, those letters *chi* and *rho* gave the appearance of a cross. It has been suggested more recently that Constantine did the faith no favour in elevating the cross in such a way. It is quite ironic that the cross of Jesus' sacrificial death became a military symbol, taken up later in the crusades and other religious or quasi-religious adventures. Even the Nazi swastika is a stylized cross.

We can well understand how many people, not just fairies, may find that black thing, which we venerate with such solemnity today, ugly and repulsive.

When I went to my sister's wedding in New Mexico I had the opportunity to visit an ancient pueblo, which was a kind of apartment house. It is such a remarkable five-storey building that those who live there, the Pueblo Indians, are named after the dwellings they designed. There I was amazed to find crosses everywhere, in their rugs, in their tapestries, carved into walls. My immediate presumption was that the Spanish missionaries had introduced the symbol to them, and that it was an expression of Christian faith. I learned from the guide, however, that the cross was a symbol for these people long before the missionaries arrived, and that Christianity began including their meanings into its prayer and theology. The cross links north, south, east and west. When upright, the cross links up and down, right and left.

The cross is God's shape, the shape of reconciliation, embrace and communion. Isn't it wonderful to think of Jesus today as God's shape, open arms and hands outstretched between heaven and earth in welcome and embrace? Our first eucharistic prayer for reconciliation uses that language: "He was nailed to a cross ... he stretched out his arms between heaven and earth in the everlasting sign of your covenant."

Jesus is shaped like God. The cross is God's shape. Jesus lives and dies shaped like God. As we listened to the passion according to St. John, we recognized and affirmed his divinity in that stance, in that position.

We bow before this ugly black thing because for us it is a thing of beauty beyond description. We touch it, we bow before it, we kiss it as an act of homage to Christ in whom we see our own destiny. To the extent that we ourselves are shaped like a cross, we are in communion with him. To the extent that our lives are cruciform, they reflect the way, the truth and the life that Jesus is and reveals.

Our experience has taught us that such a stance is anything but comfortable. Reconciliation, embrace and communion are not achieved without a high cost, which cannot be overlooked or minimalized. Death to the old and resurrection to the new arise only from generosity and sacrifice.

The liturgy of Good Friday expresses how beautiful this process can be, perhaps especially in its high cost, even in its darkness.

> We should glory in the cross of our Lord Jesus Christ, for he is our salvation, our life and resurrection; through him we are saved and made free. (Galatians 6:14)

We move forward to do just that.

Consumed in the Burning

Easter Vigil
Holy Saturday

Genesis 1.1–2.2
Psalm 104 or 33
Genesis 22.1-18
Psalm 16
Exodus 14.15-31; 15.20, 1
Exodus 15
Isaiah 54.5-14
Psalm 30
Isaiah 55.1-11
Isaiah 12
Baruch 3.9-15, 32–4.4
Psalm 19
Ezekiel 36.16-17, 18-28
Psalm 42 or Psalm 51
Romans 6.3-11
Matthew 28.1-10

Then God said, "Let there be light"; and there was light.... God made the two great lights—the greater light to rule the day and the lesser light to rule the night—and the stars. (Genesis 1.3, 16)

"Christ our light!" "Thanks be to God!"

I was hearing the confessions of the children at the local elementary school in a little reconciliation corner we had set up in the school library. During a break, I picked up a book that was lying on a table near where I was sitting. I was amazed at the facts that I picked up: The sun is so hot that it could melt in one second a column of ice two and a half miles square and stretching the ninety-three million miles from the earth to the sun. You could empty the Atlantic, Pacific, Indian Oceans and the Great Lakes into the sun without it sputtering. From every square yard of the sun's vast surface there streams continuously over one hundred thousand horsepower, enough to lift two hundred and fifty ten-ton tanks to the top of a forty-storey building in one minute.... If we had to pay some power company for the light received daily from the sun, the bill would make the national debt look like carfare.... It could supply two billion more earths like our own.

Such extraordinary energy!

Before we proclaimed the creation story, which roots this energy in the creative love of God, the Easter vigil began with the lighting of a fire out under the stars. We then moved to the lighting of the paschal candle, which in turn gave light to our own candles and led us into the church. Here we heard chanted a prayer of thanksgiving for the "Morning Star which never sets, ... Christ, that Morning Star who came back from the dead and shed his peaceful light on all humanity." Such extraordinary energy!

In word and gesture we proclaim our faith in a creative and re-creative God. The energy of the first creation becomes a metaphor for the energy of the new. Flame touches flame; life touches life towards new and quickened hope communicated from God's own fire in the Risen Jesus, communicated person-to-person in the church for newness of life.

Light of Christ. Thanks be to God.

We have celebrated the liturgy of light and the liturgy of word. Now we move forward to the liturgies of baptism and eucharist, which draw us further into communion with Christ's own way of being light and energy in his sacrificial death and resurrection. In a homily many years ago, Pope Paul VI made the connection clearly and concisely:

Christ himself says, I am the light of the world; and we are the light, we ourselves, if we receive it from him ... but how do we receive it? How do we make it shine? ... the candle tells us, by burning and being consumed in the burning. A spark of fire, a ray of love, an inevitable immolation, are celebrated over that pure, straight candle, as pouring forth its gift of life, it exhausts itself in silent sacrifice.[21]

Consumed in the burning, inevitable immolation, silent sacrifice for the life of the world.

Listen again to the Apostle Paul, in the text from Romans which we heard moments ago:

> Do you not know that all of us who have been baptized into Christ Jesus were baptized into his death? Therefore we have been buried with him by baptism into death, so that, just as Christ was raised from the dead by the glory of the Father, so we too might walk in newness of life.
>
> For if we have been united with him in a death like his, we will certainly be united with him in a resurrection like his. (Romans 6.3-5)

As we celebrate Christ's death and rising, we celebrate our own in communion with countless believers who have gone before us in faith, beacons of light and energy, each in their own way. We move to the baptistery, invoking their names as we prepare to include even more names among their number. We move forward from light to light, from life to life—knowing its cost, embracing its promise. Alleluia!

---

[21] Homily delivered on the Feast of the Presentation of the Lord (Candlemas) at which religious men and women renewed their vows.

The Waters of Eden

Easter Sunday

Acts 10.34a, 36–43
Psalm 118
Colossians 3.1–4
1 Corinthians 5.6b–8
John 20.1–18

A summer Bible camp teacher was going through the great Christian feasts with her class of nine-year-olds. She began with Easter, because it's the most important one. From their answers, it became pretty clear that this teacher had her work cut out for her.

"Easter is when all the family gets together and they have a big turkey and sing about the pilgrims and all that," replied one student.

"No, that's not it," said the teacher.

"I know what Easter is," a second student announced. "Easter is when you get this pine tree and cover it with decorations and sing lots of songs."

"That's not it," the teacher repeated.

The third child responded, "Easter is when Jesus was killed, put in a tomb and left for three days."

"He knows, he knows!" the teacher said to herself.

But the boy went on. "Then everybody gathers at the tomb and waits to see if Jesus comes out, cuz if he comes out and sees his shadow he has to go back in for seven more weeks of winter."

I'm sure that our answers would be more on target than the answers of these children. I'm sure that we'd all come up with the resurrection of Jesus and would not confuse his appearance with those of Wiarton Willie, our famous Ontario groundhog.

I'm also sure, however, that our understandings of that event would be quite diverse. We would approach the questions "What is Easter?" and "Why do we celebrate it?" very differently. Yes, these questions are more than Bible camp questions for children. I think it would be interesting, even fun, for us to organize ourselves in groups of six or eight to discuss those questions for 20 minutes and then to hear from the groups this Easter Sunday morning. Just look around at the wonderful diversity in this church filled to the rafters. But don't worry, we're not going to do it!

It seems that at this time every year Jesus makes the front cover of major newspapers or weekly newsmagazines. He was the subject of a front-page story in the *Ottawa Citizen* that outlined various current interpretations of the historical Jesus and his resurrection. Out of curiosity, I went into Chapters and looked on the Bible and Christianity shelves. There I found more than 20 books relating to this topic. For those of you who are interested, I think the discussion in *The Meaning of Jesus: Two Visions* by Marcus J. Borg and N.T. Wright (San Francisco: Harper and Row, 2000) gives a very good introduction to two approaches to the issue. In spite of their differences, both agree that the resurrection is less about an empty tomb and more about a lived experience of a living presence that reaches into today.

The resurrection stories invite us into them. The preceding chapter in John's gospel concluded the passion story on a note of solemn finality with the burial of Jesus. However magnificent he may have been in his all-too-short life and ministry, he is now dead and buried. The accustomed ways of hearing him and being touched by him are over.

The empty tomb is not the message of the resurrection. At best, it provides a context for something more. The tomb opens towards personal encounters with a living Jesus that take different forms and shapes in people like Mary, Peter, Thomas, the disciples on the road and all of us. Let's just use this morning's gospel as an example.

The Easter narrative begins early Sunday morning. There is a new week, a new first day. There is a dawning after the darkness, emphasizing from the outset that what seemed like an end is a new beginning. The stormy sky is clearing up. Misunderstanding is replaced with new realization.

After discovering the empty tomb, going to fetch Peter and the disciple Jesus loved, Mary Magdalene comes back with them and stays on behind, presumably as a sign of love and respect. Standing outside the empty tomb weeping, she had first a vision of angels and then an encounter with Jesus himself.

> Mary turned around and saw Jesus standing there, but she did not recognize him.

> Jesus said to her, "Woman, why are you weeping? Whom are you looking for?" Supposing him to be the gardener, she said to him, "Sir, if you have carried him away, tell me where you have laid him, and I will take him away." Jesus said to her, "Mary!" (John 20.15-16)

"Supposing him to be the gardener" … Especially in the context of John's mystical gospel, could this be an "Easter echo" of the Book of Genesis heralding new beginnings at a very profound level of life?

> And the LORD God planted a garden in Eden, in the east; and there he put the man whom he had formed. Out of the ground the LORD God made to grow every tree that is pleasant to the sight and good for food, the tree of life also in the midst of the garden, and the tree of the knowledge of good and evil.

> A river flows out of Eden to water the garden, and from there it divides and becomes four branches. (Genesis 2:8-10)

A gardener indeed! Mary is not visiting a cemetery, but a garden. Can we sense how early in the morning on the first day of the week a new light is dawning; a new creation is being born; a new river is flowing? A cemetery is being transformed to a garden. Eden is being restored at the hands of a new Adam, the Risen Jesus, and from his hands the trees of life and of the knowledge of good and evil are sharing their fruit.

Can we hear ourselves being invited into the garden this Easter Sunday? Can we hear the gardener of Eden calling our names?

Two babies in the front pews are today awaiting baptism. Is the Risen Christ not calling the names of these children, inviting them into the garden with us? Are not wisdom and eternal life being promised to them and to us? If not, I don't think the empty tomb and whatever first-century appearances may have taken place matter very much.

Around Remembrance Day, I read an article describing the masses of visitors who flocked to Arlington National Cemetery on the shores of the Potomac River just outside Washington, D.C. They were there for the changing of the guard. The author, who was from overseas, described her almost eerie experience of standing in an open-air amphitheatre before the tomb of the Unknown Soldier. Hundreds of strangers stood in complete silence. The slap of military cleats and the clicking of cameras were the only sounds to be heard. Boisterous teenagers and gregarious tourists of every conceivable background were transformed into respectful witnesses to this highly choreographed ritual. She was deeply impressed.

Easter isn't like that. Christians at Easter come less to Arlington and more to the Potomac, less to the cemetery, and more to the river. We are less concerned with the empty tomb and more concerned with being immersed into the life and knowledge of the Risen One whom we meet here.

Christian believers come to Easter not as spectators, however respectful, but as participants, fully expecting to meet their Risen Lord and to experience the possibilities for re-creation that his death and rising promise.

The blessing of the font into which the paschal candle was immersed last night makes clear reference to the creation/re-creation that takes place in our sacramental encounters with the Risen One. Let me just chant a few verses of that blessing before we move to the baptism of these children and to the renewal of our own vows.

Father, you give us grace through sacramental signs,
which tell us of the wonders of your unseen power.
In baptism we use your gift of water,
which you have made a rich symbol of the grace you give us
in this sacrament.

At the very dawn of creation your Spirit breathed on the
waters,
making them the well-spring of all holiness ...

Father, look with love upon your church and unseal for her
the fountain of baptism.
By the power of the Holy Spirit give to the water of this font
the grace of your Son.
You created human beings in your own likeness;
cleanse our race from sin in a new birth of innocence by water
and the Spirit.
We ask you, Father, with your Son, to send the Holy Spirit
upon the waters of this font.

May all who are buried with Christ in the death of baptism
rise also with him to newness of life.[22]

Come to the garden. Come to the waters of Eden.

---

[22] *Rite of Christian Initiation of Adults*, Ottawa: Canadian Conference of Catholic
Bishops, 1987.

The Crucible of Doubt

Second Sunday of Easter

Acts 2.42-47
Psalm 118
1 Peter 1.3-9
John 20.19-31

"Unless I see the mark of the nails in his hands, and put my finger in the mark of the nails and my hand in his side, I will not believe." (John 20.25)

The apostle Thomas was in turmoil. Others had seen. He hadn't. Others believed. He couldn't—at least not yet.

In the soul of Fyodor Dostoevsky, the great Russian novelist, there was almost continual conflict. On one hand, he felt the strong desire to be in close union with God. On the other hand, he experienced an almost violent tugging away from any contact with the Almighty. When, in his novel *The Possessed,* the atheist character Kirilov admitted that he was haunted continually by the God whom he was trying to deny, it was actually the author himself speaking. Not long before his death, Dostoevsky wrote in his diary this forceful, almost strident answer to those who ridiculed his return to faith:

> Those fools could not even conceive so strong a denial of God as the one to which I gave expression. You might search the whole of Europe for so powerful an expression of atheism. Thus it is not like a child that I believe in Christ and confess him. My hosanna has come forth from the crucible of doubt.

What he came to learn in his struggle was that faith is not the result of a long battle with doubt in which the truth of God finally wins. Faith is the beginning of an ongoing partnership, an ongoing adventure with the living God in which recurring doubts and uncertainties are

137

normal and will continue to play a part. They are a part of the adventure, part of the challenge, even part of the fun.

Faith will always include doubts or it is not faith. Doubts are the odds that faith must meet. The episode of doubting Thomas allows John to make a strong statement about what he understands true faith to be. Thomas is doubly unbelieving because he refuses to accept the word of his brother apostles and because he demands a personal experience. It is, however, from this crucible of doubt that his hosanna arises. It is in his experience of Christ that he comes to faith, that he comes to the point of declaring, "My Lord and my God."

I was on the train not long ago and had both *The Globe and Mail* and *The Montreal Gazette* with me. Coincidentally, both papers reviewed books in whose spiritual themes doubt figured prominently.

The Globe and Mail reviewed Deepak Chopra's book *How to Know God: The Soul's Journey into the Mystery of Mysteries*. It quoted him as describing his own spiritual journey in an interview. He was "looking, looking, looking and never finding," or rather was finding "bits and pieces here and there, but never truth he could hold on to." The more he explored, "the bigger the unknown became, because by nature it's infinite." As I understood his developing thought, knowledge of the absolute truth of God is not the issue. In fact, such knowledge is impossible. Savour the hints, the bits and pieces; savour the experiences of the transcendent that inevitably will come your way. For Chopra the inevitable experience of doubt and uncertainty is an invitation to delve deeper.

It is in this regard that I think Thomas was on the right track with his refusal to believe too soon or too easily. First of all, he wanted the connection between the crucifixion and the resurrection to be crystal clear by seeing for himself Jesus' hands and feet and side. More than that, he wanted not only to see the wounds of Christ but to touch them, to enter into them, to experience the crucified risen one.

Let's take an example to illustrate the value and power of experience. It may be a silly example, but it might help anyway. I have a friend who loves oysters Rockefeller. He can tell me they exist and I can believe him. He can tell me how good they are and I can believe him. He can give me a recipe and I can analyze the contents, but to appreciate what he's telling me, to believe him, I have to share his experience. I have to smell them and taste them for myself.

More seriously, a group of us went to the Holocaust museum when we were in Jerusalem a few years ago. It's one thing to believe that the Holocaust happened, quite another to enter into the experience, even in such a limited way as a museum can make possible. To appreciate Handel's *Messiah,* reading the score with his picture on the cover isn't enough. You have to drink it in with your ears, with your body and soul. Knowledge is not the issue. You know best as you become one with what you know, as you enter into its mystery. Faith is like that.

Faith is not about knowing that God exists, or that this or that truth is absolutely true. It is about a living, growing relationship, the kind of relationship that Thomas was seeking—no, demanding—as a test of the authenticity of the resurrection. The doubting Thomas enters into the experience and, from within the experience, cries, "My Lord and my God." It is an act of faith unmatched in the whole New Testament. It changes forever the direction of his life.

That day of my train trip, *The Montreal Gazette* reviewed E.L. Doctorow's latest novel, *City of God.* As the story begins, an eight-foot cross has been stolen from Saint Timothy's Episcopal Church in Lower Manhattan and has turned up across town on the roof of the Synagogue of Evolutionary Judaism. Of all places. The church's wayward priest and the synagogue's husband-and-wife rabbi team are thrown together around this mystery. In the midst of their conversations and growing relationship, Rabbi Sarah says:

> "In the twentieth century, about to end, the great civilizer on earth seems to have been doubt. Doubt, the constantly debated and flexible inner condition of theological uncertainty, the wish to believe along with rueful or nervous or grieving skepticism, seems to have held people in thrall to ethical behaviour; while the true believers of whatever stamp have done the murdering."

She's not talking about relational faith. She's talking about faith that can be sick and destructive, that has been over the centuries. She's talking about right and wrong ideas, about proudly absolute convictions that turn people against each other. God neither desires nor needs the protection of human absolutes.

"Blessed are those who have not seen and yet have come to believe," Jesus says after Thomas' great outburst of faith. We may not see as Thomas saw, but we do need to see something, to experience something as we come to faith in Jesus.

How does that happen? Without seeing, where do we meet the Lord so as to believe in him? Why not right here?

"Jesus did many other signs," John reports. There's a wonderful tradition about how Thomas gave his whole life to the gospel and established the faith in India. He himself became a sign. Is it stretching it too far to think that we could be signs to each other, motives of credibility, living invitations to faith?

Can our own stories echo the story of the wounded, risen one? Can our stories resonate with Christ's truth about the wonder of dying and rising? Can we come into contact with each other's glorious wounds and find good reason in them to believe in the ultimate victory of God's love for the world?

Foot First into the Story

Third Sunday of Easter

Acts 2.14, 22b-28
Psalm 16
1 Peter 1.17-21
Luke 24.13-35

"Are you the only stranger in Jerusalem who does not know the things that have taken place there in these days? ... We had hoped .... " (Luke 24.18, 21)

As is so often the case, the scriptures not only connect with very deep human experiences, but offer striking alternatives for thinking and behaving that reach across the ages. In some cases the scriptures are almost eerily timely.

This story is particularly wonderful. Instead of a lot of comment and application, maybe we can just find our way into the story itself, letting our imaginations fill in the blanks.

Are you the only one in Jerusalem who doesn't know what was going on there? Didn't you hear about this man Jesus? He seemed so good and so pure. He spoke with such integrity, energy and grace. He had compassion in his eyes and healing in his hands. Some of our leaders were almost crazy with jealousy and you know what can come from that. We just couldn't believe it. They got him on some trumped-up, half-religious, half-political treason charge and had him put to death. He was crucified. Didn't you know about that?

It's always like that. The only people who get ahead in this world are those with big financial or political connections, with big, loud voices and even bigger fists. That's the only way—really! Nothing else works. We thought he was terrific,

141

but he was only out of it, out of it big time. We used to hope that he was somebody who could make a difference. He wasn't; he didn't. He's gone. That's the way it goes.

And do you know what else? Some of the crazy women went out to his tomb. They thought the least they could do was offer a little respect. They said that the tomb was empty and saw angels. You know what can happen when people get overtired or stressed out—especially women? You never know what they'll see.

As for us, we're out of here. Out of that awful place. Jerusalem, bye-bye! Thank you, but no, thank you. I'm outta here. Bye-bye.

They are clearly tired, frustrated, discouraged, sad, cynical. Any spirit of hopefulness or idealism has been virtually wrung out of them. Have you ever felt something of that kind of pain? Have you ever felt that hanging in there just isn't worth it, that virtue and integrity aren't worth their cost? Have you ever felt like saying "Jerusalem, bye-bye"?

And then there's this stranger who approaches to go along with them. He begins to open their minds. They don't know who he is, but they let him talk.

Oh, how foolish you are and how slow of heart to believe all that the prophets have declared! Was it not necessary that the Messiah should suffer these things and then enter into his glory?

We can continue letting our imagination fill in the blanks about Jesus' word to them.

Where have you been all your life? You go to synagogue every week. What has the Bible been telling you? What do you expect? Don't you remember all of those wonderful stories? Don't you remember how generosity, self-sacrifice and discipline—even death—have a way of bringing life and newness? Don't you know, can't you remember, that integrity and generosity inspire in ways that power and money do not? Where have you been? Were your ears plugged in synagogue?

Have you not been observant about life? You've been missing the point. Maybe those women aren't so foolish after all. Maybe they know something you don't. How foolish you are!

In prayer or in conversation with someone you trust, have things ever come together in new ways for you? Have you been able to see differently or more deeply? Have you come to realize that not to pay the price for your own integrity is to lose everything? Are there moments when you yourself have come back to life?

> Jesus walked ahead as if he were going on. But they urged him strongly, saying, "Stay with us, because it is almost evening and the day is now nearly over." So he went in to stay with them. When he was at the table with them, he took bread, blessed and broke it, and gave it to them. Then their eyes were opened, and they recognized him; and he vanished from their sight. (Luke 24.28-31)

They recognize him in the breaking of the bread, in the great sacrament of holy communion with his own way of living fully and abundantly. In the breaking of the bread, they enter into his story. They connect with his story and, as he vanishes from their sight, realize that they have to write the next chapter of that story with their own lives. Even though it's night, there's plenty of light to hightail it back to Jerusalem.

"Hello, Jerusalem. We're back!"

Eleven kilometers is a big hike in the night, but there's plenty of light and fresh energy for the trip.

Theologian Harvey Cox is quoted as saying that we humans are creatures who not only work and think, but who sing, dance, pray, tell stories and celebrate. We are *homines festivi*. No other creatures we know of relive the legends of their ancestors, blow out candles on a birthday cake, or dress up and pretend to be something else.

He may have modified his comments had he known that other creatures do pretend to be someone or something else. There are certain types of crabs, for example, that carry clam shells over their bodies or attach a roof of living sponges to their backs to avoid being mistaken for somebody's lunch!

What would require no modification, however, is his insight that no other creatures on the planet relive the legends of their ancestors. No other creatures tell stories and relive them in their rituals. Having heard the story from Jesus, the disciples sit down at table. In broken bread, they see him and his story becomes their own.

Three-year-old Timothy had just heard his mother read his favourite bedtime story for the third time. After the third and final reading his mother witnessed a strange phenomenon. Timmy took the book, opened it on the floor, gently put one foot, then the other, on the open pages, looked down and began to cry. The mother was puzzled until her eight-year-old daughter offered the simple interpretation. Timmy really likes the book. It was then that the mother recognized that he wanted to walk right into its pages, to enter into its drama, to become a real part of his favourite story.[23]

In some way, all of this is happening right here today. The story is being told and relived in all of us who recognize the presence of the Lord in our midst and our call to communion in his body. We simply need to let our imaginations tune in to our own ways of being in conversation with the Risen Lord. We need to fill in the blanks and get our own feet into its pages. Let's name a few special ways in which it's being told and celebrated here.

• The Kuhn family is bringing Madison to share in the breaking of the bread for the first time. She'll be celebrating her first holy communion today. We're inviting her to recognize and to say "Amen" to the living presence of Jesus in the breaking of the bread. We're all hoping that Madison will grow into the story of the life, death and rising of Jesus. We're all hoping that his story and that the food and drink from this table will inspire and nourish her on whatever road she travels.

• Candidates for confirmation have given testimony this morning to their own understanding of the Christian life and their desire to participate more fully. They have spoken about their study and their service projects, their connectedness with us in the life of this

---

[23] Citation from Cox and Timmy story drawn from Herbert Anderson and Edward Foley, *Mighty Stories, Dangerous Rituals*, (San Francisco: Jossey Bass, 1998), p. 26.

community and the ways in which they are trying to give witness and to celebrate the death and resurrection of Jesus.

• We heard from Tim, who talked about flipping pancakes and about reading at mass, about how much fun it was to work in the kitchen with his parents and friends and to serve the community and about how interesting the Bible is becoming as he prepares to proclaim it publicly.

• We heard from Sasha, who told us about her experience with younger children in Sunday School and about how much they enjoy learning about Jesus.

• We heard from Diana about spending a whole Saturday morning with her friends cleaning the church. She still doesn't think it was a very glamorous job, but it needed to be done and she's proud that the church will look even better than usual when the bishop comes for confirmation.

• We heard from Stephen who visited the Medex Nursing Home and met a lady there who knew more about baseball than he did. He says he met the "Don Cherry" of baseball and she was a little old lady!

We have the wonderful opportunity and privilege to accompany these young people as they hear the stories of our faith and walk into the book through the sacraments.

In the first reading today, Saint Peter is inviting us into the story, into the heart and mind of Jesus himself.

> I keep the LORD always before me ...
> therefore my heart is glad ....
> For you do not give me up to Sheol,
> or let your faithful one see the pit.
> You show me the path of life.
> In your presence there is fullness of joy. (Psalm 16)

Have You Outgrown
the Need for Faith?

Fourth Sunday of Easter

Acts 2.14a, 36b-41
Psalm 23
1 Peter 2.20-25
John 10.1-10

A particularly striking feature in the passage from John's gospel about the Good Shepherd is the mention of voices. The sheep hear the shepherd's voice. They follow because they have come to know, recognize and trust the call of him who knows their names. They do not follow strangers because they do not recognize their voices. As usual, the text is not talking about shepherds and sheep, but about God and people: in this case, Jesus and his flock.

As amazing as it may seem, virtually unbelievable, the God of the universe bothers to know us personally, distinguishing each of us with the unique dignity of a name. The God of the universe does not call "Hey, you!" into an anonymous crowd.

Ezekiel 34 expresses God's intimate care for individuals even more surprisingly. In this text, the shepherd not only knows his sheep, but has special care for the weak ones, a clear predilection for "little ones" over and against the "fat and the strong." Wouldn't you think that making the whole flock "fat and strong" would be the whole point of shepherding? It seems not. Once again, the prophet is talking not about sheep and lambs, but about people among whom the "fat and strong" may not be all that open to shepherding.

With so many children celebrating their first communion today, we are called to welcome and encourage these "little lambs," and perhaps even to revisit our own life of faith, our own membership in Christ's flock. Some of us strong ones aren't so sure that we hear voices anymore, or that we believe God knows or calls our names. Some of us even self-destruct when it comes to religious faith, thinking we may have outgrown the need for faith.

Sophisticated adults don't find it all that easy to believe in the presence of a Good Shepherd who knows our names. It's not that easy to stand up and sing with full conviction: "Jesus loves me, this I know, for the Bible tells me so." Do you not agree? It's quite a stretch. "Little ones to him belong."

Stephen Dunn wrote a wonderful poem entitled "At the Smiths-ville Methodist Church."

He and his wife decided to "let" their daughter attend summer Bible camp at the church, although neither of them were members of the congregation, or for that matter, believers. It couldn't do any harm, they thought.

> It was supposed to be Arts & Crafts for a week,
> but when she came home
> with the "Jesus Saves" button, we knew what art
> was up, what ancient craft.

He goes on to describe how she liked her new friends, enjoyed twisting and folding paper and learning about Jesus, but when she came home singing "Jesus loves me," it was quite another matter. What could he say to her? "Jesus doesn't love you?" That just wouldn't do. Could he tell her that the Bible is nothing but an old book designed to make people feel guilty? That wouldn't do either, so reluctantly he let her go back to church, recognizing that he didn't have a story to tell that was nearly as good as the ones she was learning there. Could he say "Evolution loves you?" Evolution may be magical, but there are no heroes and besides "stinking of extinction," nothing happens for centuries. Quite a predicament!

I found Stephen's reflections as he was driving his daughter home from the final concert especially touching. He and his wife were in church where their daughter and her little friends were singing about Noah and the ark and jumping up and down for Jesus.

> I didn't have a wonderful story for my child
> and she was beaming. All the way home in the car
> she sang the songs,

occasionally standing up for Jesus.
There was nothing to do
But drive, ride it out, sing along
In silence.[24]

Isn't it true that the faith and insight of children can sometimes leave us speechless and bring us to our knees? As I read the poem, I get the sense that Stephen is nostalgic for the faith of his own childhood, which he was not able to harmonize with his development at other levels of life. He is surely not alone. He's a citizen of his time, his culture—our time, our culture.

The period of Western cultural history known as "modernity" has been characterized by a scientific way of knowing that has been very suspicious of spirituality and religion. We know something to be true by testing, experimentation and verification of data. What is real is what can be known through the methods of science.

Modernity has produced much of great value in technology and medicine, for example, but has made people skeptical about anything that is not factual, that is, not scientifically verifiable and based on historically reliable facts.

That the Lord is my shepherd or that Jesus loves me is not subject to that kind of analysis and therefore lacks "reality."

Social commentators note that our almost exclusive preoccupation with the scientific method is running out of steam, that we are on the edge of postmodernity. There's a deepening sense that the scientific method can't do it all. Holistic medicine that highlights the therapeutic value of prayer is just one example. Parapsychology, which can be weird and quirky, is another.

A renewed interest in spirituality, in levels of experience that are not subject to scientific analysis, but which are nevertheless real, is coming to light. There is a renewed sense that stories can be true without being literally or factually true. Metaphors and metaphorical narratives can be profoundly true even if they are not literally or factually verifiable. The stories of the Bible, for example, are attempts

---

[24] Stephen Dunn, quoted in *New and Selected Poems,* (New York: Norton, 1994), p. 183.

to communicate real experiences that are beyond historically factual description.

The Easter appearances are a case in point. The original authors of the New Testament, untouched and uninfluenced by our modern preoccupation with facts, consistency and verifiability, were not in the least embarrassed that their stories didn't match or seem historically consistent with one another. They were true just the same.

The Risen Christ comes through locked doors. The Risen Christ is experienced by different people in different ways. The Risen Christ is seen and recognized only gradually. This was their experience and, when we think of it, it pretty accurately represents the experiences of Christian believers even today.

Stephen Dunn's little girl is not inviting him to a childish way of thinking, but to the re-visioning of an ancient faith that has perennial value. She's waking him up to something ever old and ever new.

Perhaps we could let our children do that for us as we enter into holy communion with them today.

Spirit and Wisdom

Fifth Sunday of Easter

Acts 6.1-7
Psalm 33
1 Peter 2.4-9
John 14.1-12

During those days, when the disciples were increasing in number, the Hellenists complained against the Hebrews ... (Acts 6.1)

Come to [the Lord], a living stone ... Like living stones, let yourselves be built into a spiritual house. (1 Peter 2.4, 5)

I am the way, and the truth and the life. No one comes to the Father except through me. (John 14.6)

Beginning with a very concrete problem, all three readings today cluster around a very important universal truth. It may be obvious, but it needs to be freshly discovered again and again.

In the summer of 2001, at the end of the *Jeux de la francophonie* (Francophone Games) in Ottawa, over a hundred of the participants from abroad stayed behind, seeking refugee status in Canada. One of our better-known political and social commentators predictably began his radio talk show with a roar. As phone calls began coming in, there were equally predictable broad generalizations about what it means to be Canadian, a true Canadian, a worthy Canadian—even, finally, an honest and worthwhile human being. Few, if any, of these potential refugees stood much chance of qualifying in any of these categories. The issues of refugee status and immigration are, of course, complex and beyond the capacity of a radio talk show to solve. And yes, people have the right to their opinion and to articulate it freely. I have to admit, though, that I was troubled by the tone of this particular conversation and I hope that it was not representative of our broader society and its values and ideals.

Chapter 6 of Acts reports how, in the very earliest stages of the church's life, as in Judaism at the time, tensions were developing between two camps, namely the Hellenists and the Hebrews.

The Hellenists were those who, although ethnically and culturally Jewish, were more open to participation in a bigger world. They recognized the dominant language and culture of the Greco-Roman world, and, more open to trade and commerce, believed that their own religion and culture could flourish there. The Hebrew Scriptures were translated into Greek and even some of their wisdom literature was written in Greek and accepted for use in Jewish teaching and preaching.

The Hebrews, on the other hand, were more concerned with the danger of being swallowed up by the broader culture. They were concerned with preserving their traditional language, culture and religion in pure form. They were concerned with maintaining their identity.

As happens so often with camps, the issues move beyond theoretical discussions of language and tradition into more economic considerations. It's not only a matter of who thinks what, but of who gets what, when and how much. Somebody's widow is inevitably getting more than somebody else's and it's probably because she belongs to the other camp. It's just not fair and something's got to be done about it. Do you see how the "conversation" is escalating, how its tone is deteriorating? It won't be long before it degenerates into finger pointing, name-calling, and sweeping accusations and generalizations about good/bad, worthy/unworthy. You know how it goes. To our embarrassment, we may even have participated ourselves in such "conversations."

How we deal with differences, how we understand and deal with conflicting ideologies, how we think about and approach the integration of outsiders, how we understand justice and compassion was in the Acts of the Apostles, and continues to be, a work in progress. Final solutions elude us. We keep plugging away.

The apostles' approach to a solution in this particular case is quite remarkable and telling. They called the community together to select persons of good standing, persons of Spirit and wisdom, to deal personally with those concerned. Persons were chosen to undertake a ministry of service, justice and reconciliation. The apostles did not establish guidelines or make new laws, but opened up their own ministry to meet this particular challenge to justice and charity. The solution was not at the level of regulation or law, but at the level of personal discernment and service.

Of course, laws and guidelines are necessary and important, and eventually arose even within the church, but this was not and cannot be the ultimate solution or the final answer under any circumstances, new or old. Even the best laws and guidelines are administered by living people who can do so with or without grace, wisdom and discernment. Even the best laws and constitutions are interpreted and administered by human beings who may or may not be endowed with spirit and wisdom. In this case seven persons are chosen to be bridge-building servants, the first deacons. In this foundational Christian text, the choice of living persons who provide living witness to the possibility of reconciliation and justice is considered more significant and more effective than specific legal or administrative change.

The texts from the first letter of Peter and from John's gospel focus on the spirit and wisdom that are incarnate in the person of Jesus himself. For First Peter, the stone tablets of the law are not foundational. Jesus himself is foundational. The risen Christ is the keystone.

In the text from John, Jesus is "the way, and the truth and the life." Clearly, the way and the truth are ultimately found not in legal systems or in catechisms, but in the living Christ.

"I am the way, and the truth and the life. No one comes to the Father except through me." *No one comes to the Father except through me.* "If you know me, you will know my Father also. From now on you do know him and have seen him."

Living in the way and the spirit of Jesus gets people to God whether they know it or not. The primacy of a living relationship over a structure, the primacy of persons over things, the primacy of a living community over a tradition, which can too easily be killed by being frozen, is being proclaimed here.

Already in the earliest days of the church, temptations arose to find a neater and cleaner way and truth than that offered by Jesus himself. Even today we are tempted to idolize structures and to divinize canons and catechisms, which, as important as they are, provide only limited directions to the Way and the Truth. Laws and doctrines have their place, but are ultimately incapable of being "the way, the truth and the life." A prior Spirit and wisdom are at work in the mysterious ongoing presence of the living Christ who is "life" leading to Life.

As the Easter season draws to a close, the liturgy highlights the invisible, mysterious ways in which the risen Christ abides with the church, the ways in which Spirit and wisdom draw us to communion with each other and with all people in him. The liturgical texts and our eucharistic communion open us to ways of spirit, truth and prayer. They call us forward and draw us into the possibilities of universal communion and peace that seem so far beyond our grasp.

At the end of Mass last evening, we sang a hymn that I found quite moving. Although it is not an Easter hymn, it sings a gentle and lyrical approach to the communion that we believe exists among all people of goodwill, people everywhere in the world who have the spirit and wisdom to pray, who are mysteriously in Christ.

> The day you gave us, Lord, is ended,
> The darkness falls at your behest;
> To you our morning hymns ascended,
> Your praise shall sanctify our rest.
>
> We thank you that your Church, unsleeping
> While earth rolls onward into light,
> Through all the world its watch is keeping,
> And rests not now by day or night.
>
> Across each continent and island
> As dawn leads on another day,
> The voice of prayer is never silent,
> Nor dies the strain of praise away.
>
> The sun that bids us rest is waking
> Your friends beneath the western sky,
> And hour by hour fresh lips are making
> Your wondrous doings heard on high.

So be it, Lord; your throne shall never,
Like earth's proud empires, pass away:
Your kingdom stands and grows for ever,
Till all your creatures own your sway.

John Ellerton, 1826–1893, alt.

"The Day You Gave Us, Lord, Is Ended,"
(found in Catholic Book of Worship III, *#667)*

Advocate and Second Breath

Sixth Sunday of Easter

Acts 8.5-8, 14-17
Psalm 66
1 Peter 3.15-18
John 14.15-21

Peter and John laid their hands on them, and they received the Holy Spirit. (Acts 8.17)

In your hearts sanctify Christ as Lord. Always be ready to make your defense to anyone who demands from you an accounting for the hope that is in you. (1 Peter 3.15)

It's one thing to travel with and watch Peter and John discover an empty tomb on Easter Sunday morning. It's quite another to enter into texts such as these. As we move through the Easter season, the empty tomb seems farther and farther away. The *meaning* of the resurrection rather than the *fact* of the resurrection moves to the foreground. The ongoing presence of the risen Lord to successive generations in the church becomes more important than stories of a mysterious saviour appearing here and there.

There's quite a difference between believing that Jesus rose from the dead and believing in the risen Christ.

Believing that Jesus rose from the dead involves looking at the resurrection from a distance, seeing it as an external event that took place long ago and was proven or demonstrated to the first generation of Christians in various mysterious ways.

Believing in the resurrection suggests a more intimate personal experience. Believing in the risen Christ involves a personal relationship and the acceptance of an invitation to enter into that relationship more deeply.

Actually, it makes a lot of sense, doesn't it? Out of your own experience of faith, hope and love, would it be more important to say "I believe that my wife exists" (which is pretty obvious) or "I believe that my wife loves me"?

Would you not say instead: "I believe in my wife" or "I believe in her love for me"?

That language points to the heart. When you believe in someone, you're ready to trust that person, to dance in the dark with that person. You're ready for genuine love and commitment.

Let's take a deeper look at the gospel.

The setting is the table on the night before Jesus died. Judas has left the room. Jesus speaks—in language that is beyond time. He points to his death and resurrection, not as historical moments, but as opening moments of an ongoing event in which his friends will participate. Both his language and its content are mysterious and timeless. They deal not with facts of history, but with an ongoing adventure.

> "I will ask the Father, and he will give you another Advocate, to be with you forever. This is the Spirit of truth, whom the world cannot receive, because it neither sees him nor knows him. You know him because he abides with you, and he will be in you."

> I will not leave you orphaned; I am coming to you. In a little while the world will no longer see me, but you will see me: because I live, you also will live. On that day you will know that I am in my Father, and you in me, and I in you. (John 14.16-20)

It makes no sense to believe simply that Jesus is telling the truth here. Rather we are invited to believe in what he is saying as he promises the Spirit, the mysterious way in which he will continue to be present for all time to inspire wisdom, courage and love.

The Greek word *paracletos* is hard to translate. Our translation renders it "advocate," which may not be particularly helpful. In the Roman courts the *advocatus* was one who stood by an accused man to defend and strengthen him, to help him articulate his own truth, or even to speak for him if necessary. The Spirit is an expert and trust-worthy companion in time of trial.

Another traditional Greek word for spirit is *pneuma*, which means breath. The Spirit is a "second wind" that brings new energy for life, for love and for service.

"I believe in the Holy Spirit," we proclaim every Sunday. In proclaiming our faith in the Holy Spirit, we affirm a living experience of "advocate and second breath."

An elementary school teacher was trying to get her class to mem-orize the Apostles' Creed line by line. She explained how it was formulated in Rome in the second century and how it has twelve positive points representing the twelve apostles after which it is named. That's what she had learned when she was their age. Twelve children were picked to each be one of the apostles and each had an assigned part to say in the creed. It was fun and seemed to be working. On one particular Monday, it seemed to be going along just fine—at least to a certain point:

"He ascended into heaven," one boy said.

"And is seated at the right hand of the Father," his neighbour continued.

"He will come again to judge the living and the dead," her neighbour continued. Then, dead silence ...

The teacher looked up from her desk—

A little girl said, "Oh, Eric's the one who believes in the Holy Spirit, and he's sick today."

Oops!

What an opening for a lesson on the Holy Spirit! What a great chance for stories about how we're all accompanied through life by God's invisible but trustworthy and helpful presence, how we can catch a "second breath" if we need to! We believe in the Holy Spirit.

You may be familiar with the writings of C.S. Lewis. We have a number of them in the parish library. He came to faith only gradually in his life, and the depth of his character and his faith reflected in such works as *Mere Christianity* and his autobiography *Surprised by Joy* are remarkable.

Perhaps even better known are his *Chronicles of Narnia*, which continue to delight children. I just discovered his published *Letters to*

Children. Some of his young readers were writing to him about their questions and observations.

He described himself to one of them as a "tall, fat, rather bald, red-faced, double-chinned, black-haired man with a deep voice and reading glasses, who hated math in school, but liked writing and animals .... I don't think age matters so much as people think. Parts of me are still 12 and I think other parts were already 50 when I was 12."

In reading through these letters, I was particularly struck by how straight he is in dealing with his young pen pals, how seriously he takes them and their experience. A paragraph from a letter he wrote to Joan, who shared one of her essays with him, fits right in with the spirit of the season, especially these last Sundays. Interestingly enough, the date is Easter 1959. Joan is probably around the same age as our confirmation candidates.

Dear Joan,

Hurrah! The essay is a promising bit of work; the sentences are clear and taut and don't sprawl. As for what you are saying, I think you are exaggerating a bit at the end. Everything I need is in my soul? The Heck it is! Or if so, it must contain a great many virtues and a great deal of wisdom which neither I nor anyone else could ever find there. Very little of what I need is at present in my soul. I mean, even things of the soul's own sort, like humility and truthfulness. And it certainly does not in any obvious sense contain a number of other things, which I need at the moment: e.g. a stamp for this letter. Never exaggerate. Never say more than you really mean ... Sorry to be a pig![25]

It sounds as though he knows from his own experience how important an advocate could be for his own life, how much in need of a second opinion or a second wind he has been from time to time. He's telling it to Joan as it is and hoping she gets the message!

---

[25] C.S. Lewis, *Letters to Children* (New York: Touchstone, 1995), p. 87.

Peter and John laid their hands on them, and they received the Holy Spirit.

Our text today from the Acts of the Apostles deals with early stages in the development of the sacraments of initiation in which the Spirit of Jesus is communicated from generation to generation in the church even to our own time. Throughout the Easter Season we have been highlighting not only the truth that Jesus is risen, but that we share his life and Spirit in baptism, confirmation and eucharist, which we have been celebrating.

In our liturgical celebrations, we enter into what for centuries the church has called "sacred mysteries," mysterious and wonderful ways in which we come into living contact with God the Father, Son and Holy Spirit. When we say that we believe in God and when we come forward for communion, we are making an act of faith in God's ongoing activity within us and among us. We believe that we are being created, being raised from the dead, being inspired, literally being breathed into by the Spirit.

In the Easter renewal of our baptismal promises and in our communion every Sunday, especially during Easter's 50 days, we have been affirming that God is not finished with us yet and have been saying Amen to our ongoing transformation in Christ.

In just a few moments, I'll be chanting the following prayer in your name. Let's be especially conscious today of our solidarity in this ancient prayer:

> Father, all-powerful and ever-living God, we do well always and everywhere to give you thanks. In you we live and move and have our being. Each day you show us a Father's love; your Holy Spirit, dwelling within us, gives us on earth the hope of unending joy. Your gift of the Spirit, who raised Jesus from the dead, is the foretaste and promise of the paschal feast of heaven. (Preface for Sundays in Ordinary Time VI)

Out of This World?

Ascension of the Lord

Acts 1.1-11
Psalm 47
Ephesians 1.17-23
Matthew 28.16-20

"I went to Nova Scotia on holidays last summer and it was out of this world." "I heard Mendelssohn's *Paulus* at Lincoln Center and it was out of this world."

"Out of this world" doesn't mean what it says, does it? To say that something or someone is "out of this world" usually points to something that's very much appreciated in this world, that may not have an immediate practical value, but that has a high level of relevance just the same. To be "out of this world" is to be in the world—big time.

This funny expression may be a good starting point for entering into the mystery of the Ascension.

David Buttrick, professor of preaching at Vanderbilt University, begins his commentary on this feast with a story of a little girl being shown around the Church of the Ascension in a large city in the eastern United States. Looking up at the painting on the front wall, she asked a very important question: "Why is Jesus up in the air?"

Why is Jesus up in the air, indeed! Why and how is he "out of this world"? For modern minds, the whole scene is a bit much to take: a mountaintop, white-robed angels and Jesus riding on a cloud.

"Out of this world" language and the little girl's question are well worth considering. The theological content of these images, however mythological they may sound, is crucial to Matthew's understanding of Christianity.

As one might expect, the story of the Ascension concludes his gospel. Typically, the evangelist makes all kinds of interesting connections with what has gone before by skillfully and subtly reaching back into the gospel to pull important elements forward.

The mountaintop location calls to mind the location of Jesus' first sermon, the Sermon on the Mount. In commissioning his disciples from the mountain to "teach all things," it is clear that the substance of their teaching will be intimately connected with that first mountain proclamation. The course content and agenda are set.

That some still entertain doubts recalls other instances, such as the calming of the storm, where doubts became occasions for turning points in faith. Full authority is given even in the midst of doubt. Disciples, even doubting ones, are called to make disciples of others, to draw them into the process of coming to faith and ever-deepening conversion.

Baptism, which implies "plunging in," is "in the name of the Father, Son and Holy Spirit." The act of baptism will plunge the disciples into relationship with the dynamism of a living God, an ongoing, mysterious communion with God.

The "I am with you" in the text corresponds with "Emmanuel," the name given to Jesus at the very beginning of the gospel. It is an example of inclusion, the Hebrew literary device that unifies a text by echoing its beginning at the end. "Where two or three are gathered in my name," and "Whatsoever you do to the least of these brothers and sisters of mine, you do to me" indicate how Emmanuel's ongoing presence will be felt.

Now, what about this "going up," this being "in the air"? I would suggest two avenues to interpret this crucial imagery.

First, it is politically important for Christianity. If Jesus Christ is "enthroned at the right hand of God," then primary obedience is owed to him. Kings, presidents and dictators, as well as social and economic systems and structures, are demoted. The relationship of a believer to God in the Spirit of Jesus is absolute. This is clear throughout the gospel, where Jesus even points to the possibility of standing up to rulers and kings, even experiencing alienation from family and friends. The mythological language of the Ascension story reinforces very concrete, down-to-earth responsibilities and commitments found elsewhere in the gospel. Christians find the ultimate source and rationale for their political courage in the mystery of the Ascension. This is especially clear in the text from Ephesians, which some scholars even suggest may be a very early Ascension hymn, reconstructed to read something like this:

God raised him from among the dead
And set him at the right hand in the heavenly places
Above every rule and authority and power and dominion
And every name named, not only in this age, but in the coming one.
God put under his feet all things
And gave him to be head over all things.

Another important consideration is the "great commission," the sending of the disciples to make disciples of all nations. The commission has been all too easily interpreted as an invitation to go off to Africa or India with a catechism. That's definitely part of it, but not all of it. For us, it means a move into the world of computers, the field of biochemistry, the arenas of politics and education. Discipleship is lived in the context of what makes this world go 'round.

Jesus is lord of our world, of our here and now, or he is lord of nothing. The Sermon on the Mount can work here, or it will work nowhere. It's that simple. That Jesus is with us, not just looking over our shoulder, calls us to collaborative work where he is present, among us and within us and perhaps especially in those left behind by everybody else, "the least."

This may be another way of saying the same thing, but from a different angle. It relates to the mystery of the incarnation and the integrity and continuity of the whole gospel message.

Who is "in the air"? asked the little girl. Who is exalted at the right hand of the Father?

It is the crucified, risen one, wounds and all. The humanity of Christ is real or it isn't. One of us in all things but sin, the whole of the human experience as he lived it is exalted in his Ascension. Yes, this is the language of mysticism, if not mythology, but bear with me. It is the risen body of the crucified One at the right hand of the Father. Emmanuel goes both ways. If God is with us, then we're with God. If heaven has come to earth, then earth has gone to heaven. Something of this earth is in heaven. Heaven and earth are one, never to be thought of separately.

We are not speculating here that even risen bodies displace air, so heaven must be a place and if we had the proper spacecraft, we might be able to find it. You may remember how the first Soviet cosmonaut ridiculed that idea, when he remarked that he went into heaven and found nothing. Christians take human bodiliness with ultimate seriousness. It's all we have; somehow it mysteriously transcends space and time. Heaven will be what we make of it here on earth. It is the crucified and wounded son-friend-rabbi-healer-exorcist-social critic who is risen and ascended. And, as today's preface says, where he has gone, we hope to follow.

In light of the Ascension no detail of human life is inconsequential, because it was lived and brought along by him who is seated at the right hand of the Father. This, too, is typical of Matthew, who includes even sparrows and lilies of the field in the circle of God's eternal love and providence.

As a graduate student at Saint Paul University in Ottawa, I lived for a few months at the seminary and got to know Brother Gauthier. He had been porter or doorkeeper there since the seminary opened. He even slept in a little room off the window and wicket from which he monitored all of our comings and goings, received visitors, looked after street people, sorted the mail and did God knows what else. He had had polio as a child and was limited in every way but that of the spirit. I picked up the Christopher News Notes at the back of church last month and found this little anonymous poem, which I recognized as the one Brother had pinned to his little bulletin board.

> I have only just a minute
> Only sixty seconds in it,
> Forced upon me, can't refuse it,
> Didn't seek it, didn't choose it, but it's up to me to use it,
> I must suffer if I lose it,
> Give account if I abuse it
> Just a tiny minute,
> But Eternity is in it.

In its own way, this little anonymously authored poem proclaims the truth: Heaven and earth are one. Life matters. It matters a lot. Ascension is today. Look up and live! Jesus Christ is out of this world.

All in a Breath

Pentecost Sunday

Acts 2.1-11
Psalm 104
1 Corinthians 12.3-7, 12-13
John 20.19-23

When the day of Pentecost had come, they were all together in one place. And suddenly from heaven there came a sound like the rush of a violent wind, and it filled the entire house where they were sitting ... And at this sound the crowd gathered. (Acts 2.1-2, 6)

It was the first day of the week, and the doors of the house where the disciples had met were locked for fear of the Jews, Jesus came and stood among them ... He breathed on them and said to them, "Receive the Holy Spirit. If you forgive the sins of any, they are forgiven them; if you retain the sins of any, they are retained." (John 20.19, 22-23)

I've always pictured both scenes taking place in the same room—the upper room, the room of the Last Supper. In both instances there's air, wind, breath, spirit.

Last week I finished a book by Walter Brueggemann entitled *Texts Under Negotiation: The Bible and Postmodern Imagination* (Minneapolis: Fortress, 1993). Although it sounds pretty heavy duty, it's not as hard going as you might think, and is well worth the effort.

In his first chapter Brueggemann describes an approach to religious faith with which those of us who are 40-plus are quite familiar. It is absolute and dogmatic. It involves discussion, argumentation, even combat among various groups who understand their faith differently. The sense is that there's a right and a wrong way of looking at things. There are those who have it right and those who don't. And fortunately, we Catholics (or we Protestants, if you happen to be on that side of the argument) are those who have it right and have always had it right. Some are validly ordained, others are not. Some believe in the "real presence," others do not. Some believe in the Immaculate Conception, some do not. Catholics believe one thing; Protestants believe something else. If one is right, the other is wrong. It's that simple.

Brueggemann suggests that this kind of thinking is bankrupt. Whether people should or should not think in these terms anymore is not the point. The fact is that, by and large, they don't and, when they do, it's in a narrowly combative sort of way, which serves no one. While the conception among combatants is that the truths under discussion are eternal, absolute and unchangeable, a closer look shows them to be very much products of their own time and place.

He suggests that people have decided for themselves that these questions are irresolvable, there are no winners in the argument, it is going nowhere and it is not life-giving. He doesn't say this, but I have a feeling that even God is sick and tired of this kind of discussion, that God is bored stiff with it.

Brueggemann asks what this new situation implies for Christian thinking, preaching and teaching. Is it ultimately a problem, or is it an opportunity? He suggests that it is an opportunity to rediscover the approach that the Bible itself takes. The Bible functions less at the level of "hard facts," as we have come to understand factual truth, and more at the level of the imagination, which draws us beyond "hard facts." I can't possibly explain his thought, or do justice to his approach, but let's try to get our imaginations around today's texts. Let's negotiate with them to discover their truth.

What happens, for example, in the upper room on Easter Sunday and on Pentecost is not the clarification of abstract truth, but the reconciling breath of Jesus on the one hand and a rush of fresh spirit on the other. What occurs in these texts is Jesus breathing on his disciples and inviting them to share with him in a ministry of recon-ciliation and the forgiveness of sins. There is a rush of wind that fills the place and draws people together. Galileans, Parthians, Medes, Elamites, Mesopotamians, Judeans, Cappadocians are drawn together and taught a new language.

First of all, what are we to make of all this air, wind, breath and spirit?

God has been breathing from the very beginning. In the beginning, the breath of God was hovering over the deep in the creation story of Genesis 1. In Genesis 2, God is pictured as picking up dust from the earth, shaping it and breathing into it the breath of life.

I know that many of you have witnessed the birth of a child; many of you have given birth yourselves. I've only seen it on television, but when the infant comes forth from its mother's womb, somebody has to pick up that little person and maybe even hold him upside down and give him a little swat. There's a gasp of breath, a cry, a living voice, a person, a whole set of wonderful new possibilities, a future for the human race—all in a breath.

That God was breathing and that God still breathes is ultimately more important than being right or wrong about a point of abstract theology. It's another way of talking about faith that invites imagination and response and community about the dignity of persons and the giftedness of life.

According to John's gospel, Jesus is risen from the dead and is breathing in a new way, speaking a new word. Receive the Holy Spirit. Receive the breath of God. Receive life and courage for the forgiveness of sins. Pretty exciting stuff. It boggles the mind—as it should. It is true mystery.

In the world of the Bible, events and experiences such as these shape faith as a way of thinking and acting, of understanding life and living it. It is the religious imagination that moves hearts to prayer: Don't let me stop breathing, dear God. Don't let me choke. Don't let all of your wonderful plans be frustrated because of my stupidity, my sinfulness, my lust, my arrogance for power. Breathe in me. Keep breathing. Let me breathe.

Second, we might ask ourselves about upper rooms. Could this church or the library where the pastoral council and the finance council hold their meetings be an upper room where God's breath is blowing? Could Queen's Park be an upper room, or the House of Commons, or the General Assembly of the United Nations? God knows there's plenty of wind in all those places.

What kind of a mighty rush of wind would be required to help British Columbians, Albertans, les Québécois and Newfoundlanders know that they are, that we are, one? What kind of rush needs to fill the halls of the United Nations as members deal with issues such as the international AIDS crisis? Where's the wind going to come from? Where's the energy? Where's the fire? Keep blowing, dear God. Blow harder.

Brueggemann's sense of the postmodern situation is that narrow, more rational, doctrinal preoccupations have made religion and religious institutions unpersuasive, even incredible to most people of our time. He further contends that much of what we have considered absolute is quite distant from the spirit of the Bible and the foundational inspiration for Christianity. I think we need to consider very seriously his point of view and that of others like him. It's not an academic issue, but one that touches the lives of all of us who believe in God and in Jesus, and believe that our faith can continue to make a difference in the world.

The hymn *Veni Creator Spiritus,* ["Come, Creator Spirit"] was very much a part of Pentecost when I was growing up. "Come, Holy Ghost" is a free translation of the ancient hymn. I'd like to quote from another adaptation of the original by Edwin Hatch (1835–1889), which is a wonderful prayer for fresh breath that I think we could all make our own this Pentecost Sunday.

> Breathe on me, Breath of God,
> fill me with life anew,
> that I may love what thou dost love,
> and do what thou wouldst do.
>
> Breathe on me, breath of God,
> till I am wholly thine,
> till all this earthly part of me
> glows with thy fire divine.

Is Your God Too Small?

Trinity Sunday

Exodus 34.4-6, 8-9
Daniel 3
2 Corinthians 13.11-13
John 3.16-18

I remember being given a book shortly after I was ordained in 1968. The title of the book was *Your God Is Too Small*; its author was J.B. Phillips. He is perhaps best known for his translation of the New Testament from the original Greek into contemporary English. The King James Version, with all of its majestic solemnity, had been standard for Protestants, and the Douay-Rheims version had been standard for Catholics.

Translators discovered early on how difficult a project they had on their hands. It's not just a question of translating words, but ideas, feelings and moods. Words communicate not just concepts, but pictures, images and experiences. We spoke last Sunday on the feast of Pentecost about the limitations of rational concepts, and about the role of imagination in dealing with and communicating spiritual and religious truth. Today's text from the Book of Exodus provides us with another wonderful opportunity to carry such considerations forward.

You will remember the story of Moses and the burning bush. It just wouldn't stop burning, so Moses knew there was something sacred about it and took off his shoes. He met God in the burning bush and learned that God's name is "I am who I am," or "I will be who I will be." In other words, God's name is "Don't build a wall around me. Don't fence me in." Those of you who are regular parishioners will know that the burning bush is one of my favourite passages. God is so open, inviting and inclusive!

The text from Exodus 34, which was proclaimed today, describes an episode that took place much later. Moses had been to the mountain and had received the tablets of the covenant on which God himself had written. He found the people out of control, dancing and partying around a golden statue of a calf that they had made. In his anger, Moses destroyed both the golden calf and the tablets on which God had written. After a cooling-off period, further consultations with the Lord and appropriate acts of repentance and renewal, the LORD once again called Moses to the mountain to receive a fresh set of tablets on which the covenant would be inscribed yet again.

The NAME, meaning "I am who I am," occurs six times in this brief passage, but because of the great respect in which it is held, the NAME is translated "LORD," which I find quite limiting. For me the word "Lord" conjures up the image of a British gentleman who sits in the upper house of parliament. At any rate, it certainly does not do full justice to the NAME. It is not an adequate translation.

Among the Jews, "the Almighty" has become a very common substitute for God's name. In the Latin collects of the Roman Missal, we find *Omnipotens et Sempiterne Deus,* which we translate as "Almighty and ever-living God." *Omnipotens.* Can you hear potential in that word? "Almighty" does not mean having the biggest fist in the world, but having more potential, more possibilities than we could ever imagine. God is a God of infinite potential. To be ever living and to have infinite potential is a way of describing what "I am who I am" is like.

The doctrine of the Blessed Trinity is a way of assuring that our God is not too small. I know that I'm oversimplifying here, but one way of dealing with the Trinity is to recognize that God is indeed the creator of the heavens and the earth, the source of all that is, whom we name Father. God also appears in history, uniquely in Jesus, the Christ, whom we name Son. God likewise is discovered in our own inner being. We sense that we are not alone, that there is an inner voice prodding and testing. We name that "Holy Spirit." We say that the Father is God, but not that God is the Father. We say that Jesus is God, but not that God is Jesus. We say that the Holy Spirit is God, but not that God is the Holy Spirit. God is Father, Son and Holy Spirit, a dynamic interacting community of love and creativity whom we can discover in creation, in human history and in the depths of our consciousness. Three persons, one divine nature. Christian theologians throughout the ages have used complicated language and categories to describe God, not that they can ultimately explain God, but to "protect" God from being domesticated, tamed, shrivelled up.

Another issue about how we think and speak of God that is raised with more and more frequency today is the issue of gender. "I believe in God, the Father almighty." Is there a mother almighty? I am who I am, *omnipotens et sempiterne* is clearly not masculine, but our mental picture is masculine because of the tradition of our "Father language."

I remember a lady from a nearby parish whose 14-year-old son, Kenny, was dying. She was very angry: angry with life, with the doctors, with the drugs, with medicine. The food in the hospital was terrible, the halls were cluttered, the staff wasn't polite. Everything was wrong. She began to pray, and as she prayed, she got in touch with her own motherly passion and began understanding it as a reflection of God's own love. It gradually dawned on her that if she loved Kenny with that kind of passion and that kind of motherly energy, what about God? Could she entrust Kenny to the maternal love of God and let him go to her? It was a moment of grace. Without knowing it, she was deeply in tune with Isaiah 49, which reads, "Does a mother forget her baby, or neglect the infant nursing at her breast? Yet, even if she forget, I will not forget," says "*I am who I am.*"

I know another family where the father was physically abusive and has been living away from the rest of the family for years. His son is now 16 years old and you should see him with his mother. He torments her, teases her, plays with her: it's quite an amazing relationship. When he would pray to God who is faithful and sustaining and loving and playful and joyful and a friend and a parent, how would he image that? Would his "God picture" be male or female? For this young man, our traditional Father language may even be an obstacle to be overcome in his development of a healthy and life-giving image of God.

On a rainy vacation day last year, I was rummaging around a used bookstore and came across an issue of *National Geographic*. It featured a wonderful article about a church in Arizona, built many years ago by Spanish missionaries. They had brought their own cultural tradition with them, and the church is a masterpiece of the Spanish baroque style, in Arizona of all places. At the time the article was written, the church was undergoing the process of restoration. The Spanish had provided the architectural style, but the people themselves provided the decorative elements. The native people were the artists who actually finished the place. Particularly striking was the figure of the Good Shepherd high above the sanctuary. The painting had become very dark over the years and was being cleaned. The restoration crew got quite a surprise. The Good Shepherd was wearing a wide-brimmed hat like those the people used to make to protect them from the sun. It was tied around the chin in such a way that the figure seemed to have a beard. What looked like a beard turned out to be the bow that secured the hat. There was also a scarf that was tied around the shoulders, the corners of which fell forward over the figure's breasts. It was a she. The Divine Shepherd was female.

> God is my shepherd; there is nothing I shall want. Fresh and green are the pastures where she gives me repose. Near restful waters she leads me to revive my drooping spirit. She guides me along the right path. She is true to her name. If I should walk in the valley of darkness, no evil would I fear. You are there with your crook and your staff. With these you comfort me.

I find that quite amazing. It provides an excellent example of how our language has limited our way of understanding and picturing God. The psalm reads very differently with feminine pronouns. Our God is too small.

You have surely noticed how new hymns and even revised older hymn texts are attempting to broaden our base of images and metaphors for God. For example, Verse 3 of "Praise, My Soul, the King of Heaven" used to read: "Father-like, he tends and spares us. Well our feeble frame he knows. In his hands he gently bears us, rescues us from all our foes." Now it reads: "Father-like, God tends and spares us, well our feeble frame he knows. Mother-like, God gently bears us, rescues us from all our foes."

Trinity Sunday reminds us of how important our "God talk" and our "God thinking" are. We would not want to rally around a false God, create a golden calf, or do anything to limit the height, breadth, depth and magnificence of "I am who I am." To shrink our ideas of God is to shrink our capacity for real life.

Getting Real
About the Real Presence

Feast of the Body and Blood of Christ

Deuteronomy 8.2-3, 14b-16
Psalm 147
1 Corinthians 10.16-17
John 6.51-59

On these three great feasts of the church year—Pentecost, Trinity Sunday and the Body and Blood of Christ—I've been focusing on the importance and power of our religious imagination. I've been inviting and challenging us to be stretched, to allow the marvellous truths and traditions of our faith to open us in a fresh way to the wonder and bigness of God.

The Hebrew people, in their experience of hunger, are invited to think differently about their lives and their world.

> He humbled you by letting you hunger, then by feeding you with manna, with which neither you nor your ancestors were acquainted. (Deuteronomy 8.3)

This event, recorded in Deuteronomy, offers a very different perspective from that offered in Genesis. According to this first book of the Bible, God created humans in the divine image and likeness and gave them dominion over nature. God charged men and women with subduing the earth and sharing dominion over it. They were given another lesson in the desert. They were given another way of understanding their relationship with the earth and with nature that was very humbling for them. When you're starving, when there's no food, when there's no rain, you're not in charge. You do not have dominion over nature. Nature has dominion over you. And when the food is mysterious and "free of charge," you know that it's not really yours.

There is a wonderful little film called *Bread and Wine*. It begins with a majestic *Sanctus* that continues throughout the film. We watch a grain of wheat being planted in the ground and, with the techniques of modern time-lapse photography, we can see it germinate. We see the earth beginning to crack as life pushes forth. Then we see endless fields such as we can experience going through Saskatchewan, endless fields of golden wheat, which are then threshed. Flour is produced and, before you know it, a lady is baking bread, kneading the dough, letting it rise only to punch it down and let it rise again before it is baked, cut into slices and eaten.

> Blessed are you, Lord, God of all creation.
> Through your goodness we have this bread to offer,
> which earth has given and human hands have made.
> It will become for us the bread of life.

The same is true of the production of the wine. Grapes are grown; vines are pruned; grapes are harvested and crushed; their juice is fermented.

> Blessed are you, Lord, God of all creation.
> Through your goodness we have this wine to offer,
> fruit of the vine and work of human hands.
> It will become our spiritual drink.

The body and blood of Christ are in that—in the whole of it, in the planting, the pruning, the threshing, the crushing, the baking, the fermentation—the whole thing.

Traditional Christian spirituality has not stressed this kind of holy communion enough. The famous Chief Seattle is quoted as having advised the North American culture to "Teach your children what we teach our children. Whatever befalls the earth befalls us. The earth does not belong to us. We belong to it. We are connected. There is one blood that unites everything that lives."

> The cup of blessing that we bless, is it not a sharing in the blood of Christ? The bread that we break, is it not a sharing in the body of Christ? Because there is one bread, we who are many are one body, for we all partake of the one bread. (1 Corinthians 10.16-17)

There's a lot more in those two verses than we might realize. It expresses our faith in ways that include very natural processes. "This is my body," Jesus says as he breaks bread. "This is my blood," he says, as he offers a cup of wine. "Take this, commune with it; commune with the process that went into its coming to be; commune with nature; commune with each other; commune with me; commune with God. Know that in breaking this bread and passing this cup you are one with everything that is, one with the world and through that sign, that sacrament, one with me. This is my body. This is my blood. Believe it. Say your Amen to it."

In our liturgical actions, we reverence a piece of bread in which we discern the body of Christ! We reverence the sacrament of Christ's presence. Whether with a bow or another gesture, we reverence the grain of wheat, the harvest, the baking of the bread, the breaking of the bread, the eating of the bread. We are reverencing our own communion with each other in table fellowship. We are reverencing the Christ, who becomes bread for us. He identifies himself with bread and we reverence this sacrament of holy communion.

We reverence a cup of wine in which we discern the blood of Christ! We reverence the sacrament of Christ's presence. We are honouring the vine, the grapes, the pruning, harvesting, crushing and fermenting. We reverence wine's festivity and intoxicating energy, clinking glasses and toasting, holy communion with each other, and see in all of that the blood of Christ, the new covenant for the healing of the earth and the forgiveness of sins.

We Catholic Christians don't commonly think in this way; we have neglected this aspect of our eucharistic theology and spirituality. What happens at the altar has too often been sterilized for us, depriving us of the richness underlying the symbolic content of the eucharistic elements themselves. We need to become more "vigorously incarnational," to use a phrase I came across during the week.

I remember, for example, a communion song that we used to sing quite a lot: "Look beyond the bread you eat ... Look beyond the cup you drink ... " Maybe "looking beyond" is a mistake. Maybe "looking beyond" is not the way to go. It is in the experience itself of broken bread and poured wine shared at this table that the presence of Christ is discovered and that the body of Christ comes into being. Perhaps our "beyondly abstract" theological constructions have gotten in the way of our getting real about the real presence.

Perfume the World

Eleventh Sunday in Ordinary Time

Exodus 19.1–6a
Psalm 100
Romans 5.6–11
Matthew 9.36–10.8

Today Matthew is constructing a bridge from the great works of power that Jesus displayed in chapters 8 and 9 to his second great discourse, the Discourse on Mission, which we will be reading for the next several Sundays. This bridge has two parts featuring, first, Jesus' assessment of the situation of the people as sheep without a shepherd, followed by the listing of the twelve apostles.

Harassed and helpless, like sheep without a shepherd, the people have too often been tricked by their religious and political leaders into thinking that a new day of justice and peace was just around the corner. Their hopes were raised repeatedly and dashed repeatedly. Moving among them, Jesus senses their need for compassion. This was his prophetic reading of the moment. It was not the time for threats, judgments, or rough stuff, but for compassion. Typical of Matthew, this theme of flock provides continuity with Israel's self-understanding. The image of Israel as a flock is found consistently throughout the Hebrew Bible. There are countless allusions to dangers besetting the flock, to the possibility of being scattered, and to good and bad shepherding.

Another important image of continuity with Israel is the number twelve applied to the apostles. Ancient Israel understood itself as the confederation of *twelve* tribes descended from the *twelve* sons of Jacob, whose name was changed to Israel. Even after the structure ceased to have any political reality, the people remained very conscious of their ancestry. With the images of the flock and the twelve apostles in place, Jesus is ready to expand on his understanding of just what the mission to restore Israel will involve.

Linking these two elements and flowing out from them is the mission of proclamation, calling forward, healing and raising up that characterizes Jesus' mission to Israel. The twelve apostles and those associated with them will share this mission and carry it out in his name.

As some of you know, I taught liturgy and preaching in the seminary for a few years, both here and in Baltimore. As you can imagine, the issue of call and the potentially intimate connection between their lives and the lives of the apostles was a central concern for the seminarians. All of us share in the mission of Christ in our own time, in our own circumstances and in our own skin. For the seminarians, however, the category had a special and central place in their wondering about and discernment of a possible vocation to the priesthood.

With particular regard to preaching, I tried to encourage the students not just to repeat the words of the Bible or the truths of faith, but to find their own voices. In digesting the content of the scriptures and reflecting both on their own experience and on the historical and cultural realities of the present, most especially that of our own congregations, they would find their own voice and discover in it the breath of God. In this way the Bible becomes a living word; the living Christ becomes present in their proclamation.

I grew up in a small town in the Upper Peninsula of Michigan. For many of those years, we had but one radio station, WHDF, whose programming, needless to say, was multi-purpose. Among its regular features, however, was the Texaco-sponsored Metropolitan Opera. When we were children, my father was very interested in having us develop an appreciation for opera, so we had to at least pretend to listen. That's why I happen to know who Lily Pons was and why I was attracted to this little story that appeared as a filler in some kind of newsletter:

> A well-known mimic was entertaining at a party one night when suddenly to everyone's amazement, she burst into song and rendered an operatic aria beautifully. "I didn't know you could sing so well," her hostess remarked. "I can't sing at all," came back the prompt reply, "I was just imitating Lily Pons."

Lily Pons came alive in her voice, much to the amazement of her friends and of the mimic herself. While the example isn't perfect, it can be applied to the sense in which, as we take on Christ's mission, he comes alive in us. He gets under our skin and becomes our voice. We become his body and sing with his voice. As we move beyond our own concerns and preoccupations, as we assess the needs of others who are in any way harassed or helpless and stretch ourselves on their behalf, we become shepherds.

There's a story about a woman who had been suffering from nerves, who went to a counsellor for help. As she was leaving the office, she turned and said: "You know, Doctor, I'm a very sensitive person." In a response that couldn't have been more direct, the doctor replied, "Madam, I know that you are a very selfish person." Naturally, she left in a bit of a huff, but knew that there was enough truth in what he said to come back again for the same medicine. Depression is a reality for sure, but even many therapists come to the conclusion that the trouble with many nervous or depressed people is that they are bestowing too much thought and sympathy on themselves. They are wasting on themselves the very things—love and compassion—for which others are dying.

The 19th-century American poet Ralph Waldo Emerson believed that it was through introspection and intuition that the divine will and purpose could be discovered. He was not alone in this way of thinking, but perhaps more passionate about it than most. Not always consistent, he preferred flashes of insight and colourful metaphor to logical argumentation. He believed that people should trust their insights and recognize that what they were discovering as truth for themselves would be an asset for them in reaching out to others in understanding and goodwill. He invited divinity students, for example, to look into their own hearts for "fresh revelations that are fit for today." He is also quoted as saying that "happiness is perfume that as you draw it out and pour it out to enhance the quality of another's life, you invariably get some on yourself."

Though the pursuit of happiness is noted in the United States constitution as a universal right, we never find it by chasing after it. Happiness is found to the extent that we develop the habits and skills that give us the capacity to reach out to others.

"The kingdom of heaven has come near." Cure the sick, raise the dead, cleanse the lepers, cast out demons. You received without price; give without price.

Like Jesus, we need to make our own prophetic assessment of the circumstances of our own lives and the many ways in which the reality of the kingdom of heaven calls us out of ourselves. As limited as metaphors like singing and perfume may be, they can work in harmony with gospel invitations to enhance our sense of vocation, mission and purpose.

In the name of Jesus, cure, raise and cleanse. Sing a song. Perfume the world. Give without price. Discover your happiness.

The Winner: Truth

Twelfth Sunday in Ordinary Time

Jeremiah 20.7, 10-13
Psalm 69
Romans 5.12-15
Matthew 10.26-33

Have you ever heard the word "jeremiad"? I hadn't either until I was looking up the prophet Jeremiah in the dictionary one day just to check his dates. There it was: "jeremiad." It means "doleful complaint" and is a takeoff on the prophet's name. We have an example of one of his "doleful complaints" in the liturgy today.

O LORD, you have enticed me and I was enticed;
you have overpowered me, and you have prevailed.
I have become a laughingstock all day long;
everyone mocks me. (Jeremiah 20.7)

As he moves along, however, his mood changes. The jeremiad runs out of steam and the prophet rediscovers courage and renewed determination bubbling up in his soul.

The LORD is with me like a dread warrior;
therefore my persecutors will stumble,
and they will not prevail.
They will be greatly shamed, for they will not succeed. (20.11)

Ultimately, Jeremiah's indestructible faith and hope in God win out.

Perhaps more than any other biblical figure, the personality of Jeremiah is vividly disclosed in his writing. We get to know him as a real person. He seems to be a rather shy and timid man who is called by God to be a public figure. He is called to a career of prophetic preaching. His task was not to observe the passing scene, but to denounce moral evil and to oppose corruption at a time when political and religious leaders were ignoring reality and busily flattering each other's presumption and conceit.

For such a shy and timid man, his mission must have been sheer torture. From time to time his doleful complaints rise to God and express his utter exasperation. He gives his feelings full vent before the Almighty. He is deeply frustrated at being committed to telling the truth even though nobody wants to hear it, angry at the blind stubbornness he encounters everywhere, and fearful of the numerous enemies that he seems particularly good at making.

In his sending of the twelve, Jesus is very clear about the challenges facing them, but insists that they, like Jeremiah, will be winners if they stand up for the truth. Jesus invites them to take a prophetic stance in the midst of their community and society, to communicate truth, whatever the cost. There is simply no option, because truth is always a winner. You may as well deal with it now, because eventually it will come out anyway, however vigorously you may try to avoid or deny it.

> "Have no fear of them; for nothing is covered up that will not be uncovered, and nothing secret that will not become known. What I say to you in the dark, tell in the light; and what you hear whispered, proclaim from the housetops." (Matthew 10.26-27)

Skirting issues and trying to pretend them away may be attractive for a while, but not indefinitely. The truth to which Jesus himself bears witness is neither hidden nor esoteric. It may be difficult, even paradoxical, but is offered to all who are open to its possibilities.

We saw several times—for example, in the Sermon on the Mount—the profound realism in his vision of the world and in the ideals he presents. To pretend that there are avenues to happiness other than those that he proposes is fine, if you want to live in a dream world. To pretend that there are ways to build a house other than those that he proposes is fine, if you want it to collapse before your very eyes.

Now in his second great sermon, his Missionary Sermon, Jesus sends the apostles to echo the truth that he himself has been proclaiming. Their task will not be easy. There will be struggle involved.

An earnest young man once set out to a remote island to visit an old monk who had the reputation for great sanctity. "Do you still wrestle with the devil, Father?" he asked him. The monk answered, "Not any longer, son. I have grown old and the devil has grown old with me. He no longer has the strength. Now I wrestle with God." "With God?" the young man exclaimed in astonishment. "Do you hope to win?" "Oh, no, my son," came the reply. "I hope to lose."

In so many words, Jesus warns the twelve that there will be a certain amount of wrestling involved in their relationship with the world and with God. They will have to be alert and ready to make the right moves. There will be no easy victories. In the midst of whatever resistance they may face to the truth they have come to know and proclaim, they will be called to courage, integrity and confidence.

> "Do not fear those who kill the body but cannot kill the soul;
> rather fear him who can destroy both soul and body in hell."
> (Matthew 10.28)

The opposition here is not between flesh and spirit. The contrast is between two ways of understanding and experiencing death and dying. The body will die. It can be killed. The spirit can die, too. It also can be killed. People can be worn away and broken down physically. People can also be worn away and broken down mentally, emotionally and spiritually. We have already seen that possibility in the experience in Jeremiah, who recognizes the demons, wrestles with them and brings them to God in prayer.

We all know people who, even in the face of temptation, tragedy and death have maintained their faith and integrity. They have allowed God to win the fight with them, in them and for them.

> "Have no fear...
> Do not fear those who kill the body, but cannot kill the soul...
> Are not two sparrows sold for a penny? Yet not one of them
> will fall to the ground apart from your Father...
> So do not be afraid; you are of more value than many sparrows." (10.28, 29, 31)

Developmental psychologists insist that learning trust is one of the great building blocks to a well-integrated personality. Indeed, it is the first building block, ideally learned in infancy. From the fidelity of their parents, babies learn that they can trust their parents, and gradually learn from lived experience how to sort out the trustworthiness of others. Ultimately they learn to discern how life itself can be trusted and how God can be trusted as life, with all its complexities and struggles, unfolds.

> O LORD, my heart is not lifted up,
> my eyes are not raised too high;
> I do not occupy myself with things
> too great and too marvelous for me.
> But I have calmed and quieted my soul,
> like a weaned child with its mother;
> my soul is like the weaned child that is with me.
> O Israel, hope in the LORD from this time on and forevermore.
> (Psalm 131)

In times of tension and temptation, it is this kind of prayer that eventually arises out of "doleful complaints," out of jeremiads. It is this experience of God that gradually becomes foundational for moving forward with courage and humility amidst life's challenges and complexities.

Can you see yourself in all of this? Does it reflect something of your own experience? There may not be high drama, but anyone who seeks to live a life of integrity will resonate with these themes.

You may want to take this prayer of Saint Ignatius of Loyola on the road with you.

> Teach us, Lord,
> To serve you as you deserve,
> To give and not to count the cost,
> To fight and not heed the wounds,
> To toil and not to seek for rest,
> To labour and not to seek for any reward
> Save that of knowing that we do your will.

Discipleship and Hospitality

Thirteenth Sunday in Ordinary Time

2 Kings 4.8-12a, 14-17
Psalm 89
Romans 6.3-4, 8-11
Matthew 10.37-42

Today we continue with Jesus' Missionary Sermon. Jesus is sending the twelve with a mission to echo his own teaching and way of
commitment to the kingdom of heaven.

The text is in two parts. The first deals with being a disciple, the
proper attitude for disciples and the costs involved in seeking first the
kingdom of heaven.

> "Whoever loves father or mother more than me is not worthy
> of me; ... and whoever does not take up the cross and follow
> me is not worthy of me. Those who find their life will lose it
> and those who lose their life for my sake will find it."
> (Matthew 10.37, 38-39)

The situation in Matthew's community at the time the gospel was
written was very tense and difficult. The split between Christianity
and Judaism was widening, even though the majority in this particular
community were of Jewish origin. Christians were formally excluded
from participation in the worship and other activities of the synagogue.
Even families were divided. It's difficult to exaggerate the pain that
both sides must have experienced, which accounts for the strength of
the rhetoric found here and elsewhere in the gospel.

Let's take a careful look at the text itself. The Greek word for love
in this case is *philein*, which is commonly defined as a state of mind
compelled naturally by sense or emotion. It reflects the natural bond
that exists between family members and friends. Under the circumstances that I just described, those who hear the gospel are being

reminded that certain critical issues in life may call persons beyond even these most basic human relationships. That other people, even family members, may not understand the convictions and concrete decisions arising from those convictions is the chance a conscientious person has to take.

The verse about losing and finding our life, which is found five times in the synoptic gospels (Matthew, Mark and Luke), is a very important one. Losing our life is not just an image; we need to understand it in its broadest sense. If a person's total preoccupation in life is finding herself—i.e., seeking personal fulfillment that entails preserving herself from tension, opposition, conflict and sacrifice—her life is already lost. She is as good as dead already. If a person is preoccupied with comfort, ease and the "good life," he is already as good as dead. He has lost his life.

There may be tough decisions with equally tough consequences. In extreme circumstances, people may literally lose their bodily life. The ultimate price for integrity may have to be paid, the supreme sacrifice offered. This is central to the meaning of the cross, to the way in which Jesus embraced the cross.

In its root, the word *martyr* means witness; witnessing to truth and goodness is always costly.

> "Those who find their life will lose it, and those who lose their life for my sake will find it." (Matthew 10.39)

In ways large and small, an attitude of readiness to give the totality of our person is essential to authentic Christian witness. In that kind of witness, master and disciple become one. The cross of Christ continues to be borne by his disciples.

In Canadian cartoonist Lynn Johnston's comic strip about family life, *For Better or for Worse,* Lizzie, the middle child, rejoices as she tells her big brother, "Look! I got nine dollars an' eleven cents to spend on Christmas!" Lizzie's brother, Michael, replies. "You can't buy something for everyone with nine dollars an' eleven cents, Lizzie!" But with supreme confidence, Lizzie replies, "But, I'm gonna try!" Walking away, Michael answers sarcastically, "Well, they're gonna be cheap presents." "Nothing is cheap, Michael," Lizzie replies, "if it costs all you have."

Even in heavy matters such as cross-carrying, the spontaneous wisdom and generosity of this little one can hit the target dead centre. Lizzie has a wisdom and generosity beyond her age. She has caught the spirit of Christ himself and is bearing witness to it.

The second part of the gospel concerns the issue and challenge of hospitality, the proper attitude or dispositions exercised towards others.

"Whoever welcomes you welcomes me, and whoever welcomes me welcomes the one who sent me." (Matthew 10.40)

This statement is repeated and amplified in the great judgment scene at the end of Matthew's reporting of Jesus' fifth great discourse. This passage maintains that our treatment of a disciple is to be regarded as the practical equivalent of our response to Christ and, ultimately, to God.

"Just as you did it to the least of these who are members of my family, you did to me." (Matthew 25.40)

A true story, *Baptism,* captured this in film for presentation to children. Although it appears to have little to do with the church's ritual, it has everything to do with being church.

A little Mexican boy was badly burned, so badly burned that his face was totally disfigured. His family—parents, brother and sister—had all been killed in the same terrible fire. He alone was left. He had no home. He was a beggar, living like a frightened animal. One day he heard sounds of children laughing and playing. He looked over a wall to see the children in an orphanage. They had a home. He saw the priest, the father, walking one day in a neighbouring field. If you've ever seen the film, you will remember how the camera caught little Alfredo as he ran and fell at the feet of the priest, burying his face in his hands. The priest accepts the little boy, and starts teaching him and caring for him on the sidelines. He wants to receive this little one into the community, but wonders how and if the other children will accept him. The scars are that terrible. He hides Alfredo in his own room and gathers the children, explaining to them the story. "You have never seen anything like this boy. I will leave it to you to decide." Alfredo was brought in and the children looked with horror on his scars. He was bowed in the agony of the moment. You can read his feelings in his stooped posture, afraid to lift his head. After an eternity of silence, one boy moved. He extended his hand to Alfredo and said in Spanish: "You are my brother." The film moves very quickly into music and dancing, even fireworks, until you see at the end a smiling Alfredo with his brother. One little boy was the Christ, recognizing and receiving the Christ in another little boy.

In a very similar spirit, Hasidic masters in the Jewish tradition tell the story of the rabbi who disappeared on the evening of every Sabbath to commune with God in the forest, his congregation presumed. One Sabbath they chose one of their own to follow the rabbi at a distance, thinking that they might gain some insight into his life of prayer. Deeper and deeper into the woods he went until he came to the cottage of an old woman, sick to death and crippled into a painful posture. Once there, the rabbi cooked for her and carried her firewood and swept her floor. Then, when the chores were finished, he returned immediately to his little house next to the synagogue and began his prayers. Back in the village, the people demanded of the one they'd sent to follow him, "Did our rabbi go up to heaven as we thought?" "Oh, no," he said after a thoughtful pause. "He went much higher than that."

We really do find our lives by giving them away, don't we?

"Truly I tell you, none of these will lose their reward." (Matthew 10.42)

The great sermon on mission seeks to stretch our consciousness into recognizing the spirit of Christ himself in our own minds, hearts and bodies as we go about our task of the gracious generosity, even sacrificial living, which characterizes our life of faith. It likewise seeks to stretch our consciousness into recognizing Christ in those who join us along life's way. Let yourself be stretched.

Channelling Our Restless Energy

Fourteenth Sunday in Ordinary Time

Zechariah 9.9-10
Psalm 145
Romans 8.9, 11-13
Matthew 11.25-30

John Donne, the famous metaphysical poet and religious thinker of 17th-century London, wrote and preached a remarkably personal confession about his struggles with faith, prayer and commitment at the funeral of a friend.

> Scattered and tormented, I throw myself down in my chamber and I call in and invite God and his angels thither ... at the same time, I neglect God and his angels for the noise of a fly, for the rattling of a coach in the streets, for the whining of a door. I talk on in the posture of my praying, but if God should ask me when I thought last of God in that prayer, I cannot tell. Sometimes I find that I had forgot what I was about, but when I began to forget, I cannot tell. A memory of yesterday's pleasures, a fear of tomorrow's dangers, a straw under my knee, a noise in my ear, a light in my eye, or anything, a nothing, a fancy, a chimera in my brain, troubles me—distracts me—scatters my prayer, my commitment, my life ....

Have you ever felt that way? Scattered, distracted, at loose ends, empty?

> "Come to me, all you that are weary and are carrying heavy burdens, and I will give you rest. Take my yoke upon you, and learn from me; for I am gentle and humble in heart, and you will find rest for your souls. For my yoke is easy, and my burden is light." (Matthew 11.28-30)

These verses, surely among the best known and loved of the scriptures, are spoken by Jesus at a time of personal struggle and frustration. His message is being met with lack of understanding and acceptance among the wise and influential of his time. Matthew presents Jesus responding in the classical form of his ancestors in praise and thanksgiving to the God of the universe.

> "I thank you, Father, Lord of heaven and earth, because you have hidden these things from the wise and the intelligent and have revealed them to infants; yes, Father, for such was your gracious will." (Matthew 11.25-26)

Even in the midst of discouragement and pain, there is praise. Perhaps it is out of Jesus' pain that purification, enlightenment and thanksgiving can emerge. He invites his disciples into this total experience before they come to him.

What is this insight about God's will and God's ways that leads to praise? In the common understanding of Jesus' time, religion and spirituality were rather specialized pursuits. The recipients of divine revelation or divine insight would be those learned, wise and understanding in Torah. They would have the capacity to absorb and process truth and wisdom. Other possible candidates for wisdom would be the great heroes of the past whose lives and work could be studied, or community leaders thought to be specially chosen by God for this purpose, or perhaps a particular charismatic sage whom the Lord might raise up for this purpose.

There was also, however, another strain in the tradition that Jesus seems to have been making his own. Divine revelation, true wisdom, would come to the lowly and the humble. He had already made that quite clear in the Sermon on the Mount. There is a wonderful wisdom already at work in simple and uncluttered lives, which we have probably experienced personally, perhaps even in our own children, restless energy and all. This restless energy may even be part of what moves them and us towards growth and true wisdom.

Ironically, one of Jesus' deepest frustrations came out just verses earlier when he was complaining about "children" of another sort.

"To what will I compare this generation? It is like children sitting in the marketplaces and calling to one another,
'We played the flute for you, and you did not dance;
we wailed, and you did not mourn.'
For John came neither eating nor drinking, and they say, 'He has a demon'; the Son of Man came eating and drinking, and they say, 'Look, a glutton and a drunkard, a friend of tax collectors and sinners!' Yet wisdom is vindicated by her deeds." (Matthew 11.16-19)

We could probably sum it up by noting the difference between being childlike and being childish. Being childlike embraces growth, discovery and newness. Being childish is stubborn, foot-stamping rigidity.

Gerald May, a medical doctor who notes how this restlessness is rooted even in our bodies, says:

Authentic spiritual wholeness, by its very nature is open-ended. It is always in the process of becoming, always incomplete. Thus we ourselves must always be growing and incomplete. Children know that. It is their lived experience. Adolescents want to rush the process. Some adults want to halt it and stick with the tried and true. It is a precious restlessness that leads us to God. Such restlessness is mediated and manifested even through our physical being, through the combined minute strugglings of the cells of our brains and bodies as they seek harmony and balance in their endless adjustment to circumstances. Our fundamental dis-ease, then is at once a precise neurological phenomenon and a most precious gift from God. It is not a sign of something wrong, but of something more profoundly right than we could ever dream of. It is no problem to be solved, no pathology to be treated, no disease to be cured. It is our true treasure, the most precious thing we have, it is God's song of love in our hearts.[26]

---

[26]   Gerald May, M.D., quoted in James W. Cox, *Minister's Manual* (San Francisco: Harper Collins, 1997), p. 230.

Our restlessness is God's song of love in our hearts. The minute strugglings of the cells of our brains and bodies as they endlessly adjust themselves in their search for harmony and balance signals the greatest gift given to human beings. A neurological phenomenon signals a spiritual gift.

Especially when we are distracted, scattered, at loose ends and empty, we need to hear again the Lord's invitation, "Come to me, all you that are weary and are carrying heavy burdens." If I'm not mistaken, the thing called a yoke was actually used to direct and steer beasts of burden. It was designed for their guidance. "Take my yoke upon you and learn from me," Jesus says. "Let me channel your restless energy in ways that are sound and true," he seems to be implying. "It is much wiser," he seems to be saying, "to take my yoke upon you than to think you can carry the weight of the world on your shoulders." "I will give you rest."

Eleanor Roosevelt, who always delighted in challenge, carried a little prayer in her purse. "Our Father, who has set a restlessness in our hearts and made us all seekers after that which we can never fully find, keep us at tasks too hard for us, that we may be driven to thee for strength."

Abraham Lincoln is quoted as having said: "I have been driven many times to my knees by the overwhelming conviction that I had nowhere else to go. My own wisdom, and that of all about me, seemed insufficient for the day. On my knees I knew that I was alive."

Although they don't use explicitly Christian language, they too had to come to terms with the wisdom of being open to divine guidance and direction.

"Come to me, all you that are weary and are carrying heavy burdens."

Keep Sowing

Fifteenth Sunday in Ordinary Time

Isaiah 55.10-11
Psalm 65
Romans 8.18-23
Matthew 13.1-23

Every good story should have a moral, shouldn't it? The parables are terrific stories, but offering a single meaning or a clear moral does not seem to be Jesus' intention, even in Matthew's version, which includes not just the parable itself, but an extended explanation that one would think should clarify matters.

The explanation arose from a question the disciples felt they had to ask: "Why do you speak to them in parables?" Jesus answered:

> "To you it has been given to know the secrets of the kingdom of heaven, but to them it has not been given. For to those who have, more will be given, and they will have an abundance; but from those who have nothing, even what they have will be taken away. The reason I speak to them in parables is that 'seeing they do not perceive, and hearing they do not listen, nor do they understand.' With them indeed is fulfilled the prophecy of Isaiah that says:
> 'You will indeed listen, but never understand,
> and you will indeed look, but never perceive.'"
> (Matthew 13.11-14)

What sense can we make of that as a prelude to the explanation and interpretation of a story that's supposed to have a moral that's clear and accessible to the people? What kind of a teacher is that? What kind of teaching is that? Very mysterious indeed!

In efforts to work out the meaning of the parable, I've often heard extensive discussions on the soil, its quality and its readiness to receive the word. In this line of thought, we are the soil and the moral of the story is that we need to be open and well-prepared to hear, receive and respond. There is the arduous task of plowing. The ground needs to have been broken so that there's a spot for the seed to take root. Sharp prongs of a plough or a pitchfork are pictured penetrating the firm and hardened earth, puncturing, loosening and turning over the soil. It's broken open and shaken free. You can easily see how this kind of imagery can work well to describe various psychological processes in a person opening up to something new.

I've even heard the analogy of niche used. We have to dig out a niche in our heart for the seed, niche being a modern word for a "place in the market" or an old word for a place in the pantheon of our heart for another statue. That doesn't work very well either.

Looking at the parable more closely, however, we see something different. "Listen," Jesus says in its initial telling, "a sower went out to sow." In its further elaboration, Jesus continues: "Hear, then, the parable of the sower." The story is less about the soil, or even about the seed and more about the sower.

Jesus tells the parable right after he has met serious resistance both to his teaching and to his person. The gospel reader can even sense Jesus' frustration and disappointment in telling the parable, especially in the awkward and ambiguous section of the text that I just reread. I hope that my tone of voice in proclaiming the text in the first place communicated those feelings, which I think are so important to a proper understanding of the parable and its place in the gospel.

The sower goes out to sow the seed with great liberality—and the results are predictable.

Notice the typical Hebrew symmetry or parallelism, which Matthew uses. There are three states of loss and three states of gain.

There is the immediate loss of the seed sown on the path, the gradual loss of the seed sown among rocks and the ultimate loss of the seed sown among thorns. In a further elaboration of the parable, Jesus further describes the circumstances surrounding the loss in all three instances and applies them to categories of persons.

There are three corresponding degrees of gain in the good soil: thirty, sixty and a hundredfold. Notice, however, that no interpretation is given to these three degrees of fruitfulness. If the point were soil preparation, wouldn't you think that he would have elaborated on various ways and qualities of being prepared to receive the seed and describe three corresponding categories of persons?

Isn't it true that, typically, it's easier to explain why things go wrong than why things go right? I sense a certain continuing irony in Jesus doing what is expected. He analyzes failure, but not success.

I like to think that, in these circumstances, Matthew is picturing Jesus as talking to himself. Jesus may, in fact, be talking to himself. He may be insisting that instead of trying to understand how and why things go right and things go wrong, it's time simply to move on, to move ahead. He may be telling himself—and letting his disciples overhear him—that whatever the odds might be, "Keep sowing."

To keep sowing in spite of complications and heavily unfavourable odds is to image God, who keeps sowing among us humans with unwavering hope and confidence in the inherent energy and vitality of the gift.

"As the rain and snow come down from heaven,
  and do not return there until they have watered the earth,
  making it bring forth and sprout,
  giving seed to the sower and bread to the eater,
  so shall my word be that goes forth from my mouth;
  it shall not return to me empty,
  but it shall accomplish that which I purpose,
  and succeed in the thing for which I sent it." (Isaiah 55.10–11)

One way of looking at the overall scenario might be that in telling the "Parable of the Sower," Jesus is inviting the disciples, and us with them, to picture ourselves with him as fellow sowers.

The seed is good. There's no time like the present. Whatever the odds, keep sowing.

Let's imagine this more concretely.

Parents may need a great deal of determination to resist measuring their own or their children's worth by academic success or personal popularity. There's another word to be spoken, another way of seeing. Whatever the odds, "Keep sowing."

Career people may find it very difficult not to function as if cleverness, political savvy and the manipulation of others were the most important tools at their disposal. There's another word to be spoken, another way of seeing. Whatever the odds, "Keep sowing."

A person who has been ill for years may find it very difficult not to be bogged down in self-pity and consider himself only a drain on his family and on society at large. There's another word to be spoken, another way of seeing. Whatever the odds, "Keep sowing."

Could it be that Matthew is letting us in on Jesus' own way of thinking about and interpreting his own ministry in the midst of both cultural obstacles and personal frustrations?

Could it be that, in overhearing him, we're being invited into the mystery of hope?

Stop Before You Weed

Sixteenth Sunday in Ordinary Time

Wisdom 12.13, 16–19
Psalm 86
Romans 8.26–27
Matthew 13.24–43

Jesus' third great sermon, the Sermon of Parables, continues. Parable after parable! Master teacher that he is, Jesus talks about things that he and his listeners experience daily. He refers to wheat and weeds, mustard seeds, a shrub, a tree, leaven and dough—all of which point beyond themselves to the kingdom of heaven.

> Jesus told the crowds all these things in parables; without a
> parable he told them nothing. This was to fulfill what had
> been spoken through the prophet:
> "I will open my mouth to speak in parables;
> I will proclaim what has been hidden from
> the foundation of the world." (Matthew 13.34–35)

Here is a wonderful description of a parable: "A parable is a metaphor or simile drawn from nature or common life, arresting the hearer by its vividness or strangeness and leaving the mind to sufficient doubt of its precise application to tease it into active thought."[27]

Jesus isn't talking about wheat, weeds, shrubs and leaven. He's talking about people. He's prodding his listeners to probe the human condition and to recognize in the parables something of their own lives and experience. The parables don't solve anything, but aim to offer a lens through which we can look at life, a fresh perspective, an approach to creative human living. Parables are not put before the crowds to answer their questions, but to invite them to question in a

---

[27] C.H. Dodd, *The Parables of the Kingdom* (New York: Scribner's, 1961), p. 5.

new and deeper way. Parables are not proposed to clarify issues, but to further destabilize the situation. They tease our imaginations into action.

We approach parables in different ways depending on our situation, our age, our maturity, even our mood at the time of a particular hearing. If I were to go down the aisle and ask the children in the congregation about the readings they heard today, I'm sure that few would remember anything about the first or second reading, but that many would remember the wheat and the weeds and would have some ideas of their own about the meaning of the story.

I remember hearing about my grandfather Eddy who thought he was being helpful one afternoon by doing some weeding. He pulled out what were probably snapdragon seedlings and left a nice little row of weeds happily waving in the breeze. My father, who had planted the snapdragons, was not amused.

We have to know what we're doing and be pretty sure of ourselves before we undertake the weeding process. Sometimes we may be in too big a rush to clean up the garden and may wind up doing more harm than good.

Think of it in terms of your own families, your children and the friends and connections they make, some of which may well trouble you. You are naturally anxious to protect them from anything and anyone that may lead them astray or corrupt the values that you have tried so hard to pass on. How do you handle what look like bad weeds? A quick clean-up may not be the way to go and may even be counterproductive to what you are trying to achieve.

Sometimes even in the development of our own personalities we can look back over our lives and see persons and circumstances that we may have weeded out of our lives as threatening and dangerous, but in retrospect were good opportunities; they challenged us to ongoing maturity. To have faced these situations head on and to have lived with them and through them would have given us wonderful opportunities for growth.

If weeding out the bad is our principal metaphor for a good way of life, we may need to consider alternatives.

We have within the Catholic community certain people for whom weed-pulling is their primary mission in life. The possibility of doing some patient analysis of this or that trend in liturgy, catechetics or morality, of presuming good faith and asking genuinely open questions is not the methodology of weed-pullers.

What is righteousness, what is the kingdom of heaven, what is holiness and how are these profound values fostered in the midst of new circumstances and a complex culture? The parable doesn't have an answer, but does provide one angle. Perhaps it suggests teasing the imagination into not making premature judgments and acting too hastily against anything that seems foreign or strange. It certainly doesn't give a total answer to complex issues of parenting, teaching, pastoring, or administering institutions and organizations, but it does offer a caution against premature weeding operations.

The text from Wisdom, which is the companion piece to the gospel parables, is quite striking in its description of the ways of God.

> For neither is there any god besides you, LORD, whose care is
> for all people,
> to whom you should prove that you have not judged unjustly...
> For your strength is the source of righteousness,
> and your sovereignty over all causes you to spare all.
> For you show your strength when people doubt the com-
> pleteness of your power,
> and you rebuke any insolence among those who think they
> know it.
> Although you are sovereign in strength, you judge with mildness
> and with great forbearance you govern us ...
> Through such works you have taught your people
> that the righteous must be kind. (Wisdom 12.13, 16-19)

Let me give you an example of this approach in action. Not long ago I went to Montreal for a concert that was being held at Notre Dame Basilica in a chamber music festival. The subway train was very crowded and I was standing up, holding on to one of those posts. Right next to me were two young people. They had green and yellow striped hair and earrings in very unusual places. You can probably picture the sort they were. They were arguing and using colourful language. Right next to me was a religious sister. She had a ring and a little silver cross and very white hair ... a sharp contrast. There was so much commotion going on that I was concerned that she was getting bumped around, especially by these two "bad" weeds. She made the sign of the cross, said a little prayer and began talking with them. She saw something in them that I hadn't seen in my preoccupation with their appearance and my frustration with their inappropriate behaviour. My sense that somebody should kick these kids off the subway train was instantly invalidated. I was being teased into seeing them differently, invited by Sister's grace to imagine something underneath the green hair, something beyond nose and navel rings. In the words of the Book of Wisdom, my own insolence was being rebuked, not theirs.

This is surely not the definitive reading of the wheat and the weeds. There is no such thing, but if it leads us to reflect the wisdom and patience of God who is "slow to anger and rich in kindness," it has done its job—for today. Next time, something else.

Treasure Hunters All

Seventeenth Sunday in Ordinary Time

1 Kings 3.5-12
Psalm 119
Romans 8.28-30
Matthew 13.44-52

The search for buried treasure is the stuff of which the old pirate stories are made. They fascinated us as kids. As fantastic as these stories are, they continue to fascinate because there is something about them that is real life. There's a bit of the treasure-seeker in all of us.

In our continued reading of Matthew, we come to the end of the Great Discourse of Seven Parables and read three short ones that are unique to his gospel. The third of these, about the net catching good and bad fish, matches the parable of the wheat and the weeds that we dealt with last Sunday, so let's stick with the first two today. They are twins, very similar in structure and significance.

The first is about a farm worker plowing another's land. Invasions, revolts and other catastrophes, which are unfortunately still not all that uncommon in some parts of the world, sometimes led people to bury their valuables. If they died without telling their heirs about their buried treasure, it would remain buried until someone like this lucky worker dug it up. Overwhelmed with his good fortune, the man in the story did not hesitate a moment before selling all he had to buy the field. It must have been quite a treasure!

Did you ever think, though, that this is another of Jesus' "immoral heroes"? Why did he go out and buy the field? If the rule were "finders, keepers," he could have taken the treasure away without buying the field. If not, selling all of his own property and buying the field, then casually digging up the treasure and going off with it are not going to sit very well with the previous owner or the broader community. Perhaps it would be legal, but what about its morality? Wouldn't you think, too, that even the process of liquidating his assets to buy this small patch of land would have aroused suspicion? With notoriety, animosity and even anger in the community all around him, I wonder if he could have enjoyed his treasure and lived "happily ever after." I doubt it.

Somewhat different is the merchant who is consciously on the lookout for pearls, which were considered to be among the most valuable substances in the ancient world. What brings the men together is their enthusiasm and absolute commitment to take full advantage of their find. Although the treasure and the pearl in the parables sound like material things, we know they aren't. Even the highly questionable judgment and morality of the man in the first parable is designed to make the case for an immediate and urgent need to get to the treasure. All other considerations need to be put aside. Do it fast, straightaway, with no detours. All bets are off. The risk is worth it. If nothing else, these guys are determined! The first of these twin parables in particular may match Jesus' comment elsewhere that the children of darkness are more determined and energetic than the children of light.

Let's see if these parables can't tease us into the kind of active thought we explored last week. What are we to say about searching for treasure—about treasure-hunting?

Curiosity characterizes humanity; it's part of the human condition. We are creatures on the lookout. Sometimes discoveries are made almost by chance and at other times they come at the end of a long, hard process.

A specific intention to search and discover has led people into the desert, into the mountains, into space, to the ocean floor and below. Our own generation has been privileged to share firsthand in phenomenal adventures and discoveries. Those of us who were not watching television the Sunday in 1969 that the Apollo spacecraft landed on the moon may remember where we were at the time and how we heard about the first steps taken by Neil Armstrong on the surface of the moon. I was at a recital at the National Arts Centre that afternoon. Joan Sutherland herself made the announcement from the stage. Jacques Cousteau's adventures in an ocean underworld continue to fascinate millions as we share them via television. Somehow it doesn't matter that they're reruns.

The challenge and fascination of research has led people to extraordinary investments of time and energy. Researchers have accomplished feats as remarkable and varied as unlocking secrets from the Bible and developing more effective antibiotics. Some of us will remember Jonas Salk's discovery of a vaccine against polio that protected most, but not all, of my own generation. Polio was still quite a scare for parents when I was a preschooler.

We search in ways great and small, in ways substantive and trivial. Kids play hide and seek, search for Easter eggs and organize treasure hunts. People search for the most satisfying career, the best schools for their children. We search web sites for this, that and anything. I was talking with a lady in the checkout line at Loblaws who thinks she has discovered a diet that's going help her lose 20 pounds in time for her daughter's wedding.

The other day I heard a radio interview with the personnel director of a major corporation. He was complaining about the job applicants he was dealing with. "What salary do you offer?" "Do you have a dental plan?" "What is your pension plan?" "When do I retire?" were their questions, in that order. He admitted that he was exaggerating somewhat, but was clearly frustrated that so few applicants seemed fired up to do the job. Few seemed to have an urge to excel, to invest themselves in other people or on behalf of a common cause. He wondered about their long-range well-being, about whether they had any depth.

Did it ever occur to you that the greatest treasures are always found in the depths? A pearl is buried in an oyster bed. Diamonds are hidden in crystallized form far under the surface of the earth. The rarest of orchids are hidden in the depths of the forest. Human life in its embryonic stage is entrusted to the depth of a mother's womb. We speak of the secrets of human personality as buried deep in the psyche.

"Where your treasure is, there your heart will be," Jesus said in an earlier discourse. The heart, for Matthew, is the place of one's deepest convictions. Perhaps it is digging and exploring the heart itself that will uncover what needs to be brought more clearly to the surface, the treasure which is already yours, the kingdom of heaven which is already planted there by your creator. The real issue for most of us might be searching in the right place for the right treasure.

There's More to Eating than Eating

Eighteenth Sunday in Ordinary Time

Isaiah 55.1-3
Psalm 145
Romans 8.35, 37-39
Matthew 14.13-21

There is a traditional story of Francis of Assisi and Masseo, one of his brothers, who were journeying from town to town. As usual, they begged for their daily bread. Francis would take one street and Masseo the next. Francis was small of stature and looked like your run-of-the-mill beggar. Masseo was tall and handsome. Francis got scraps while Masseo landed a whole loaf of freshly made bread. They met near a fountain outside the town to share the alms they had been given. Masseo took note of what was lacking—meat, vegetables, a knife to cut the bread. Francis, as he broke and shared the bread, could only exclaim joyfully: "We're not worthy of this vast treasure, bread, a table of stone, clear water and God to serve us."

The spirituality of Saint Francis rests on his point of view, the way in which he sees and understands the events of life, great and small, and how everything comes together around praise and thanks to God.

We just heard another story, the story of how five loaves and two fish became food for thousands in the hands of Jesus.

> [Jesus] ordered the crowds to sit down on the grass. Taking the five loaves and the two fish, he looked up to heaven, and blessed and broke the loaves, and gave them to the disciples, and the disciples gave them to the crowds. And all ate and were filled. (Matthew 14.19-20)

Bread, like rice in other cultures, is a rich, natural symbol of life. Even apart from its being featured in biblical stories and its liturgical use, broken bread bears a message. It speaks of people being drawn together in a shared experience of being human, being family, being part of the earth. It is a sign pointing beyond itself to deeper truths and values.

In the summer liturgy institute at Saint Paul University in Ottawa, one of the students in my class spoke up and said, "You know, there's more to eating than eating." We all knew what she meant. She was absolutely right. The breaking and sharing of bread in Christian liturgy, for example, has come to be called holy communion, the sacrament of the body of Christ.

As part of that same class we read the following passage. Listen carefully and see if it doesn't sound familiar.

> On the day, which is called the day of the Sun, we have a common assembly of all who live in the cities or in the country and the memoirs of the apostles or the writings of the prophets are read, as much as there is time for. Then, when the reader has finished, the one presiding provides in a discourse, admonition and exhortation to imitate these excellent things. Then we all stand up together and say prayers and after we finish the prayers bread and wine are presented. He who presides offers up prayers and thanksgiving to the best of his ability and the people express their assent by saying Amen and there is the distribution and participation by each one in those things over which thanksgiving has been said and these are sent, through the deacons, to those not present. The wealthy, if they wish, contribute whatever they desire and the collection is placed in the custody of the president and he helps the orphans and the widows, those who are needy because of sickness or any other reason and the captives and the strangers in our midst; in short, he takes care of all those in need.[28]

The description of a Sunday morning in his "parish" was written by St. Justin, who was martyred for the faith in the year 150. You got it! What we're doing this Sunday goes back a long way. Note how inclusive his description of the proceedings is. Justin is not talking only about what goes on *in* church, but what goes on *as* church. He cannot

---

[28]   Justin the Martyr, quoted in Kenan Osborne, O.F.M., *The Christian Sacraments of Initiation* (New York: Paulist Press, 1987), pp. 179-180.

separate the two. The sharing of bread and wine over which a prayer of thanksgiving (a eucharistic prayer) is offered moves outward and forward. Communion is brought to the housebound and a collection is taken to assist both needy members of the community and strangers alike. In the case of our parish, his description would include not only the Mass, but pastoral care and the food bank ... never one without the others.

In connection with that same liturgy class I taught, I read a contemporary description of another parish's sense of bread ministry. The parish is in the heart of one of our large cities and the person reporting is doing just what Justin did. She is describing what goes on, what she sees in her parish some 18-plus centuries later.

> There are two events that prompt the people to come together, the eucharist on Sunday and the evening meal served below the church. Once a week a motley assembly lifts up bread and blesses it and distributes it in memory of the life and death and continued life of Jesus. The poor are there and those who do not yet know how to become poor. The marginal are there: minorities, persons of other denominations, resigned priests, the homeless, alcoholics, the mentally disturbed. All are welcome and linked in a chain of solidarity as hands are joined and the Lord's Prayer is sung. If anyone is uncomfortable at that table, it is those who are over-dressed, over-fed and over-versed in liturgical matters. Everyone at that celebration of bread comes to know the connection between the liturgy upstairs and the daily evening "liturgy" downstairs. When the doors are opened hospitality and friendship are served along with fish and bread. There may be five hundred on a given night. The cooks and servers may be young or old, black or white, sinner or redeemed, newcomer or old-timer. But the spirit is that of the eucharist; a community meal, the free gifts of God and always enough for everyone.[29]

---

[29] Quoted in Joan Puls, O.S.F., *Every Bush Is Burning* (Mystic, CT: Twenty-Third Publications, 1985), p. 3.

This single illustration, multiplied in many churches in many parts of the world, may be sufficient to let us see how Jesus is still breaking bread. He is still multiplying loaves and fishes. He is still feeding people, drawing them into communion with one another and with the whole world in a spirit of grateful praise in and through the life and ministry of the church, in places just like this.

Liturgy and life are still coming together around breaking bread. We must see to it that it continues, in all its rich and wonderful dimensions. Our own ongoing development and renewal as a parish community depend on how we handle this simply magnificent gesture.

Hang in There

1 Kings 19.9a, 11–13a
Psalm 85
Romans 9.1–5
Matthew 14.22–23

There's so much drama in the Elijah stories. Do you remember his competition with the prophets of Baal? They set up an altar and so did he. Everything was ready. All that was left to do was light the fire— and that was going to be God's project. The priests of Baal danced and sang until they were hoarse and limping. Elijah taunted them, suggesting that perhaps their God was taking a nap, or had gone for a little walk. It is quite funny. Elijah, to make matters worse, had four jars filled with water to pour out over his sacrifice. He did this three times until twelve jars had been poured over the altar so that water was running in the trench around it. He invoked the God of Abraham, Isaac and Jacob, and the "fire of the Lord fell and consumed the burnt offering, the wood, the stones and the dust, even licked up the water that was in the trench."

What a spectacle! Elijah and his God were clearly vindicated and the prophets of Baal were brought down from the mountain and summarily executed. Wouldn't you think that, after such a triumph, Elijah would be heralded by the whole people as a great prophet and hero? Not on your life. The event so enraged Queen Jezebel that she vowed never to be satisfied until Elijah met the same fate as the prophets of Baal.

Before long, Elijah set out for Mount Horeb to hide out there, asking himself all along what this was all about. It's just not worth it! It's no fun being a minority of one! After a 40-day adventure on his way to the mountain,

The word of the LORD came to him, saying, "What are you doing here, Elijah?" He answered, "I have been very zealous for the LORD, the God of hosts; for the Israelites have forsaken your covenant, thrown down your altars, and killed your prophets with the sword. I alone am left, and they are seeking my life, to take it away." (1 King 19.9b-10)

At this point we begin the section that was read today. It describes another wild theophany. This time it's not a fire coming down to eat up Elijah's offering, including the rocks and the dust of the altar itself, not to mention licking up the water in the trenches. This time it's a mountain-splitting wind, an earthquake and another fire that doesn't seem to have any special purpose except to pass by and dazzle poor Elijah huddling in the makeshift shelter he has set up for himself in a cave.

What follows is as striking as it is obscure. The Lord was not in the wind, the earthquake, or the fire, but in the "sound of sheer silence" that followed. Elijah heard the silence, wrapped his face in his mantle and stood at the entrance to the cave, ready for the word of God. Elijah heard the silence and it was out of the silence that the Lord God spoke to him.

Fleeing to escape both notoriety and his ongoing responsibilities, Elijah is confronted with a message, which we have all needed to heed from time to time: "Be still and know that I am God."

The Lord's message was what we might have expected to come out of this newfound silence.... "Hang in there, Elijah."

God did not pull up a chair and tell Elijah how much he sympathized with him. He did not agree with him that things were tough and unfair out there all by himself. God did not commiserate with him. He simply sent him back to work, reminding him, by the way, that he wasn't alone, but that there were seven thousand Israelites who had remained faithful and had not bowed to Baal. His thinking was getting way too negative, and as self-pity and despair threatened to turn Elijah in on himself and to consume him, God turned Elijah outward once again to tasks still undone.

In Matthew's gospel, the feeding of the multitude is followed by the episode known as the "walking on water." Jesus sends his disciples ahead of him to the other side of the lake, while he withdraws into the hills to pray. The disciples are up against a strong headwind. Late in the night, Jesus comes to them, walking on the sea. He calms their terror and, as he enters the boat, the winds cease.

As a companion to the Elijah story, it is very interesting to pay attention to the rich texture of scriptural allusions in the gospel passage. In the psalms, for example, the chaos of wild and turbulent waters, the waves of death are opposed by a divine figure. In Exodus the waters of the sea are opened and closed by the power of God, by the might of his word, by the wind of his breath. In the midst of storm and turmoil, Jesus speaks: "Take heart, it is I; do not be afraid." His words echo similar assurances throughout the scriptures. His word "It is I," even reminds us of the very name of God. "I am"—"I am who I am" with its corresponding challenge to pick up courage, to believe and to trust. "Be still and know that I am God." "Hang in there." "Keep paddling."

All of this leaves us asking ourselves where and how in the sounds of silence we hear the word of God. When, in the winds and waves of darkness, do we meet the Lord walking on the water? Where and how do we pick up the message "I am with you. Hang in there"?

John Greenleaf Whittier (1807–1892), the American Quaker journalist and poet, was a champion of the anti-slavery movement and suffered from mob violence and political hate. In one of his hymns, he writes of an experience of prayer into which all of us need to be led:

Drop thy still dews of quietness
Till all our strivings cease;
Take from our souls the strain and stress,
And let our ordered lives confess
The beauty of thy peace.[30]

---

[30] John Greenleaf Whittier, quoted in James W. Cox, *Minister's Manual* (San Francisco: Harper Collins, 1997), p. 109.

Getting the Best of Jesus

Twentieth Sunday in Ordinary Time

Isaiah 56.1, 6-7
Psalm 67
Romans 11.13-15, 29-32
Matthew 15.21-28

"It is not fair to take the children's food and throw it to the dogs." (Matthew 15.26)

There's just no excuse for this kind of behaviour, under any circumstances. Surely it flies in the face of our normal image of a welcoming and compassionate Jesus, so human in his approach to people. It is even more inappropriate of Emmanuel or the Son of God. He seems feisty, narrow, even mean-spirited in the face of this woman kneeling at his feet.

This anonymous woman, however, is something else. Along with having character, she must have *been* quite a character. In the circumstances of the time, she's got everything going against her except her character, her spunk, her passion, all of which Jesus finally calls "great faith."

She is a Caananite, a representative of the original inhabitants of the land and one of Israel's ongoing antagonists. Jesus turns a cold shoulder towards her and addresses her in hostile terms. The reference to Gentiles as dogs was not uncommon, but no less an insult when offered to the woman's face. She is not deterred. Her daughter is possessed by a demon and she wants her to be released, to be free. Respectfully but clearly, she acknowledges the priority of Israel, but will not withdraw her claim. It takes extraordinary courage for her to renew her plea for help. Her persistence pays off. She is the only person in the gospel who gets the better of Jesus in an argument. She is the only person in the gospel who is said to have great faith.

We cannot gloss over or explain away this attitude on Jesus' part. It is an important occasion for taking full cognizance of his real involvement with the ingrained approaches and attitudes of his time. The evangelist Matthew is struggling with this issue in his own community. He is encountering the Jewish-Christian majority's suspicion of and resistance to full inclusion and incorporation of Gentiles. He may be using this story to say something like, "Look, even Jesus struggled with this issue. He changed. So can we. Let's be like him. God-in-Christ is being faithful to Israel precisely by making our faith a 'light to the Gentiles,' by making its riches available to the world."

Last Sunday I was at a cottage up in Michigan's Upper Peninsula and went to Mass in Copper Harbor. You'll remember that the gospel was about Jesus walking on the water. The priest told a funny story, which I think is even more appropriate in connection with this gospel.

Three men in their late 50s or early 60s were out on the lake fishing. No, it wasn't a priest, a minister and a rabbi. Just three guys! It was very early in the morning, before daybreak. In fact the almost foggy mist that characterizes early morning was still hanging over the surface of the water. Suddenly they saw a light rising in the horizon, which would have been fine except it was coming out of the south, not the east. It wasn't the sun. It was something else. They were so stunned that they were virtually paralyzed. What were they to do? What could they do? Just sit and quake with fear. You got it. It was Jesus. He walked right up to the side of their boat, dissolving the mist as he moved. Needless to say, they were surprised, but not so sure they were thrilled. If he was coming to point the way to the big fish, fine, but maybe he had come to take them home, and in their heart of hearts, they weren't sure they were ready to go.

Jesus spoke with them as a friend, asking them about their lives and their families. He told them that he had a little system for doing this once in awhile to assure the world that he really was around. To prove it, he would do a favour for each of them, anything they asked.

One of them said: "Lord, I've had this kidney problem and it recurs—stones that I'm sure are the size of baseballs. I don't think even you know how painful that can be."

Jesus admitted that he hadn't lived long enough to develop anything like that, but bent over and put his hands on the man's waist.

The man felt the healing power—and knew that there would be no more kidney stones.

The second man said, "Lord, when I was a kid I injured my elbow and shoulder playing football. Now that I'm getting a little older, arthritis is setting in; it's a nuisance and sometimes so painful that I go nuts." Once again Jesus admitted that he had never played football and that he hadn't been around long enough to develop arthritis, but reached out his hand, touched the man's arm—healing went out—and the man knew that there would be no more arthritis in that arm. He was wishing that Jesus had touched him all over.

Finally Jesus turned to the third man. He said, "Lord, I'm very honoured that you have come down here for us. I am very honoured and all that, but Lord, I think you should go home now. Anyway, don't touch me. I'm on a 100% disability pension."

Some of us might be more like him than like the woman in the story. We are not at all sure that we want to be any different than we are right now. There is something in all of us that stands back and says: "Please, God, don't love me too much. Don't touch me because I'm enjoying my disabilities. I'm enjoying my limitations. Don't open my mind too much because I enjoy this little space that I'm in. Please don't touch me, Lord. I'm enjoying my disability."

Have you noticed that, in many of the biblical stories, there's a passion for healing, freedom and transformation in human persons that serves as a foundation for God's action? There are interesting examples among people of great, even driving, faith in the God of new possibilities. Such is certainly the case in this instance. This is one determined lady! Whatever his mood, location or operative theology that day, Jesus is virtually jolted into action. He has almost no choice in the matter. She's gotten the best of him. The healing of her daughter arises out of her determination, her passionate, even crafty, faith.

Perhaps too few of us very enthusiastically seek the possibility of growth and transformation in ourselves and in the world. We like our little demons. It has even been suggested that some of us are passive-aggressive when it comes to real change in the world order. At one level, we may be a bit scandalized that Jesus calls this Caananite woman a "dog," but we're not all that sure we want the Caananites of our own world treated even with minimal foundational human dignity—

except, perhaps, in theory. There's no real passion for it, because underneath, perhaps even unconsciously, we recognize that it would cost us a lot. Our own priorities and style of life would have to change. Please don't touch us, Lord. We're enjoying our privileged status.

Great faith inspires us to work with Matthew's community and with Jesus himself towards freedom from demons of every kind.

"Have mercy on us, Lord, Son of David."

Shouldering the Keys
to the Kingdom

Twenty-first Sunday in Ordinary Time

Isaiah 22.15, 19-23
Psalm 138
Romans 11.33-36
Matthew 16.13-20

I will place on his shoulder the key of the house of David ...
(Isaiah 22.22)

"I will give you the keys of the kingdom of heaven ..."
(Matthew 16.19)

The image of a key is a powerful one, even in our own day. You may have read lately of a young woman who grew up on a small reservation near a northern Ontario village. There had always been a certain amount of friction between the people of the reservation and the people of the town. This young woman won a medal at the Olympics. To honour the occasion the town council organized a celebration to present her with a key to the town. Residents of the town and of the reservation were drawn together. The giving of the key was a very moving token of respect signalling a real desire on the part of the council that the two cultures be "at home" together. For her to accept the key to that town was to accept an invitation to be at home in both worlds.

You may remember experiences of giving and receiving keys: receiving the keys to your first home, giving the car keys to your 16-year-old daughter for the first time. Big and important moments. Growing up and a certain independence can be symbolized by the keys in both instances.

I will call my servant Eliakim … I will place on his shoulder the key of the house of David; he shall open, and no one shall shut; he shall shut, and no one shall open. (Isaiah 22:20-22)

The short text that we heard from Isaiah today doesn't give us the whole story. A man named Shebna had been appointed master of the household of Hezekiah, who was a king and religious reformer who lived towards the end of the eighth century. Isaiah is expressing God's disgust with him for using precious resources to design and build a richly ornamented tomb for himself. Imagine!

Shebna is deposed and Eliakim is chosen in his place. The text refers to his official dress and to the authority it symbolized. The key symbolizes the official's unique responsibility to grant or prevent access to the royal household. He holds a position of great trust. The kind of key used by such a functionary was a much larger implement than what we use today, making the description of him carrying the key on his shoulder not merely symbolic, but practical as well. His weighty responsibilities had to be shouldered.

The symbol—and the reality—of being the holder of keys continues in the gospel.

"Who do you say that I am?" …"You are the Messiah, the Son of the living God." …"I will give you the keys of the kingdom of heaven, and whatever you bind on earth will be bound in heaven, and whatever you loose on earth will be loosed in heaven." (Matthew 16.15-19)

Matthew's gospel is especially interested in the role of the apostle Simon, renamed Peter. There can be little doubt that Matthew's concentration on episodes in which Peter figures prominently reflects Peter's importance in the early church. His prestige and distinctive leadership are likewise clear in the Acts of the Apostles.

Peter's answer to Jesus' question about his identity prompts a response that expresses the basic beliefs of the early church. The builder of their "assembly" or church was the Lord himself, but Peter's role was unique and fundamental. The functions of binding and loosing represent the rabbinical language and tradition about decision-making authority within the community of faith. As holder of the keys, Peter is placed in a position of trust. He is given the responsibility of opening the kingdom of heaven in sharp contrast to other leaders whom Jesus will address later: "Woe to you [who] lock people out of the kingdom of heaven. For you do not go in yourselves, and when others are going in, you stop them" (Matthew 23.13). He cannot become a leader like that.

> "Blessed are you, Simon son of Jonah! For flesh and blood has not revealed this to you, but my Father in heaven. And I tell you, you are Peter, and on this rock I will build my church, and the gates of Hades will not prevail against it." (Matthew 16.17–18)

Just after his bold profession of faith, Simon, son of Jonah, is given a new name. The play on Peter's name is especially interesting. In Greek, and even more clearly in Aramaic, it is almost the same as the word for "rock," but its meaning is not as clear as it may appear. *Kephal/petros* refers to a smallish stone, such as one might throw, rather than bedrock, which would serve as a solid foundation for a building. "Upon this rock." Is Jesus being ironic?

Jesus' gesture of offering the keys to Peter is less about what kind of rock he is and more about Christ's regard for Peter's potential and for human potential in general. It's less about Peter's faith in Christ and more about Christ's faith in him. Christ accepts him as he is, trusts him and is ready to let him grow into the kingdom of God. Throughout Matthew's gospel, Jesus is often critical of persons and institutions, but he never writes them off. He continues to trust their potential. The gospel has, in fact, been called the "gospel of the church."

An example of how shaky Peter's rockiness is comes just a few verses later. We'll hear next Sunday how Peter took Jesus aside to rebuke him for suggesting that he go to Jerusalem where he would suffer, die and rise again.

> [Jesus] turned and said to Peter, "Get behind me, Satan! You are a stumbling block to me; for you are setting your mind not on divine things but on human things." (Matthew 16.23)

Yet another name! It arises this time not from Peter's faith, but from his lack of insight into the real costs of faith. The kingdom of heaven will cost Jesus' life and eventually Peter's own. When Peter says, "God forbid it, Lord! This must never happen to you," (v. 22) he does not know what he is saying, which makes one wonder whether he knew what he was saying in the first instance when he proclaimed, "You are the Messiah, the Son of the living God."

Within the Catholic tradition, we see our church founded on these and other events of challenge and promise. It's not so much Peter's checkered history or, for that matter, the checkered history of the church or of the papacy over the ages that is at issue. It is instead God's fidelity to human beings and God's insistence that human beings can be trusted to carry out his will.

Peter's unworthiness is not the core of the story. The consistency or inconsistency of his "rockiness" is not the bottom line.

Almost in spite of himself, Jesus gives Peter the "keys to the car." God entrusts human beings and human institutions with the opportunity and responsibility to unlock for others the kingdom of heaven, to invite people into a place where healing and reconciliation can be found, where love and mercy can be celebrated, where a festive table is set. Only in time will Peter discover what it means to "shoulder" that key.

In a sense we're all given keys to the kingdom of heaven. All of us open and close doors. All of us bind and loose. All of us have within ourselves the potential to open certain doors and to close others, to bind wounds, to loose from fear and guilt, to invite others to share the feast that we have already begun to taste ... or to do something else.

In Jesus, God trusts us with choices. In Jesus, God entrusts the future to us.

Our psalm refrain expresses beautifully what could be at the heart of our prayer today as we recognize our own call to shoulder keys to the kingdom of heaven: "Your steadfast love, O LORD, endures forever. Do not forsake the work of your hands."

Get a Life!

Jeremiah 20.7-9
Psalm 63
Romans 12.1-2
Matthew 16.21-27

What will it profit a man if he gains the whole world and loses his soul?

I remember this text being preached often. You may remember it as well. It was a favourite during Lent, or for retreats and parish missions. Its usual application was to divine judgment and to the reality of heaven and hell as eternal reward or eternal punishment. Time was contrasted with eternity in popular preaching. Illicit delights of this world, however enticing and pleasurable, were fleeting compared with the punishment of hell. Sacrifices and hardships endured in this life were nothing compared with the eternal reward of heaven. There surely is a certain clarity and logic about this line of reasoning, but it is not what the text itself means to say. We heard a more accurate translation of the original Greek in today's gospel: "For what will it profit them if they gain the whole world, but forfeit their life?"

In its context it reads:

> For those who want to save their life will lose it, and those who lose their life for my sake will find it. For what will it profit them if they gain the whole world but forfeit their life? Or what will they give in return for their life? (Matthew 16.25-26)

In an even wider context, it deals with Jesus' immediate experience of the demands of personal integrity, real purpose, his "life." The text describes a turning point that will be decisive for him—a life-and-death moment of choice.

We see that turning point clearly in verse 21, which notes that "From that time on, Jesus began to show his disciples that he must go to Jerusalem and undergo great suffering ...."

The words "from that time on" indicate a turning point. There can be no looking backward. The issue is not heaven and hell, but immediate and long-range consequences of personal choices and way of life. It's about integrity, about being a person in the now.

Peter's reaction is intense. Jesus' rebuke to him is even more intense. The profundity of their disagreement is reflected in Jesus' final accusation: "Get behind me, Satan. You are a stumbling block to me; for you are setting your mind not on divine things, but on human things." Initially named "Rock," Simon is renamed "Satan." He's getting in the way of Jesus being who he is, of Jesus being true to himself. He is a stumbling block in Jesus' path. This very important metaphor is central to the text. The image is of two persons, one of whom is walking on a path to reach a particular goal when the other places in his path a rock or snare that causes the first to stumble or fall, putting the person's goal out of reach. We could call it a "booby trap." For Jesus to call Peter a stumbling block or a booby trap is serious stuff!

It is typical of Matthew to make the very practical choices and actions of life the measure by which persons are judged. It is not a question of counting up individual acts and weighing the good ones over and against the bad ones. It is the whole tenor of life, one's overall style of life or sense of direction that will count at the end. The final judgment scene itself in Chapter 25 does deal with all kinds of specifics, but the unifying spirit is the choice of doing or not doing in favour of the least. "Just as you did it or did not do it to one of the least of these, you did it or did not do it to me." It represents choosing and living out an overall approach to making life decisions.

In the same way, it is in the overall process of losing, thereby finding, life that the Christian comes to ultimate peace in this world and the next, however challenging or costly the experience might be.

It's very dramatic at this moment in the narrative as Jesus faces his ultimate sense of purpose and direction, the ultimate consequences of being who he is and who he is to become for the world. It's very dramatic as he looks forward to embracing his cross.

In our lives, the experience may not be that dramatic, but in his story we recognize something important about our own. We know deep down that it's his style of being, his way of being that characterizes human nature at its best. There's so much more to life than being comfortable about things. With full awareness, we are capable of choosing what is right, what is best, even at great personal cost. When we do so, we are at our best.

Let me give a very concrete example. There are couples in this parish whose marriages are very strained by sickness and disease, such as Alzheimer's. Wouldn't it be much easier if ... ? may well cross the primary caregiver's mind, but cannot be the operative question. Deep down, they know that it's not the only or the best question and if they simply answered yes and moved down the easiest path, they could not live with themselves. Paradoxically, in cases like this, people find themselves by losing themselves.

The prophet Jeremiah gives us another example. Any portrayal of an ideal person of faith in terms of all-pervasive calmness, serenity and peace just has to be unreal. We may never reach the heights or the depths of Jeremiah's experience of the cost of integrity, but we do glimpse something of the dynamism of a relationship with God that is real and costly. In a beautiful image, Jeremiah talks of having eaten the words of God that have become part of him and nourished his life. Initially they had been joy and delight to him, but no longer. In his pain and frustration over the cost of speaking the truth, he is in a quandary. In spite of the cost, however, he discovers that he can do nothing other than speak up.

> If I say, "I will not mention him,
> or speak any more in his name,"
> then within me there is something like a burning fire
> shut up in my bones;
> I am weary with holding it in,
> and I cannot. (Jeremiah 20.9)

Jeremiah finds new energy by knowing who he is at his best and by believing in his best capacities. He knows that to lose or abandon core values would be to abandon everything. It doesn't matter what he might appear to be gaining by giving in to external pressure. He would be losing his soul. I think that we can all identify in some way with his experience.

> "If any want to become my followers, let them deny them-
> selves and take up their cross and follow me." (Matthew
> 16.24)

When Jesus says, "Take up the cross," he's saying, "Get a life!"

> "For those who want to save their life will lose it, and those
> who lose their life for my sake will find it." (Matthew 16.25)

Risk Telling the Truth

Twenty-third Sunday in Ordinary Time

Ezekiel 33.7-9
Psalm 95
Romans 13.8-10
Matthew 18.15-20

The word of the Lord came to me: ..."So you, mortal, I have made a sentinel for the house of Israel; whenever you hear a word from my mouth, you shall give them warning from me." (Ezekiel 33.1, 7)

"If another member of the church sins against you, go and point out the fault when the two of you are alone." (Matthew 18.15)

The texts today deal with aspects of our human, civil and religious life that most of us find delicate and difficult to deal with.

In the first case, Ezekiel recognizes the imminence of catastrophe. Jerusalem will be utterly destroyed. He senses that his knowledge and foresight oblige him to spread the bad word. The issue is not principally Israel's impending military loss, but the moral decay that led up to her weakness, instability and vulnerability.

In time of war, sentinels are appointed by the appropriate authorities to keep sharp watch for danger and to sound an alarm in emergencies. The situation implies, first, that the sentinel is up to the responsibilities entrusted to him, that he won't doze off or lose his concentration; second, it assumes that the people will be ready to pay attention to his signals and act quickly. This is not, however, the reality of Ezekiel's situation. He has sensed divine appointment to this post in the midst of a people unready to hear his message or to act upon it. His joyless task and responsibility are to proclaim tough love to a people unready to accept God's discipline.

In the second case, the situation is rather more personal. An individual who experiences sin is challenged personally to take the initiative to point out the fault to an erring sister or brother with the hope that the situation can be rectified.

For most of us, this kind of activity comes across as very negative: minding somebody else's business, sticking one's neck out, or dealing with "Who do you think you are?" questions is not a lot of fun. It's no fun being a sentinel, even a divinely appointed sentinel. The scriptures, however, take a longer view. They reach forward to the best possible outcomes of such admittedly uncomfortable situations.

Take, for example, the call to Ezekiel. It becomes clear to him he's doing the people a real favour by challenging them. Although it doesn't feel like it and may not be accepted as such, his ministry of naming their sinfulness is a positive service.

If people are ignorant, how can they grow? If Ezekiel's own personal watchfulness provides insight, even painful insight, and he refuses to share it, he's *de facto* condemning the community to remain in ignorance.

On a more personal level, which seems closer to what Matthew is driving at, if you don't warn a person and she falls, you share responsibility for the fall. If you warn her and she falls anyway, at least you've done your part. Your taking the risk of telling someone the truth, especially when it's painful, is an act of deep respect, an act of hope, an act of tough love. In proposing even hard challenges, you are showing respect and confidence in that person's ability to learn, grow and change.

The text from Matthew, as familiar as it is, deserves to be even more familiar, and its traditional application broadened. Matthew believes in the possibilities of goodwill, of common sense and wisdom and of the power of community, not just in special cases, but across the board, even times of tension, conflict and sin. The text suggests that if there's something wrong, deal with it. Deal with it head on, face-to-face. If there is something wrong, deal with the person face-to-face. Be respectful enough of the person and respectful enough of your own competence to deal quietly and privately with another human being. Believe in the power of truth to set free and the possibilities of goodwill to set right. If that doesn't work, maybe you have some friends with broader experience who can help you. If that doesn't work, there may be some wisdom in the shared experience of the community that can help you to resolve this matter. It's not a question of judgment or condemnation. It's a question of growth, justice, protection from harm, keeping relationships intact, keeping the community together. The approach Jesus offers takes courage, to be sure, but is fundamentally positive, respectful and generous.

You may have had to take such tough decisions in your own lives. As a professional person, you may have had tough conversations, perhaps even with a boss. With family members, you may have had to risk initiating tough conversations around their academic work, the friends they choose, drug or alcohol use, or sexuality. You may even have had to involve others in your conversations. It's not easy—not fun, not fun at all—but can you just let stuff go? A lady was telling me just last week about a painful conversation she had with her elderly father who really shouldn't be driving anymore, but who insists that he's quite capable. If people are afraid to intervene in difficult situations, to exercise the role of sentinel, parent or responsible friend, the consequences could be disastrous. Something in us, too, would like to avoid these situations completely. Ignore them and get out of town for a few days. Close your eyes or roll them around in your head. The scriptures have another approach that demands courage and responsibility.

I'd like to suggest that today's scriptures might even need to be stretched a bit. Beyond the crisis moments, political or personal, that provide their immediate context, might they suggest broader potential application? As sentinels, for example, could Ezekiel be stretched to suggest that perhaps we need to be watching out for one another in more positive ways? For us, as members of a community, might Matthew's gospel be stretched to suggest that we find more creative ways of positive collaboration in our ministry of healing and reconciling, binding and loosing?

I may not have all the details of this example correct, but this is the gist of a story that I heard a month or so ago. A high-school-age boy was arrested on possession of marijuana. It was clearly more than he would be carrying for his own use and he admitted to the police officer that he was delivering most of it to someone else and was keeping some as a commission. It was not a big deal, but he was part of chain—a weak link in the chain: his first time in that kind of adventure, his first offence, at least the first time he was caught. He was detained for the weekend. But a young woman who was the court-appointed lawyer, apparently for his defence, developed a plan. She gathered his mother, the police officer, someone from his school's guidance office and a young man who had a history of drug trafficking but had the guts and determination to go straight. They literally surrounded this young man with "tough love," with "proactive hope." "You're not a piece of junk," they were telling him as they developed with him a very concrete and exacting plan for the next couple of weeks before he would meet the judge. By doing so, they were not judging him or condemning him for what he had done, but were respecting his potential for what he could become. Sentinels and creative collaborators. There's more to "watching out" than condemnation or even "sin naming." Even more than making him pay the price. It's about hope and redemption.

How Good Do We Have to Be? by Rabbi Harold Kushner is very strong on the point of healthy religious faith involving genuine community and mutual responsibility for ongoing growth and conversion in individuals and in society. Here are two short paragraphs that give a sample of his thinking along these lines.

> If anyone tells you that one mistake puts you at risk of losing God's and our friendship and you believe it, then you will inevitably define yourself as a sinner…. If religion tells you that even angry and lustful thoughts are sinful then you will come to think of yourselves as sinner…. By that definition and that approach everyone of us does something wrong probably every day and we'll never make it. If nothing short of purity and perfection permits us to stand before the throne of God, then none of us ever will.

> But when religion teaches us that God loves the wounded soul, the chastised soul, that out of experience has learned something about its own fallibility and its own limitations, when religion teaches us to stand together in those experiences, when religion teaches us that being human is a complicated challenge and

that all of us will make mistakes in the process of learning how to do it right and that we need to stand together in that process, then we become participants in a wonderful adventure. Our mistakes are no longer emblems of our unworthiness, but invitations to grow. We will be brave enough to live and to share the life.[31]

In our own desire to live well ourselves and to be effective and compassionate sentinels for one another, it seems to me that we hear in Kushner a call to the kind of proactive hope implicit in today's scripture texts.

The great sentinel Ezekiel recognizes God's call in his sense of responsibility for the well-being of the community and proclaims God's presence in his experience of being vigilant and watchful. Matthew, looking beyond crisis moments, invites believers to come together in seeking truth and justice, and to recognize Christ's own wisdom and energy at work in their gathering.

"Truly I tell you, whatever you bind on earth will be bound in heaven, and whatever you loose on earth will be loosed in heaven. Again, truly I tell you, if two of you agree on earth about anything you ask, it will be done for you by my Father in heaven. For where two or three are gathered in my name, I am there among them." (Matthew 18.18-20)

Our celebration of the eucharist today invites our participation in this way of being in communion with each other and with Christ. "Protect us, Lord, from all anxiety as we wait in joyful hope"—as we watch and wait in proactive hope for the coming of the "kingdom of heaven."

---

[31] Harold S. Kushner, *How Good Do We Have to Be?* (New York: Little, Brown and Co., 1996), pp. 38-39.

Winners in the Numbers Game with God

Twenty-fourth Sunday in Ordinary Time

Sirach 27.30–28.7
Psalm 103
Romans 14.7-9
Matthew 18.21-35

Forgive your neighbour the wrong [that is] done and then your sins will be pardoned when you pray … (Sirach 28.2)

Remember the end of your life, and set enmity aside … (28.6)

The Book of Sirach is a second-century book of wisdom sayings named for its author. Sirach had wide readership in the early church and great influence in the development of common-sense wisdom that should characterize the life of a faithful, God-fearing person. It had strong influence, for example, in Saint Benedict's *Rule for Monasteries,* which continues to be highly regarded for its balance and well-integrated humanity.

The example found in the liturgy today is a case in point. It takes a lot of energy to stay mad. Letting grudges and anger go is humanly more liberating than having old debts paid. The fact is, they can't be paid anyway. So let go. It's the only way. You'll feel a lot better.

Think, for example, of the case of Timothy McVeigh, who admitted to the terrorist bombing in Oklahoma for which he showed no real remorse. The evening before he was executed, various survivors and relatives of survivors were interviewed. You may have seen some of those interviews yourselves. I was struck with the sense that those who thought his execution was going to bring them a sense of closure and peace were deceiving themselves. Far more reasonable was the "unreasonableness" of a father whose daughter was killed in the disaster. He had already come to peace and closure. He had found the grace to let it go and believed that Timothy McVeigh should not suffer the death penalty. For this grieving father, even McVeigh's life sentence was not to punish him, but to give him a chance, perhaps gradually, slowly, to see the light and to repent of his crime. He remarked that he and his family had no more energy for vengeance and retribution. They had to go on living and wanted McVeigh to have the same chance.

Listen to another verse of Sirach's wisdom: "Remember the end of your life, and set enmity aside."

Closer to home, I'm sure you're familiar with the Anglican priest in Alberta whose child was killed in a school shooting. He became an eloquent spokesperson for forgiveness and for the possibility of healing and rehabilitation for the murderer. For him, anything less than that would be a goal unworthy of his Christian faith.

Quite remarkable! But, in a way, isn't it sensible? Isn't it healthy? I believe that's what Sirach would think about it.

In our journey through life, we're all invited in various ways to enter into this mysterious and wonderful path that uniquely reflects God. In the traditional language of Christian theology, we call it the paschal mystery, centred in our experience of the power and grace of the dying and rising of Jesus.

In his spirit, we let go of a lot of stuff, and, in letting go, find that we hold something greater in our hands.

In Christ we find mysterious energy to move beyond anger to serenity, beyond hatred to love, beyond apathy to energy, beyond selfishness to sacrificial living.

To stand in judgment of others denies our common frailty and distorts our common humanity. To seek vengeance cuts off all possibility of a creative relationship with the one against whom vengeance is sought.

How much of this can be expected of us mere mortals, and for how long? Good question!

"Not seven times, but, I tell you, seventy seven times ...."
(Matthew 18.22)

"Should you not have had mercy on your fellow slave, as I had mercy on you?" (Matthew 18.33)

Think, for example, of today's gospel invitation. Once again Peter figures prominently. In Chapter 16 he is the spokesman for both God and Satan. Matthew once again brings him in as a dialogue partner with Jesus in a way that is entirely consistent with the rest of his gospel. Jesus had given Peter the keys, which makes the subject of forgiveness here in Chapter 18 especially appropriate. "How many times do I have to forgive?" Peter asks. "Seven?"

How many times do we have to rise above our own pain and our own very limited capacities for reflecting God's own mercy? Seven times?

No, seventy-seven times—and from the heart.

Clearly impossible!

What is required is not frequent forgiveness, but limitless forgiveness. Imagine the dying and rising that would take place in you if you had to forgive somebody seventy-seven times. Consider your hurt, your pain, your dignity, your rights, your struggle with the future of that relationship and the meaning of your own life.

The number seventy-seven is as exaggerated as the numbers in the parable that follows. Linda Maloney of the Franciscan School of Theology at Berkeley comments on the absurdity of the "numbers game."

> To get some grasp on how much money ten thousand talents represented, we need only point out that the entire revenue of Herod's kingdom for a whole year was about nine hundred. If this man were the overseer of Herod's property, he would have had to abscond with the whole proceeds for over ten years! (In other words, this is an exaggerated sum, the highest conceivable number.) Its exorbitancy matches the seventy-sevenfold forgiveness prescribed in the introductory dialogue with Peter. Clearly such a debt could never be repaid; the sale of family and property could serve as punishment but would never recover what is lost. The top price for a slave was only about one fifth of a talent. In modern terms, it would be rather like asking one guilty individual to repay the entire losses of

the savings and loan fraud of the 1980s. The king is extraordinarily generous. In light of this, the slave's attitude towards his fellow slave who owes him a sum equal to about a hundred days wages for a labourer, is shocking beyond words. It's a substantial amount, to be sure, but not relative to the amount forgiven. One hundred denarii is one hundredth of a talent. Let's put it in dollar terms. Relative to the ten thousand dollars forgiven, a hundred denarii is one cent. The proportions are wild.[32]

The parable clearly puts Peter's numbers question in perspective. Before the whole story is over, the issue of forgiveness in Peter's own life will move from the theoretical level to the deeply personal and practical level.

> He began to curse, and he swore an oath, "I do not know the man!" At that moment the cock crowed. Then Peter remembered what Jesus had said: "Before the cock crows, you will deny me three times." And he went out and wept bitterly. (Matthew 26.74-75)

By personal experience Peter would learn for himself what it means to be forgiven and, out of that experience, would learn the formula for the forgiveness of others in the church and beyond.

The whole point in all of this is that mercy and forgiveness can't be a numbers game, especially with God. When you're dealing with God, numbers just don't add up and it's a good thing.

"Remember the end of your life; remember the commandments; remember the covenant with the Most High," advises Sirach. See yourself in those terms and "set enmity aside; overlook faults."

In a numbers game with God, you'd be a sure loser. In communion with Jesus himself, you forget about the numbers and learn what it means to be a winner—in what Jesus calls the kingdom of heaven that begins already here and now, and just keeps unfolding.

---

[32] Linda M. Maloney, *Pentecost 2, Proclamation 5, Series A* (Minneapolis: Fortress, 1993), p. 58.

No Fair!

Isaiah 55.6-9
Psalm 145
Philippians 1.20-24, 27
Matthew 20.1-16

For my thoughts are not your thoughts,
nor are your ways my ways, says the LORD.
For as the heavens are higher than the earth,
so are my ways higher than your ways
and my thoughts than your thoughts. (Isaiah 55.8-9)

John Milton, in his epic poem *Paradise Lost,* appealed to the spirit for aid in the task to which he had set himself:

What in me is dark,
Illumine, what is low raise and support;
That to the height of this great argument
I may assert eternal Providence,
And justify the ways of God to men.

It's quite a bold prayer, isn't it? Do God's ways need justification? Milton certainly seems to think so. The parable today may be a case in point. It doesn't seem fair.

The principle of fairness is one of the most basic standards that guides decent people in their dealings with others. Decent people hold themselves and others to basic standards of fairness, which just don't seem reflected in God's ways.

I certainly don't expect that I will be able to justify the ways of God in this short homily, but together we can probe the mystery. As always, the context of the parable is crucial. Listen to the last few verses of Chapter 19, which set the stage for Jesus' telling of the parable. Once again, Peter figures prominently. He sets Jesus up.

> Then Peter said in reply, "Look, we have left everything and followed you. What then will we have?" Jesus said to them, "Truly I tell you, at the renewal of all things, when the Son of Man is seated on the throne of his glory, you who have followed me will also sit on twelve thrones, judging the twelve tribes of Israel. And everyone who has left houses or brothers or sisters or father or mother or children or fields, for my name's sake, will receive a hundredfold, and will inherit eternal life. But many who are first will be last, and the last will be first.
>
> For the kingdom of heaven is like a landowner ...." (Matthew 19.27–20.1)

Notice how Peter, as spokesman for the others, is asking what's in all this for them. Jesus responds that it will be clarified only at the "renewal of all things." It's clearly about God's ways, God's ultimate judgment. They can be assured of a hundredfold—eternal life besides, but the parable follows as a warning not to get mixed up thinking that these "rewards" are somehow earned and can be calculated ahead of time.

Notice, too, how the parable is framed. "But many who are first will be last, and the last will be first" introduces the parable, and "So the last will be first, and the first will be last" concludes it. The framing, however, strikes me as a bit odd because the parable doesn't match the saying except for the reverse order in which the workers are paid. The point is more like "Last and first will be equal." In the mixed communities of Jews and Gentiles for which Matthew was writing, the parable may have been directed towards Jewish Christians who were inclined to despise latecomers, the Gentile Christians. Its overall application and impact, however, is more far-reaching.

I've referred to Linda Maloney's commentaries before, and find her remarks about today's parable especially interesting. Although not its original intention, she suggests that its real sting for today's audiences is recognizing God as an "Affirmative Action Employer." She writes:

Those who oppose affirmative action are driven by a feeling that, somehow, they themselves are being cheated if other people "get something for nothing" or receive "unfair advantages," no matter what advantages they themselves have unconsciously enjoyed, they and those like them for generations past. The conviction is strong in all hearers that we have a right to what we have "earned." The idea behind this parable, that whatever we receive is essentially gift, meets with strong resistance. It comes too close for comfort to Marx's dictum: "From each according to ability, to each according to need." What an uncomfortable business it would be to be forced to admit that Karl Marx understood the gospel message better than we.[33]

The envy harboured by the grumblers is likewise serious business. The word "envy" is more accurately translated "evil eye." "Are you envious because I am generous?" is more accurately translated "Is your eye evil because I am good?" The frustrated first-hired workers respond to this unacceptable situation by casting an "evil eye." The Middle Eastern understanding of this expression is that it implies wishing evil on another person, wishing that person's destruction, even death. Envy is too mild a word to capture the strength of its negative energy. We know from our own recent history how an evil eye can become a suicide bomber, or the perpetrator of the Montreal massacre where engineering students were gunned down just because they were women.

As it stands, the parable can't be applied directly to economic issues, contracts, seniority, appropriate benefit packages, or affirmative action. It is about God's free generosity that transcends all such categories. We cannot afford, however, to leave it on that high and distant shelf. The way of God's ultimate generosity and ultimate judgment needs to touch, influence and colour our own ways so that they better reflect the kingdom of heaven already mysteriously present. The principles in this parable and those like it call for real and concrete application. Not easy, is it?

---

[33]   Ibid., p. 65.

Ultimately the ways of God can't be "justified to men" as Milton may have hoped. Instead God's ways stagger human imagination, keep us humans off balance, keep us from being too sure that our ideas about justice and fairness are right and godly.

The grace and the love of God transcend our human assessments of what is fair, and we cannot bind God or understand God solely in terms of the principle of fairness. If we stop to think about it, the same is true in our own relationships with one another. The love and graciousness that we show to family and friends cannot be understood, calculated or evaluated merely in terms of fairness.

Let's get back to the issue of God's free love and grace in the final judgment that we'll all face one day. I think Karl Barth, the great German Lutheran theologian, has a pretty good answer for Peter's initial question, "What's in this for us?"—the question that got the whole discussion started in the first place. Barth is speaking about himself:

> Certainly it is a lovely thing when someone has faithfully performed something in his life, be it great or small. Why should he not be permitted to rejoice at this? I too know such a person who has been fairly diligent, has written books, fat tomes some of them, has taught many students. Goodness, why not? Only one thing is quite certain: he too has his time and not more than his time. One day others will come who will do the same things better. And some day he will be completely forgotten—even if he should have built the pyramids or invented atomic fission. And one thing is even more certain: whether the achievement of a man's life is great or small, significant or insignificant—he will one day stand before the eternal judge and everything that he has done and performed will be no more than a molehill and then he will have nothing better to do than hope for something he has not earned: not for a crown, but quite simply for gracious judgment which he has not deserved. That is the only thing that will count then, achievement or not.[34]

---

[34] Karl Barth, quoted in J.W. Cox, *Minister's Manual* (San Francisco: Jossey-Bass, 1999), p. 318.

No Vengeance!

Twenty-sixth Sunday in Ordinary Time

Ezekiel 18.25-28
Psalm 25
Philippians 2.1-11
Matthew 21.28-32

In one of my attempts to clean out my office, I came across a friend's ordination prayer card from the early 1970s. It reads:

Champion the right to be yourself;
Dare to be different
And to set your own pattern;
Live your own life
And follow your own star.

There's surely something to be said for the point of view reflected in the card. The "I will" and the "I will not" of today's gospel parable fit in with that sense of human potential, our capacity to set standards for ourselves, and to take responsibility for our decisions. It stresses, too, that people have the freedom to change, and to move in new directions—for better or for worse.

What do you think?

"A man had two sons; he went to the first and said, 'Son, go and work in the vineyard today.' He answered, 'I will not,' but later he changed his mind and went. The father went to the second and said the same; and he answered, 'I go, sir'; but he did not go." (Matthew 21.28-30)

Ezekiel also emphasizes personal decision-making, personal responsibility for decisions, and the possibility of change for better or for worse. God takes that kind of movement seriously, and seems to judge it at face value.

When the wicked turn away from the wickedness they have committed and do what is lawful and right, they shall save their life. Because they considered and turned away from all the transgressions that they had committed, they shall surely live; they shall not die .... Are my ways unfair? (Ezekiel 18.27-28, 29)

"Life for the righteous; death for the unrighteous." Fair enough? The norm applies not only regardless of one's family history, but regardless of one's personal history, if the past has really been put behind and there is genuine change of heart. Nobody is stuck in the past. Nobody is determined by his or her past, for better or for worse. There is clearly a great emphasis here on the dignity and freedom of the individual and on the reality of individual responsibility. God deals with and searches the hearts of individuals.

I'd like to suggest, however, that we take a closer look at another side of the question, the long-term social consequences of past decisions and patterns of past decisions on our own lives and the inevitable influence of our decisions and patterns of decision-making on succeeding generations. As important as individual responsibility and individual salvation might be, there is more. There's a lot more to eternal life than individuals getting to heaven when they die. The issues are deeper than the possibility of a death-bed conversion, on the one hand, or on the other, the issue which may have troubled some of us as kids: that one unconfessed mortal sin could send us to hell.

All of us have memories, memories that live. Our parents and grandparents may well be in heaven, but they live on in us. It's not only the genetic bloodline either, is it. Important persons other than family members live on in their effects and influence. Decisions that were made and events that took place long ago still "live." Witness tensions among various national, linguistic and ethnic groups that are traced to age-old stories of injustice and war.

In a culture that has tended to focus on individual rights and responsibilities, today's parable and Ezekiel's prophetic voice are challenging, to be sure, but fit in rather well with our overall way of seeing things. They call us to be careful and discerning in the individual choices we make in regard to God's judgment, but they are not all we need to hear.

Prophetic voices raised today may have to take a different emphasis. You may remember hearing the ancient biblical proverb that reads: "The fathers have eaten sour grapes and the children's teeth are set on edge." Very descriptive, isn't it?—and real. Our personal decisions and way of life have enduring consequences. Our personal decisions are not taken apart from their consequences for the community. The results can offer a blessing or a curse to future generations. In today's circumstances, prophetic voices may need to remind us more about the father who eats sour grapes and sets his children's teeth on edge than about the individual son who changed his mind about working in the vineyard.

We've all heard about and perhaps even experienced certain family patterns that endure across the generations. In a family where one parent was an alcoholic, for example, chances are good that alcoholism could feature in the next generation. Part of it may be genetic, but certainly not all. Children of parents who read to them at a very young age, to offer another example, will normally have a higher success rate in their early days of school. It's not just that they already recognize certain letters and have already begun to learn to read. They have ingrained convictions about the value of reading and a personal desire to get into the books. Patterns of behaviour, coping skills, or lack thereof, are communicated and passed from one generation to the next.

To say that people are all equal, that the playing field is level, that everyone can pick themselves up by their bootstraps is naive, although the exception proves the rule. Some remarkable people do just that. For the most part, however, the proverb about the fathers eating sour grapes proves true.

In terms of the biblical experience of ethics and morality, solidarity in both good and evil was common wisdom. Children are affected by the decisions of their parents—punished, as it were, or rewarded accordingly.

In Ezekiel's thought, it is the "as it were" that needs further comment. A text in the Torah connected with the Ten Commandments pictures God "visiting the iniquity of the father upon the children from the third to the fourth generation." It is this kind of thinking that Ezekiel is trying to qualify or nuance. For him, the thought that God punishes from one generation to the next is clearly unfair. The thought that God has a long memory, that God personally takes out grudges on successive generations, or that God issues vendettas, was unthinkable for Ezekiel. Such was unworthy of a God of justice and mercy. Human decisions and actions, good or bad, affect society and even bounce down the line to future generations. It is not God who from his heavenly throne rewards or punishes future generations because of our decisions and actions. Our decisions and actions carry within themselves the power to influence the future. "The fathers have eaten sour grapes and their children's teeth are set on edge."

We clearly are personally responsible for our actions and will be judged accordingly, but we need to be increasingly attentive to their broad effects and consequences.

> Make me to know your ways, O LORD;
> teach me your paths.
> Lead me in your truth, and teach me,
> for you are the God of my salvation... (Psalm 25)

Look Beyond the Walls
of the Vineyard

Twenty-seventh Sunday in Ordinary Time

Isaiah 5.1–7
Psalm 80
Philippians 4.6–9
Matthew 21.33–43

Let me sing for my beloved
my love-song concerning his vineyard ...
And now I will tell you
what I will do to my vineyard ...
I will make it a waste; ...
I will also command the clouds,
that they rain no rain upon it. (Isaiah 5.1, 5, 6)

Doesn't that sound excessive to you—a love song for a vineyard
and then all that vindictive energy levelled at a patch of ground? The
matter is clarified only at the end of the passage when we discover
what the vineyard stands for and who its lover is.

For the vineyard of the LORD of hosts
is the house of Israel,
and the people of Judah are his pleasant planting;
he expected justice,
but saw bloodshed;
righteousness,
but heard a cry! (Isaiah 5.7)

There's a difference between a parable and an allegory. The story
of the vineyard would have been a parable had it been left open-ended.
We would have been left to puzzle over it and might have come up

with multiple layers of meaning. When a parable is interpreted and its elements are given a specific meaning, it becomes an allegory. Its meaning is pinned down; its message is clear.

In this case, the prophet's beloved is God, who created the earth and all people. The vineyard is Israel. The good grapes, which they are supposed to produce, are right moral behaviour and works of justice and mercy. The wild grapes, which they actually produce, are bloodshed and crying. It's clear—we can move on now to something else. That's the problem with allegories like this. They refer to someone else in some other time and place.

In addressing a parable to the chief priests and elders of the people in his own time, Jesus does what the prophet Isaiah did before him. In fact, he begins by quoting directly from the prophet and expanding the metaphor in his own way and for his own purposes.

> "There was a landowner who planted a vineyard, put a fence around it, dug a wine press in it, and built a watchtower."
> (Matthew 21.33)

> (Visitors to Israel can still see remnants of just such operations.)

At this point Isaiah's parable is expanded and reworked to include his leasing it to tenants. His slaves, and eventually his son, are sent later to collect the produce. Not only did the tenants not turn over the produce, but they beat the slaves and killed the son. Once again, the parable becomes an allegory when its meaning is clarified, pinned down.

Jesus said to the chief priests and the elders of the people: "Listen to another parable" ... but at the end he continued:

> "Therefore, I tell you, the kingdom of God will be taken away from you and given to a people that produces the fruits of the kingdom." (Matthew 21.43)

The tenants are the chief priests and elders themselves and those who have gone before them. The slaves are the prophets, Jesus himself is the son and the new tenants are the Christian church made up of Jews and Gentiles alike.

We could just stop here, couldn't we? We know exactly what these parables mean. They are allegories referring to somebody else in some other time. Interesting to a point, they have no further bearing on us or on our own times.

As allegories, one parable fulfills the other. The rejection of Jesus by the Jewish leadership of his time is the end of a long and tragic series of rejections detailed in the Old Testament. Are we supposed to simply note that we are now God's vineyard and that the Jews are not? Can we use this as a proof text that the Jews had their chance and blew it? Do these passages reach into our own time to suggest superiority for us who are fortunate enough to be Christian? Does the solemn liturgical reading of these texts contribute to self-congratulation and anti-Semitism? In the history of Christian preaching and interpretation, the passages have, in fact, been read in this way. You may have heard them so interpreted yourselves.

Luke Timothy Johnson, in an extended commentary on these texts, proposes another approach, which is well worth examining.[35] He suggests that the original allegorical meaning of the text by no means exhausts its meaning or potential to address successive generations of believers. The texts continue to be God's living word for all generations. They continue to hold prophetic energy.

To tap into this energy, we could begin by making a shift in our usual way of hearing these texts. We need to imagine Isaiah speaking directly to us. The text as living word, after all, underlies our basic theology of liturgical proclamation. The *Constitution on the Sacred Liturgy* from the Second Vatican Council couldn't be clearer on this point when it declares: "Christ is present in his word, since it is he himself who speaks when the holy Scriptures are read in the church" (7).

Isaiah addresses not only the Israel of the past, but all who seek kingdom life and accordingly bring themselves under the grace and judgment of the Almighty. We could stretch the reading of the vineyard of the Lord to include not only the covenanted relationship of the Lord with the people on the land of Israel, but also the covenanted

---

[35] Luke Timothy Johnson, *Pentecost 3, Proclamation 5, Series A* (Minneapolis: Fortress, 1993, p. 11.

relationship of God with all of humanity on the planet earth. When we make this stretch, we discover ourselves in the parable as caretakers of creation, stewards of the earth.

Another stretch would be to hear Matthew's parable not simply as an allegory of the rejection of Jesus by the chief priests and elders of his time, but as an ongoing challenge to all to whom the kingdom is given. The owner of the vineyard still seeks the appropriate produce in due season—seeks fruits of justice and righteousness in the land. It is quite possible for successive generations to reject God's messengers. It is even conceivable that Christians could turn on Jesus himself and reject him. In doing so they would be abandoning their own identity as Christians.

If we make adjustments such as these, the allegories become parables once again and we hear them in a more pressing and powerful fashion, perhaps even with frightening directness.

Invited into the parable, perhaps we can discover that the vineyard of the Lord is not simply Israel, or even the church. The vineyard could be all of creation, over which God has placed us as stewards. God has charged us with responsibility for its well-being and fruitfulness. Humanity has been coming to that realization more fully in recent times, but only slowly, painfully slowly, and largely as a result of disasters, which have served as wake-up calls.

Prophets are at work even now, reminding us of modern forms of envy, greed and pride that lead us to the misuse and waste of the earth's natural resources. Johnson is especially clear on this point when he writes:

> It is not necessarily a cause for congratulations that we who have exploited the poor and the earth in order to support our needlessly, heedlessly opulent style of life, have come to our senses not because God's word has convicted us, but because we are now in danger of eliminating the sources of our pleasure. Our pillaging of the vineyard is in danger of making it a wasteland. It is, we must admit, our fear and not our faith that

has moved us at last to make the first small steps towards ecological consciousness.[36]

Ouch!

Dostoevsky, the renowned Russian novelist, writes in *The Brothers Karamazov*:

> Love all God's creatures, the whole and every grain of sand in it.
> Love every leaf, every ray of God's light.
> Love the animals; love the plants; love everything.
> If you love everything, you will perceive the divine mystery in things.
> Once you perceive it, you will begin to comprehend it better every day
> And you will come at last to love the world with an all-embracing love.

We share today in the eucharist that comes to us in the form of fragile gifts from God—"fruit of the earth and work of human hands," to be received in thanksgiving and used as a blessing. Let us say "Amen" out of faith and genuine commitment to all-embracing love for the world and for the Lord of the vineyard.

---

[36] Ibid., p. 11.

Come to the Feast

Twenty-eighth Sunday in Ordinary Time

Isaiah 25.6-10a
Psalm 23
Philippians 4.10-14, 19-20
Matthew 22.1-14

On this mountain, the LORD of hosts will make for all peoples
a feast of rich food, a feast of well-aged wines,
of rich food filled with marrow,
of well-aged wines strained clear. (Isaiah 25.6)

Once again this Sunday, a vivid image in the prophet Isaiah is brought forward into the Gospel of Matthew. Last week it was the vineyard of the Lord, this week it's a feast catered by the Lord of Hosts.

Deuteronomy 12 refers to feasts of rejoicing that the people would enjoy in Jerusalem if they observed the commandments and rules of the Lord. The feast would flow out of their fidelity to God; it would be a thanksgiving celebration of God's blessing, a gift to be sure, but somehow appropriate, fitting—almost a prize. The blessing of such a feast couldn't be earned, but would somehow be appropriate because of the dispositions and ethical behaviour of the people that would lead up to it and bring it about. Their fidelity to the covenant with God would occasion such a festival.

In the case of Isaiah 25, however, the situation was quite different. Not only were the people unworthy of a great feast, they were *very* unworthy. Their performance had not been impressive. The promised feast follows upon repeated condemnations of the people for their failure in keeping the covenant. The blessing of a feast was based not on performance, but on God's stubborn fidelity to his own promises. Rather than threatening punishment, or offering a reduced vision of hope, the prophet elevates expectations; he ups the ante; he raises the rhetoric. The prophet promises a feast of fine food that surpasses any possible temporal realization.

> On this mountain, the LORD of hosts will make for all peoples
> a feast of rich food ...
> he will swallow up death forever ...
> will wipe away the tears from all faces. (Isaiah 25.6-8)

The promised feast is clearly not grounded in human accomplishments or human worthiness. It is God's free gift, extending beyond Israel, clearly beyond any reasonable expectation. Actually, it is inconceivable. Its language is so appealing, comforting and consoling that this text is often chosen for funerals.

As he did with the vineyard, Matthew takes this prophetic feast metaphor and reconstructs it for his own purposes. A simpler, more straightforward version of the parable exists in the Gospel of Thomas, an ancient manuscript which, although not part of the New Testament, is an important source for understanding how Jesus' teaching was being communicated in the earliest stages of Christian history.

In the Gospel of Thomas, Jesus speaks simply of a man who sent his servant out with dinner invitations for four friends. Each of them declined, pleading a prior commitment. When the master heard of their regrets, he commanded the servant to "go out to the roads" and bring back for dinner whomever he could find. Told this way, it's a genuine parable, open to interpretation in many and various ways.

The story may have something to say about now-or-never opportunities. It could refer to revisiting plans and priorities that may not be the right ones. It could be about openness and flexibility. It could mean that one must be ready to respond immediately to an invitation to move beyond what seems important at the time to something new and mysteriously larger.

In its telling by Matthew, the simple parable of the feast, like that of the vineyard, is transformed into an allegory. It is extended and interpreted. The host is the king and the occasion for the feast is his son's wedding. The two sets of servants sent by the king represent God's messengers and prophets who were sent out to Israel over the centuries and were rejected, some of them killed. The great destruction must refer to the destruction of Jerusalem and its temple, which would already have occurred at the time of the gospel's writing and could be interpreted as God's judgment on the Jews for not heeding the invitation. The king's subsequent invitation to others represents the foundation of the church open to Jews and Gentiles alike.

To stop here, however, would be to stop before Matthew stops. He adds a coda to the parable. He adds the wedding garment metaphor. In doing so, he precludes any such clear or simple interpretation or application of the allegory. This addition transforms the allegory back into a parable, ambiguous and open to further probing, open to the ongoing project of interpretation.

In the climate of troubled relationships between Jews and Jewish Christians, Matthew seems to lock the parable in the past until he raises the issue of appropriate clothing and decisively opens the door into the present. He turns the parable into a challenge for those who accepted the invitation. It is for the church of his time and of all times in which there co-exist good and bad, ready and unready, faithful and unfaithful members.

Would it be stretching things to see some hint of liturgical practice here? Could the wedding robe refer to the baptismal garment? After baptism, persons, even infants, are clothed in a white robe, which symbolizes the dignity, purity of heart and readiness for public witness that the Christian life entails. On the feast of the Baptism of Our Lord, I cited Pheme Perkins, who suggests such liturgical connections in Matthew. She finds references to the baptismal liturgy in the questioning of Jesus before his baptism and in the baptismal formula, both of which are found in this gospel. This may be another allusion, this time to the robe of baptism. Those so clothed who, in the words of the liturgy, "keep it unstained" have honoured places at the feast. Listen to the admonition offered to the newly baptized when they are clothed in the white garment:

> You have become a new creation and have clothed yourself in Christ. Receive this baptismal garment and bring it unstained to the judgment seat of Our Lord Jesus Christ, so that you may have eternal life.

In the liturgy we anticipate the great feast of eternity towards which Isaiah directs our gaze. Our acceptance of Christ's invitation to come here today signals our readiness to enter into the spirit of that great celebration. The question of our "baptismal clothing," however, is an open one. Just because we're here doesn't mean that we're as ready as we might be. Even though we're here, our hearts and minds might still be at home, or on the farm or with the business—not at this "wedding feast." We may have mental reservations about being here, other priorities that keep us from being fully present.

In his letter to the Colossians, Paul puts it beautifully:

> If you have been raised with Christ, seek the things that are above.... When Christ, who is your life is revealed, then you also will be revealed with him in glory.... As God's chosen ones, holy and beloved, clothe yourselves with compassion, kindness, humility, meekness and patience .... Above all, clothe yourselves with love, which binds everything together in perfect harmony. And let the peace of Christ rule in your hearts, to which indeed you were called in the one body. And be thankful. (Colossians 3.1, 4, 12, 14-15)

Paul is describing the style and texture of the wedding robe, the baptismal garment. The pall, with which we clothe the casket at funerals, also represents the baptismal garment in which the person enters eternity. Let's all believe that we can be dressed like this both in life and in death. Let's picture each other in baptismal robes as we come forward for communion today.

Come to the feast. Enter into the mystery of eternal life.

One Allegiance—and Then Everything Else

Twenty-ninth Sunday in Ordinary Time

Isaiah 45.1, 4-6
Psalm 96
1 Thessalonians 1.1-5b
Matthew 22.15-21

Thus says the Lord to his anointed, to Cyrus,
whose right hand I have grasped. (Isaiah 45.1)

Isaiah's prophecy is remarkable in its reference to Cyrus, the pagan Persian king whose right hand was grasped by the God of Israel. Not only is the prophetic word located in the world of politics, it is so located in a decidedly odd way.

The gods of the ancient near East were usually associated with a particular people and its land. In the Second Book of Kings, for example, Naaman the Syrian is converted to the God of Israel, and takes back some Israelite soil so he can worship Israel's god at home. The God of Israel was originally experienced as the powerful one who led Israel out of slavery, stronger than the gods of the nations. As Jewish thought developed, its understanding moved towards radical monotheism. Its thought developed to a point where Israel understood their God to be the only God, the creator of the universe. This passage takes them a further step down that path. The historical setting is the Babylonian exile. The Jews had been carried off into exile under Nebuchadnezzer in the sixth century BC and, at this stage, were being rallied by the prophet for a return to Jerusalem under God's guidance. The rhetoric was high in energy, but low in specific content—a typical political convention speech.

Suddenly, surprise—it's happening. The promises weren't just rhetorical. Liberation is upon them, *but not under God's guidance as they may have thought*. There's no pillar of cloud by day or pillar of flame by night. There's no mysterious passage through the sea. Instead, the Persians beat the Babylonians in battle, and the winning king decides to send them home. It's not God's work at all—instead, warfare and statecraft have won the day for them.

The prophet makes a logical stretch in his thinking. If the Lord is not a tribal deity, but the only true God, the ultimate source of all that is, then the Lord is at the source of this historical turn. The God of Israel, who is the God of the universe, is also the God of history. God's personal providence and protection extend beyond the boundaries of Israel and its people to Cyrus, the ruler of a powerful pagan nation. The God of Israel is the God of creation. The God of Israel is likewise the God of history, the God of all nations. Mysteriously, the Lord has chosen Cyrus, and has anointed this unbelieving foreigner as shepherd to carry out his purpose. The prophet's faith makes it possible for him to see beyond a politician's success to the presence and action of God, who can use anyone, anything, anywhere, to achieve his purposes.

In all of this, two distortions are possible. I'm sure you can see them already.

The first is to quickly generalize and universalize God's hand in things. Everything is God's direct and effective will from the rising of the sun to a devastating earthquake, from a win by our city's hockey team to an election victory in the House of Commons. Isaiah is making no such claims, but is suggesting that a discerning believer can discover a purposefulness beneath the seemingly random events of history. It's very tricky, though. Greater minds than ours have struggled with the interpretation of history in accordance with divine providence.

The second possible distortion would be to equate power with legitimacy. If he has power, he must be respected. In earthly terms, no human exercises as much effective power as an absolute monarch or emperor. Throughout history the temptation has existed to attribute divinity to such figures. The divine right of kings is idolatry; it is contrary to the first commandment, yet it has showed up from time to time in the structures and practices of the church. Relating temporal power and authority to that of God is tricky business, too.

The logic is clear. The God of Israel is the God of the universe and the God of history, but how that works out in practice is quite another matter.

> "Teacher, we know that you are sincere, and teach the way of God in accordance with truth, and show deference to no one; for you do not regard people with partiality. Tell us, then, what you think. Is it lawful to pay taxes to the emperor, or not?" (Matthew 22.16–17)

The Pharisees and Herodians are opening this very large can of worms to trap Jesus, in the temple at Jerusalem of all places, and during the Passover festival of all times! The stakes couldn't be higher. At this place and time, countless Jews gathered in the city to celebrate their freedom from slavery, often in a frenzied combination of patriotic feeling and rebellion against ongoing foreign domination.

If Jesus says yes to the legitimacy of taxation by the hated Romans, he will seem disloyal to the traditions and ideals of his own people and will be rejected, possibly even stoned, by them. If he says no, he could be reported for treason and punished, even crucified by the Romans as a fomenter of revolution.

Jesus sees through their malice and deals with their question brilliantly. With a coin of the realm taken from the hands of his questioners, he says:

> "Whose head is this, and whose title?" They answered, "The emperor's." Then he said to them, "Give therefore to the emperor the things that are the emperor's, and to God the things that are God's." (Matthew 22.20–21)

His answer can be read in a number of ways. First, it is crafty. His questioners have the coin of the realm in their hands. They are implicated and involved in the system themselves, which uncovers the hypocrisy of their question.

Second, some theory of politics may be at work. Recognizing civil authority and participation in public life is clearly appropriate. There is no necessary opposition between political involvement and religious faith, even though political life will never perfectly reach the ideals of the reign of God. Difficult compromises may have to be made. Greater and lesser goods may have to be weighed in the balance along the line. Believers who engage in politics and struggle to discover and achieve the best that is politically possible deserve a lot of credit.

Finally, Jesus' answer is a prophetic statement of the profound difference that exists between allegiance to Caesar and allegiance to God. Next week we will hear him say:

> "You shall love the Lord your God with all your heart, and with all your soul, and with all your mind." (Matthew 22.37)

No one but God can claim our absolute allegiance. As for the rest, we're all responsible for sorting stuff out as best we can. There are no easy formulas for discovering how the God of Israel, of the universe, and of history works. Instead we are invited to an ongoing conversation with the Sermon on the Mount and the wonderfully provocative parables Matthew has been offering us. Together we are invited to an ongoing dialogue with Jesus himself. Join the conversation with grace and courage.

Be a Law-abiding Citizen

Thirtieth Sunday in Ordinary Time

Exodus 22.21–27
Psalm 18
1 Thessalonians 1.5c–10
Matthew 22.34–40

When the Pharisees heard that Jesus had silenced the Sadducees, they gathered together, and one of them, a lawyer, asked him a question to test him. "Teacher, which commandment in the law is the greatest?" (Matthew 22.34–36)

We enter today into another situation of conflict, so typical of Matthew's perspective on the gospel story. The stakes are high; the question is designed to test Jesus. Like the question about taxation and the image of Caesar on the coin, it is designed to trip him up and embarrass him.

The text is so familiar that we all know Jesus' answer ahead of time. Had I stopped reading, you would have been able to finish the text from memory. It's precisely because the text is so familiar and so basic that it requires a fresh look from time to time. We need to reconnect with its original energy, the gutsiness of Jesus' answer and its ongoing importance for our way of life. Let's start by taking a look at just where the lawyer was coming from.

The Jewish people were expected to follow 613 laws on the books or, better, in the *book*. The word of God in Torah is clear that the people must deal with the "whole law," that they absorb it all, that they teach their children the "whole law." Six hundred and thirteen is a big number of specific regulations. One of the ways of trying to deal with such a number was to break it down into smaller units, to find ways to make the project of learning and keeping the law less daunting and, ultimately, less discouraging.

Here's one strategy that was offered. Over the years some rabbis broke down that number in a very interesting way. First of all, they found that there are 248 positive laws. "Thou shall" occurs 248 times.

At the time of this insight, the common understanding was that there are 248 body parts. To maintain one's body and to keep all the parts in some kind of harmony is clearly necessary. If we can keep our 248-part body going and well-integrated—which we must; if we can take care of ourselves—which we must; if we can walk and jump and sing and eat and sneeze, surely we can integrate these 248 laws into our ethical and spiritual lives. We may not be able to memorize them, but with practice, we can integrate them into the fabric of who we are. So, if we can keep our own physical complexity going; if we can walk and jump and sing and eat and sneeze, surely we should be able to integrate these 248 divine expectations into an ethical-spiritual way of life.

If you subtract 248 from 613, you get 365. That's the number of days in a year, which is also a manageable number. It's life-size, not larger than life. These same rabbis found 365 "Thou shalt nots." There was no question of getting them all down at once, but we humans live day by day. With practice and the passage of time, all 365 will become second nature. The law of God is not beyond human grasp, beyond our reach.

This is just an example of what the lawyers were trying to do. They were looking for ways to deal with the law, perhaps establishing priorities, perhaps just finding ways of communicating it and teaching it that were manageable and doable for people who sincerely wanted to live and grow as devout and observant Jews.

The complexity of such attempts to simplify and streamline matters is behind the question that the lawyer hoped would trip Jesus up, and makes his provocative summary response even more interesting.

> "'You shall love the Lord your God with all your heart, and with all your soul, and with all your mind.' This is the greatest and first commandment. And a second is like it: 'You shall love your neighbour as yourself.' On these two commandments hang all the law and the prophets." (Matthew 22.37–40)

In fact, Matthew has Jesus *misquoting* the text from Deuteronomy which, according to our translation, reads:

"Hear, O Israel: The LORD is our God, the LORD alone. You shall love the LORD your God with all your heart, and with all your soul, and with all your might." (Deuteronomy 6.4-5)

Jesus substitutes "mind" for "might." Is Matthew suggesting the need for a more critical approach to the whole project of religious faith? I don't know for sure how much should be made of this substitution, but it strikes me as very important. Might and mind are quite different energy sources.

Is Jesus suggesting that "thou shalt" bring a critical approach along with you as you deal with your understanding of faith, life, religion? Is he suggesting that it's not his role to sort out all these commandments? Is he suggesting that if "thou dost" love the Lord your God with your whole heart and your whole soul and your whole mind, you'll be able to sort them out yourself?

Jesus was only asked for the greatest commandment, but he goes on to give a second, which "is like it." This second commandment is on equal footing and needs to be dealt with in an equally serious manner. Here, too, Jesus quotes Torah, literally this time, but lifts this commandment out of a long list of other regulations. He highlights it, underlines it, makes it bold on his computer and proclaims it as different from the others, central, like the first and greatest. Listen to it in its context:

"You shall not hate in your heart anyone of your kin; you shall not reprove your neighbour, or you will incur guilt yourself. You shall not take vengeance or bear a grudge against any of your people, but you shall love your neighbour as yourself: I am the LORD.

You shall keep my statutes. You shall not let your animals breed with a different kind; you shall not sow your field with two kinds of seed; nor shall you put on a garment made of two different materials." (Leviticus 19.17-19)

The list goes on. There is no apparent hierarchy of values or regulations, except in terms of your own values. From the long list, Jesus selects one value that transcends the others and includes the most important of the others. It's almost as if he is demonstrating what it means to love the Lord with the whole mind. He is discerning priorities and making distinctions among greater and lesser prescriptions of the law. He is not simply counting. He is making value judgments. A human person's response to the law of God is not mindless. Obedience, justice and love are not exercised without discretion. Just the contrary is true. The two great commandments engage our whole humanity in an ongoing conversation with God and with each other. To keep them well requires a passionate, heartfelt, soulful and mindful commitment to the God of the universe and to God's created world.

Jesus is inviting us to commit with our whole being. There's nothing mechanical, boring or humdrum about being a "law-abiding citizen"—at least not according to Jesus. It's a passionate love affair with God and the whole of humanity.

Grounded in a Bigger Picture

Thirty-first Sunday in Ordinary Time

Malachi 1.14b–2.2b, 8-10
Psalm 131
1 Thessalonians 4.13-18
Matthew 23.1-12

When an old farmer who was very hard of hearing finally arrived late for a political meeting, he had to take a seat at the back of the hall. There he sat in silence for about a half hour while the tireless man on the platform went on and on. At last he turned to a friend who was sitting next to him and asked, "Zeke, what's he talking about?" Zeke thought for a moment and replied, "Don't know, Jake. He ain't said yet."

We know what that's all about. Windbags are always with us! William Gillette, of razor blade fame, was a stenographer as a young man. He was living in what he described as a "boarding house of the better class," and decided to practise his shorthand every evening by taking down every word that was said in the drawing room after dinner. I don't know what the others must have thought of him, ensconced in the corner with pad and pencil in hand, but that's what he did. Years later, he told a friend, "I went over my notebooks and found that in four months of incessant conversation, no one had said anything that made any difference to anybody."

In Matthew's gospel, Jesus is reported as being very critical of the teachers of his day, who seemed far more impressed with their teaching and their titles than he was. Their ministry is regarded as a ceaseless quest for personal, religious and social standing and prestige. Even worse, their teaching is inconsistent with their own behaviour. In its context, however, Jesus' teaching is directed to his own followers, to people like me, whose ministry is to be one of humble service to people, in obedience to the Lord, uncorrupted by the self-importance that can come from status, titles and degrees. "You are not to be called rabbi or father—you are all students and there is but one Father." The whole context of the passage strongly reflects Matthew's own circumstances, where Jewish and Christian teachers had become hostile competitors, and where Christians, too, were subject to the temptation to exercise a self-serving ministry.

It strikes me that a solid life of honest prayer is the best and perhaps the only way out of and beyond our human temptation to stratify ourselves, to take ourselves too seriously and to overemphasize our experience, our age, or our qualifications over and against others. Prayer is a process by which we review who we are, what we have and what we do. Prayer is both affirming and humbling as we reflect on the gift of life. So much of life, including family, friends, health and material goods, is not of our own personal doing. Life is gift.

I could have been the starving baby in the Sudan whose picture was in the newspaper recently, but I am not. Born in 1942, I could have been an infant thrown into the fire at Auschwitz, but I was not. In light of who I am, I have to take responsibility for my life as best I can, with humility and grace. So do we all.

That kind and level of prayer and reflection grounds us in reality, in God's reality, as participants in a story bigger than our own and in a time frame larger than our own span of life.

The Haudenausanee, the Six Nations Iroquois confederacy, had developed its own system of laws and procedures for decision-making. Their perspective is broad and far reaching. For example, it is written in their law that "In every deliberation we must consider the impact of our decisions on the next seven generations." Leadership in the tribes must respect their obligation to those who would live 150 to 200 years in the future. Such a perspective in our own centres of political power would serve the world well.

Once I met a Christian Brother who told me about the devotional objects he kept in his room as an aid to prayer. Many of us use a cross, a rosary, or an icon. He had a little collection of fossils: a small trilobite, an ancient marine animal, and a recently found tiny fish that's 600 million years old. He looks at them and handles them as he prays. They ground him.

Such people invite us beyond an all-too-common perspective that overvalues "places of honour at banquets and the best seats in synagogues, being greeted with respect in the marketplaces and having others call you by a distinguished title." Such concerns are too often not only superficial, but self-serving and community-destroying.

"You have one Father—the one in heaven.... You have one instructor, the Messiah. The greatest among you will be your servant. All who exalt themselves will be humbled, and all who humble themselves will be exalted." (Matthew 23.9-12)

Live Today As If It Were Your Last

Thirty-second Sunday in Ordinary Time

Wisdom 6.12–16
Psalm 63
1 Thessalonians 4.13–18
Matthew 25.1–13

> The Lord himself, with a cry of command, with the archangel's call and with the sound of God's trumpet, will descend from heaven … (1 Thessalonians 4.16)

Most scholars and commentators on the New Testament suggest that eschatological language such as St. Paul is using here serves a parenetic function. Take that! Does that sound parenetic enough for you? It's definitely eschatological, but parenetic?

As unreal as words like "eschatological" and "parenetic" sound, they're worth investigating. Eschatology has to do with the end times, the very end times, the end of the world, which, at this stage, we know will happen, but presume to be a long way off.

But—be ready for it! You never know what's coming your way or when it's coming, so be ready for anything at any time. That's parenetic. The word suggests that the inevitability of future judgment is about today. The fact of final judgment should colour our experience of the now. To bring it down to the "bumper sticker level" we could say: "Live today as if it were your last." Live with the intensity that comes with a judgment perspective. Don't drift, wait around, or kill time.

The apostle Paul's own convictions about all this run along these lines. God's ways are unpredictable. Therefore it's a good idea for us to focus on just and generous ethical behaviour now, so we won't be caught short later. Paul was in no better position to know the exact stages of the end time than we are. Indeed, his letters contain several versions that are not altogether consistent with each other. The scenario that he presents in today's text depends on standard apocalyptic images: the descent from heaven, the cry of command, the archangel's call, the blast of the trumpet and the gathering of the dead and the living in the cloud. His concern is twofold: first to remind his readers of the enduring power of the resurrection of Jesus and second to insist that they not get lazy, bored, or discouraged as they await his final coming. His eschatological language is parenetic.

The meaning of Jesus' parable about the wise and foolish virgins also runs along these lines. It harmonizes with the categories of the wisdom literature of the Old Testament, which are eminently down-to-earth and practical. The foolish women in the parable presumed that their time of waiting for the bridegroom would be short and that their supplies would hold up, but were caught short and ultimately left in the dark and the cold. The wise women recognized their calling to be bearers of light for this splendid occasion and took their responsibilities seriously, organizing their supplies for the long haul. Don't be caught short.

Let me give you a couple of examples of wise and prudent women who had more than enough oil for their lamps.

Movie buffs may recall the film *I Remember Mama*. The story concerned a Norwegian family living on the edge of poverty near the Golden Gate Bridge in San Francisco. The one bright spot in the family's existence was their belief that mama had a bank account downtown for big emergencies. Emergencies came and went, but never the " big" one that had been anticipated. The family never had to turn to the account for rescue, but knowing it was there gave them courage and inner strength to take the necessary risks to move ahead. Years went by. The children grew up and were on their own. They were all quite successful. "Now, Mama," one of them said, "we don't need to worry anymore. You go downtown, take the money out of the bank and do something special for yourself." Mama shook her head and smiled gently. "There was no bank account," she said.

When a man named Nathaniel Hawthorne lost his job at the customs house where he had been working, his wife, Sophia, surprised him by observing with a smile, "Now you can write the book you've been dreaming about."

"Right," he answered sarcastically, "and what shall we live on meanwhile?" She opened a drawer and pulled out a hoard of cash, which she had been secretly saving. She knew how desperately he wanted to write and had been taking money out of their household budget every week and putting it aside. There was enough cash in that drawer for them to survive for almost a year. It was during that year that Nathaniel Hawthorne wrote *The Scarlet Letter*.

What wise and wonderful women these were! Oil in their lamps and oil to spare! I love the way the first reading today describes the way in which Lady Wisdom seeks out such persons with such style and grace.

> Wisdom is radiant and unfading,
> and she is easily discerned by those who love her,
> and is found by those who seek her.
> She hastens to make herself known to those who desire her.
> One who rises early to seek her will have no difficulty,
> for she will be found sitting at the gate.
> To fix one's thought on her is perfect understanding,
> and one who is vigilant on her account will soon be free from care,
> because she goes about seeking those worthy of her,
> and she graciously appears to them in their paths,
> and meets them in every thought. (Wisdom 6.12-16)

What is interesting to me about the passage is that the wise seek Wisdom, and Wisdom seeks the wise. Wisdom is not some*thing*, but some*one* with whom we enter into a relationship. She is the source of the oil and fire we need to light our lamps and keep them burning as we await and seek out the comings of the bridegroom in the meantime.

God's final judgment will come in God's own good time. In the meantime, we have the choice of just hanging around or of living our days with energy, creativity and grace. Let's choose Plan B. Lady Wisdom and we can have lots of fun playing hide and seek with each other. That would be parenetic—hugely paranetic!

Alert!!

Thirty-third Sunday in Ordinary Time

Proverbs 31.10-13, 16-18, 20, 26, 28-31
Psalm 128
1 Thessalonians 5.1-6
Matthew 24.36; 25.14-30

Now concerning the times and the seasons, brothers and sisters, you do not need to have anything written to you. For you yourselves know very well that the day of the Lord will come .... (1 Thessalonians 5.1-2)

The "day of the Lord." That's not an idea that fits very well into the modern—or is it postmodern—scheme of things.

He will come again in glory to judge the living and the dead, and his kingdom will have no end ....
We look for the resurrection of the dead, and the life of the world to come.

In his very interesting and useful commentary on these last Sundays of the church year, Luke Timothy Johnson remarks:

Our lack of eschatological expectation may be connected to a more fundamental collapse within the structure of our Christian faith. If we believe in a living God who creates the world and us anew at every moment and who has raised Jesus from the dead to be present to us in the Spirit, what should shock us about a future encounter? But if our belief is constrained by the limits of enlightenment rationality, even the concept of a living God appears mythical and the hope of a future "coming" of God only a future mystification of the delusion.[37]

In the tradition that we Christians have shared in every age, we affirm that God is not finished with us yet. We fully expect God's continued activity in the world to the very end and await a final and all-consuming encounter with him. It is in light of this truth that Christians watch and wait.

Listen again to Paul:

> You, beloved, are not in darkness, for that day to surprise you like a thief; for you are all children of light and children of the day; we are not of the night or of darkness. So then let us not fall asleep as others do, but let us keep awake and be sober... (1 Thessalonians 5.4-6)

The distance between the symbolic world of scripture and the one we inhabit is clear, but the biblical texts and creedal statements with which I began this homily simply won't go away. Nor can they be dismissed as marginal to the tradition. Johnson continues:

> The contemporary reader is therefore forced to make an unusually sharp decision. The texts should be abandoned because they are meaningless and scandalous; our contemporary ethos should be adjusted to conformity with our sacred texts; or, we must find a way to negotiate the space between these ancient symbols and ourselves without destroying either them or us.[38]

Let's see if we can make a move here towards negotiating that space.

Paul calls his community to a continuous state of alert. He suggests that settling into a comfort zone is very dangerous. To keep saying "peace and security" as a mantra can be hypnotic. It can dull people's sensitivities. It would be something like Canadians saying, "This is the

---

[37] Luke Timothy Johnson, *Pentecost 3, Proclamation 5, Series A* (Minneapolis: Fortress, 1993), p. 50.

[38] Ibid., p. 50.

best country in the world" over and over and over and over, falling into a trance that produces lethargy and allow for virtually no movement or change.

"Let us not fall asleep as others do, but let us keep awake and be sober." Do not be a child of the night, who gets drunk at night and sleeps it off during the day—who is never fully alive.

Paul is certain of the approaching end time because ours is a living God who will ultimately make his claim on all creation. Humans have no choice in the matter. That is simply how things are and how things will be. The issue is in the quality of waiting for that day, the spirit in which we live in the meantime.

The parable of the talents illustrates this point very concretely. The talents are distributed according to each one's ability. In the master's absence no one was expected to perform beyond capacity. The amounts of money, however, are quite large. A denarius was an ordinary labourer's daily wage. One talent, the smallest amount in the story, was worth 600 denarii. In other words, you'd have to work 600 days and spend nothing to have a talent in your pocket. Five talents would be the equivalent of 3000 denarii.

All three slaves are placed in a position of trust; all are entrusted with considerable resources; all are expected to produce. Of particular interest is what the master has to say to the servant who simply buried his talent to preserve it.

> "You wicked and lazy slave! You knew, did you, that I reap where I did not sow, and gather where I did not scatter? Then you ought to have invested my money with the bankers, and on my return I would have received what was my own with interest. So take the talent from him, and give it to the one with the ten talents. For to all those who have, more will be given, and they will have an abundance; but from those who have nothing, even what they have will be taken away." (Matthew 25.26–29)

The statement is especially powerful if we recognize the talents in the story as a metaphor for spiritual gifts. In English, the word talents itself works very well. Talents are real only to the extent that they are shared. In being shared they come to life. Love grows by being given away. Hope shows itself in adventurous risk taking.

A talent to be invested may even be an apt metaphor for the gift of faith itself. Simply to preserve "the faith" in some exaggerated preoccupation with orthodoxy isn't being faithful. Our Christian history can teach us a lot about what happens when faith is ossified, protected in its own little space, rather than invested, brought into dynamic contact with the world so that it can be productive and life transforming.

The industrious pioneer woman of whom we read in the book of Proverbs is herself a wonderful metaphor for how talented persons and communities function in faithful, hopeful and loving ways. It's very much about being in this world in creative and energetic ways.

> He will come again in glory to judge the living and the dead, and his kingdom will have no end.... We look for the resurrection of the dead, and the life of the world to come.

It's probably true that most of us don't think very much about these things. Despite the distance from our consciousness of any traditional expectation of the end time, the liturgy today speaks of the urgent need for vigilance and preparedness for the future. It challenges us to take a long view. It does so with energy and great conviction.

The texts don't waste any time on the how or when of final judgment, but focus instead on its inevitability. They invite individuals and communities living in a particular time and space to recognize their relationship with universal history and a common universal destiny. Not to live creatively and intensely "in the meantime" is to bury our heads in the sand as we bury our talents there.

Incarnate in the Least

Christ the King

Exodus 34.11-2, 15-17
Psalm 23
1 Corinthians 15.20-26, 28
Matthew 25.31-46

In this very dramatic and familiar judgment scene, we reach the climax of Jesus' preaching, his last major word before the passion. It has even been suggested that, in Matthew's account of it, all of Jesus' teaching is summarized in this great event.

The most amazing element in the story is the utter unawareness of both the righteous and the accursed of the ultimate meaning of how they chose to live their lives. Neither group recognized the king himself in the lost, the stray, the injured, or the weak.

Each group chose or failed to choose reaching out to others as the primary direction of their lives. They either did or did not devote themselves to service of others as their foundational orthodoxy, their core spirituality.

If the text is indeed so crucial for the gospel, I was on the right track as a very young priest at another parish in Ottawa. It was a Saturday morning and the pastor thought I was crazy even to talk with these people, much less invite them into the house. Whoever they were, they had lots to say about God and were very sure of themselves. After listening for a while, I asked them if they were interested in what I thought. They weren't, but couldn't admit it. I turned to this text from Matthew and read it from beginning to end with no comment. They finally remarked that I was oversimplifying things "terribly." I was wise enough, at that stage of my life, to stand up and, as graciously as I could, show them the door.

Sad to say, I've since had similar encounters, even with Catholics, which have turned into lengthier and more combative discussions on this, that and everything. I realize now that in most cases, I would have been better off turning to Matthew 25:31-46, and reading it without comment.

The utterly disarming simplicity, clarity and profundity of this text may, in fact, be best without comment, but somehow, I can't help myself. I guess it's an occupational hazard!

I know that it's a little early to start talking about Christmas. It's not even Advent yet, but I want to tell you about an experience I had with the children over at the local elementary school last year as Christmas started to become their horizon. They had gifts on the brain, as you can well imagine. One of the teachers had suggested that because it's Jesus' birthday, he's the one who should be getting the gifts. The discussion turned to the kinds of gifts that might please Jesus. There were suggestions about love and caring for each other, about being more helpful at home when things are especially busy, about working hard to make the Christmas exchange and food collection a success. It became clearer and clearer that we couldn't think of anything that we could give Jesus directly. We were actually giving gifts to others and trying to see him in them. We sang the familiar song "Whatsoever you do to the least of my brothers/sisters, that you do unto me." (We did try to alternate "brothers" and "sisters" verse after verse, but got a little mixed up sometimes!) Women in prison, for example. Some of them couldn't picture that. It finally dawned on one little boy that since we give gifts to everybody on Christmas because it's Jesus' birthday, it must somehow or other be *everybody's* birthday, including his own and he was going to be quite excited and happy to get his share of whatever's going around. He was ready to get down to business and make his list. The relentless logic of children!

This text of divine judgment centred on "whatsoever you do to the least you do to me" provides a wonderful link between Ordinary Time and the Advent–Christmas Season. It is about the Incarnation, isn't it? Emmanuel, God-with-us in the poor and the needy.

In Matthew's first chapter, Joseph learns in a dream that "the virgin shall conceive and bear a son and they shall name him Emmanuel— God is with us." This Emmanuel's last words according to the same gospel are: "Remember, I am with you always, to the end of the age." (Matthew 28:20) One of the ways, perhaps the chief way, in which

Christ remains Emmanuel is in the least of the brothers and sisters. In them he remains incarnate. There can be no separation between divine revelation found in Joseph's dreams so long ago and today's concrete ethical demands.

We could turn to John Ruskin (1819–1900) as an example of one of our ancestors in faith who insisted that believers "keep it all together." He struggled throughout his life with traditional forms of orthodoxy and church life, which he found unpersuasive, even empty. He was, however, deeply attached to the Bible and to his faith in God's omnipresence and God's incarnation. By profession he was an art critic, which, in his mind, included being a social and political critic and activist as well. For him, nothing truly beautiful made sense or could survive in a world that was out of order. In his writings, he stressed nobility and aesthetic development as the only lasting wealth of a civilization, but for such nobility and beauty to be accessible to people there were certain social requirements, including a system of national public education, the organization of labour and old-age pensions. Although many of his concrete projects failed in his own time, his ideals live on. Apropos of this last Sunday of the church year, listen to what he says about divine judgment.

> For us every day is a day of judgment—every day is a *Dies Irae* and writes its irrevocable verdict in the flame of its West. Think you judgment waits till the doors of your graves are open? It waits at the doors of your houses—it waits at the corners of your streets; we are in the midst of judgment.[39]

I think that the evangelist Matthew would be quite at home with both Ruskin's thought and his rhetoric.

Especially today, as we come to the end of Matthew's year, I hope that we can appreciate his overall style, approach and message. Time and time again, over the course of the year, we have discovered in our liturgical celebrations that faith-morality-judgment is less about the separation and distinctions that make for greater conceptual clarity than it is about the integration and ambiguity that push us to greater active

---

[39] John Ruskin, quoted in J.W. Cox, *Minister's Manual* (San Francisco: Jossey-Bass, 1997), p. 197.

charity. At its best, the spiritual and religious tradition we inherit from Matthew is less about definition and more about wonder.

Using all the skill inherited from his Jewish forebears, Matthew presents Jesus to us as a provocative itinerant rabbi, to be sure, but as more than a rabbi. Jesus is Emmanuel: God-with-us. In his teaching and in his person, heaven and earth are one; past and future are one; we and the neighbour are one; God and humanity are one.

For Matthew, this same Jesus, in his rising from the dead, proclaims himself God-with-us in a new and definitive way until the end of the age. Emmanuel is our ever-living Messiah, Teacher, Shepherd and Judge. Emmanuel is our conscience and our neighbour. Emmanuel is our beginning and our end—God with us—all in all. Amen.

AGMV Marquis

MEMBER OF SCABRINI MEDIA

Quebec, Canada
2001